War-Path and Bivouac

GENERAL GEORGE CROOK

Reproduced from photograph by courtesy of
the National Archives.

WAR-PATH AND BIVOUAC

The Big Horn and Yellowstone Expedition

By John F. Finerty

EDITED BY

MILO MILTON QUAIFE

UNIVERSITY OF NEBRASKA

PRESS

Lincoln and London

The Bison Book edition of *War-Path and Bivouac* appeared as No. 53 in the Lakeside Classics, published in 1955, and is reprinted by arrangement with the Lakeside Press, R. R. Donnelley & Sons Co., Chicago, who are the sole proprietors of its special contents.

First Bison Book printing: 1966

Most recent printing indicated by first digit below:
5   6   7   8   9   10

International Standard Book Number: 0–8032–5059–2

Manufactured in the United States of America

CONTENTS

v

Contents

ILLUSTRATIONS

ILLUSTRATIONS

vii

HISTORICAL INTRODUCTION

IN 1641 two zealous Jesuits from the mission of Sainte Marie in modern Ontario accompanied some dusky guides to the outlet of Lake Superior, where they gave to the Rapids and the River Saint Marys the name they still bear. They also learned from their hosts that nine days' journey to the westward of Lake Superior lived the Sioux or Dakota nation. "These people till the soil in the manner of our Hurons," the Fathers recorded, "and harvest Indian corn and tobacco. Their villages are larger and in a better state of defense, owing to their continual wars with other great nations who inhabit the same country. Their language differs from the Algonquin and Huron tongues."[1]

In this thumbnail sketch we are given our first description of the nation which was to play so large a role in the subsequent history of the western country. In it the Jesuit Fathers merely recorded, of course, the information given to them by their Chippewa hosts at the Sault. The latter, however, who lived around the shores of Lake

[1] The quotation is from Father Lalemant's relation, dated at Sault Sainte Marie in Huronia, June 10, 1642. It is printed in Vol. 33, Chap. 12 of the *Jesuit Relations,* edited by Reuben G. Thwaites.

Superior, had excellent reasons for knowing whereof they spoke. They were a militant Stone-Age people who warred upon the Sioux and the Foxes to the westward and resisted as best they might the aggressions of the Iroquois from the East. To the latter the Chippewas applied a name meaning "adders," or enemies. The same name, accompanied by the diminutive "little," was applied to the Sioux—Little Adders, or lesser enemies.

Their warfare with the Sioux lasted for over 200 years, being terminated only by the White Man's government in the middle decades of the nineteenth century. In its course the Chippewas, early obtaining guns and ammunition from the White Man, gradually drove the Sioux westward to the Plains region of the upper Missouri. From a timber-dwelling people living in fixed dwellings and habituated to the use of the canoe, they developed a horse-buffalo economy, utilizing moveable lodge-pole tepees and with the passage of time gradually losing almost all knowledge of woodcraft and boatmanship.

In 1668 the Jesuit Fathers established a mission at Sault Sainte Marie where they soon came to learn much more about the troublesome Sioux, who were objects of dread to all their neighbors. An affair which occurred at the Sault in 1674 serves to illustrate some of the reasons for this state of mind. Although as yet the Sioux had no guns, every warrior carried two knives, one fastened to his belt, the other suspended by his hair. To terminate a period of warfare with the Chippewas which had been raging for some years, a Sioux embassy of ten warriors accompanied by two women journeyed to the Sault. Upon making their mission known they were warmly welcomed by the Chippewas. However, a party of Crees who lived north of Lake Superior and were bitter enemies of the Sioux chanced also to be paying a visit to the Sault. Determined to prevent, by any means, the peace from being concluded, they threatened to kill the ambassadors. The latter were given protection in the house of the missionaries, where industrious Father Druillettes promptly set about converting them to Christianity.

The Sioux had no choice save to listen docilely to his preaching, since the savages gathered outside were clamoring for their blood. An attempt was made to disarm all who entered the house, but amid the confusion half a dozen Crees armed with knives slipped in. One of them, knife in hand, taunted a Sioux warrior with being afraid. "If you think I am," replied the Sioux, "strike straight at my heart."

The Cree struck, and the tumult began. The nine surviving Sioux, supposing the Chippewas had conspired with the Crees against them, fell upon Crees and Chippewas indiscriminately, and since all save the half-dozen Crees were unarmed they killed several and drove the rest in panic from the mission house. Finding a store of guns and ammunition in the house they opened fire from the windows upon all who ventured within range. Despite this, the frenzied mob succeeded in firing the building. Compelled to abandon it, the Sioux seized possession of a hut nearby, within which they continued to defend themselves, "and ceased not to slay while powder and ball lasted them." Only when the supply of ammunition was exhausted were the besiegers able to overcome them. At length all were slain, but not until they had inflicted a four-fold loss upon their attackers. "It was a horrible spectacle," continues Father Druillettes, "to see so many dead, in so small a space; and horrible to hear the cries of those who warmed to the battle and the groans of the wounded amid the tumult of an exasperated rabble that scarcely heeded what it did."[2]

Upon the missionaries the melee inflicted a two-fold loss. Their mission house with its precious records was destroyed: more important, upon the conclusion of the affair the Algonquins at the Sault promptly fled, to escape the reprisals of the Sioux when they should learn the fate of their ambassadors, leaving the missionaries alone to

[2]Father Druillettes' recital of the affair is printed in *Jesuit Relations,* Vol. 58, pp. 257–63.

face the expected enemy. . . . "thus" concludes Father Druillettes, "besides the danger of being massacred, to which they are continually exposed not only at the Sault but in every other place where they set up their mission . . . the progress which the Gospel was beginning to make by these means has been seriously arrested for some time."

We have related this affair of 1674 at some length for the light it sheds upon the character of the Stone-age Sioux warrior at the moment of his entrance upon the page of recorded history. Almost exactly two hundred years later a mere handful of warriors, entrapped in a den at the Slim Buttes battle and encumbered by their women and children, fought the encircling white soldiers with a desperate determination which evoked the ungrudging admiration of the latter. Let the reader compare their story as related by our author and the parallel accounts of Captain Bourke and General Charles King,[3] and decide for himself whether the ancient reputation of the Sioux for valor in warfare had suffered deterioration during the two centuries from 1674 to 1876.

Although Sioux warriors from the upper Mississippi participated as allies of the British in the American Revolution and the War of 1812 the

[3]John G. Bourke, *On the Border with Crook* (New York, 1891) and General Charles King, *Campaigning with Crook, and Stories of Army Life* (New York, 1890).

nation was chiefly occupied during these early decades with its interminable warfare with the neighboring Indian tribes. During the War of 1812 Robert Dickson, an influential British Indian trader among the Sioux, led various contingents of warriors eastward to support their British "Father" in that conflict. They shared in the downfall of Mackinac in July, 1812, the opening blow of the war, and in General Procter's attack upon Fort Meigs, near present-day Toledo, the following year. When this failed, almost all of the Sioux set out for their distant homes, refusing to aid their white ally in the ensuing attack upon Fort Stephenson.[4]

The termination of the war with England involved the necessity of restoring peace between the United States and Britain's Indian allies. In the summer of 1815 over a score of treaties were concluded with as many different tribes, the con-

[4]At present-day Fremont. To this desertion Dickson subsequently ascribed rather extravagant consequences: the loss of the British fleet (Battle of Lake Erie), the evacuation of Amherstburg and Detroit by Procter, and the destruction of his army in the Battle of the Thames. Doane Robinson, *History of the Sioux Indians,* in *South Dakota Historical Collections,* II, 87. One of the warriors who participated in the attacks upon Fort Meigs and Fort Stephenson was the Sauk chief, Black Hawk. Upon the failure of the latter attack he prudently decided, like the Sioux before him, to go home to his wife and family. For his own story of these affairs see his *Life,* the Lakeside Classics volume for 1916, pp. 52–58.

tents merely reciting that whereas the two parties had been engaged in war, peace was now restored, with mutual forgiveness of any hostile acts committed by either.

One of these treaties with several bands of Sioux was concluded at Portage des Sioux near the confluence of the Missouri and the Mississippi rivers. Meanwhile the intertribal warfare in the upper Mississippi area was resumed, and in 1825 in a treaty concluded at Prairie du Chien the United States sought to terminate it by establishing boundaries which the tribes concerned agreed to respect. Despite this effort, however, intermittent warfare between the Sioux and their ancient enemies continued to be waged. Outstanding among these were the Chippewas and the allied Sauk and Foxes. In 1832 when Chief Black Hawk's ill-conceived war upon the whites collapsed, Sioux warriors from the upper Mississippi joined with the white army in destroying the fleeing followers of the Sauk chieftain.

By now, however, the westward flood of white settlement was overflowing the country between Lake Michigan and the Mississippi, before whose onset the Sioux nation was doomed to destruction. Modern Chicago—a wilderness outpost in 1832, whose denizens trembled in fear of Indian massacre—dates its birth in 1833. Milwaukee's founding followed close upon the heels of Chi-

cago, and in 1836 Wisconsin Territory with a
white population of 12,000 was organized. A year
later by the Treaty of Washington, concluded on
September 29, the Sioux began ceding their lands
in Minnesota to the United States.

The process, long since made familiar eastward
of the Mississippi, of whittling away the Indian
lands by successive cessions to the whites, was
about to be repeated west of the great river.
Minnesota Territory was organized in 1849. Further extensive sessions of Sioux lands were made
during the next half dozen years. By 1857 the
white population, insignificant in 1849, had increased to 157,000, and Statehood was achieved
a year later. In short, the relentless sweep of white
settlement across the continent which began at
Jamestown and Plymouth over two centuries earlier was now crowding the Sioux from their Minnesota homeland, and the resentment thus en-
gendered found expression in the futile uprising
of 1862.

Even earlier, however, serious trouble with the
Brule and Ogalala tribes had developed. The discovery of gold in California was followed by the
storied trek of the Forty-niners, thousands of
whom traveled the Oregon or California Trail,
which led through the hunting grounds of these
tribes. They resented the intrusion with its consequent destruction of the buffaloes and other

wild game, and their resentment found expression in a persistent harrying of the emigrants, with frequent abduction of their live stock and occasional killings of the emigrants themselves.

To terminate these depredations and to define and protect the rights of the Indians themselves, a great Council, attended by 10,000 Indians representing half a dozen tribes. was convened at Fort Laramie in the summer of 1851. The sessions continued for twenty-three days, in whose course agreement was reached upon a treaty establishing boundaries for the several tribes concerned in it, and promising peaceful relations for the future between them and with the white people. The latter were guaranteed right of way and protection while traversing the Indian country. In return, the United States Government agreed to provide the Indians $50,000 in goods annually for ten years, with the proviso that any tribe found guilty of violating the treaty should be deprived of its share in the distribution of the goods.

The comment of General Harney that this was a "molasses and cracker" treaty proved only too accurate.[5] The promises of peaceful relations for the future were promptly disregarded by all the parties to the pact. Although a garrison had been

[5]"It was scarcely so binding in its operation as good molasses." Doane Robinson, in *South Dakota Hist. Colls.*, II, 223.

established at Fort Laramie in 1849 its presence had no effect in restraining the depredations upon the emigrants. In fact, it seems to have exerted a contrary influence, for parties of Sioux would lie in wait about the fort for parties of emigrants approaching or leaving that rendezvous.

From this situation grew the first open warfare between the Sioux and the United States since the War of 1812. On August 19, 1854 Lieutenant John L. Grattan led a detachment of 29 soldiers from Fort Laramie to a Sioux encampment a few miles distant, intent upon arresting a warrior accused of killing a cow belonging to a Mormon emigrant. The Sioux had assembled to receive the allotment of goods promised to them by the treaty of 1851. Grattan was young and inexperienced, and his conduct of the mission proved sadly inept. Since the Sioux declined to surrender the culprit Grattan resorted to force, and in the ensuing melee his entire contingent of soldiers was slaughtered.[6]

Provoked by this affair and by the depredations upon the emigrant trains, the Government in the spring of 1855 dispatched a punitive expedition of 1200 men, commanded by General William S. Harney, against the Sioux. He marched from Fort Leavenworth on August 5, intent upon ascending

[6]For the Grattan tragedy see A. E. Sheldon, *Nebraska, The Land and its People* (Chicago, 1931), I, 133–34.

the Platte as far as Fort Laramie and from there turning backward through the heart of the Brule and Ogalala country to Fort Pierre on the Missouri. On September 3 he came upon Little Thunder's band of Brules at Ash Hollow near the emigrant trail, and in the ensuing battle killed 136 warriors, with a white loss of only 13 men.

Doane Robinson, South Dakota historian, characterizes Harney's victory as a shameful massacre, as needless and barbarous as any inflicted by the Sioux upon the whites. Caught between encircling lines of Harney's infantry and cavalry, they wished only to surrender. Denied the opportunity to do so, they fought to the end with characteristic Sioux valor.

Following the battle, Harney completed his march as he had planned it, and the troops went into winter quarters at Fort Pierre and adjoining locations.[7] In March, 1856, he negotiated a treaty with the Teton tribes. Its terms required the Indians to respect the right of travel upon the Overland Trail and upon a road from Fort Laramie to Fort Pierre, in return for certain annuities in goods.[8]

[7]Documents showing the difficulty encountered in securing suitable quarters for the troops are printed in *South Dakota Hist. Colls.*, I, 381 and following.

[8]The entire Sioux confederacy numbered three major divisions: the Santee, or eastern group; the Yankton, or middle group; and the Teton, or western group. The

General Harney also devised a plan of government for the Teton tribes, based upon the principle of the warriors themselves policing their camps with sufficient soldiers to restrain the young men from acts of violence against the whites. To carry out the plan 700 warriors were to be uniformed and maintained by the Government. But the Indian Department, which in this period was commonly at loggerheads with the army, withheld its approval. "In later years." observes Robinson, "the campaigns against the Sioux cost money enough to have supported the Harney scheme for a century."[9]

Whether with or without the Harney plan, however, the destruction of the Sioux as a nation was inevitable. Like the buffaloes upon which they depended for existence, their way of life was incompatible with that of the white man. The situation was never stated more clearly than by Lieutenant G. K. Warren, of subsequent Civil War and Gettysburg fame, who served as chief topographical engineer on the Harney campaign of 1855.

Soon afterward he was assigned the task of conducting a preliminary survey of the Black Hills. From Fort Laramie he proceeded north-

latter included the Brules, Ogalalas, Sans Arcs, and several other tribes.

[9]*South Dakota Hist. Colls.*, I, 226.

ward with a small party as far as Inyan Kara
Peak, where he encountered a large band of
Sioux. They objected strenuously to his further
advance, giving reasons whose justice he could
not refrain from recognizing.

The Sioux were encamped near herds of buffaloes whose hair was not yet sufficiently grown
to make robes. No one was permitted to kill any
animals in the large herds for fear of stampeding
the others, and only such were killed as strag-
gled away from the main bands. Thus the whole
range of buffaloes was prevented from traveling
southward, the intention of the Indians being to
retain them in the neighborhood until the hair
would answer for robes, and then to kill the animals by surrounding one band at a time and
completely destroying it. In this way no alarm
was communicated to the neighboring bands,
which often remained quiet, almost in sight of
the scene of slaughter.

"For us to have continued on, then" wrote
Warren, "would have been an act for which certain death would have been inflicted upon a like
number if their own tribe had done it; for we
might have deflected the whole range of the buffaloes 50 or 100 miles to the west and prevented
the Indians from laying in their winter stock of
provisions and skins upon which their comfort, if
not their lives, depended. Their feelings toward

us under the circumstances were not unlike what we would feel toward a person who should insist upon setting fire to our barns. The most violent of them were for immediate resistance when I told them of my intentions, and those who were most friendly, and most in fear of the power of the United States, begged that I would take pity upon them and not proceed."

Another objection to Warren's survey, advanced by the Sioux, was no less compelling. They said that the treaty recently concluded with General Harney permitted the whites to travel along the Platte and along the White River between Fort Pierre and Laramie and to make roads there, and to travel up and down the Missouri in boats; but it guaranteed to them that no white people should travel elsewhere in their country and thus drive away the buffaloes by their careless manner of hunting them; and, finally, that Warren's party was about to examine the country to see if it was of any value to the whites, and to search out roads through it and places for military posts. But having already given up all of the country they could spare to the whites, the Black Hills must be left wholly to themselves. "I was necessarily compelled to admit to myself the truth and force of their objections," concludes the white spokesman.[10]

[10]Lieutenant Warren's report, quoted in *South Dakota Hist. Colls.*, II, 227–30.

As a consequence of the Sioux outbreak in Minnesota in 1862, several military expeditions, led by Generals Sibley and Sully, invaded the upper Missouri area (chiefly comprised in present-day North and South Dakota) during the next three years, and in their course parties of Sioux were several times encountered and defeated. Other issues aside, a crisis was precipitated about the close of the Civil War by the opening of the Bozeman Road through the heart of the western hunting grounds of the Tetons, or western Sioux, as the shortest route for emigrants from the East to the Montana gold fields.[11]

The resultant rush of gold-seekers to the Virginia City mines served merely to intensify the depredations of the Sioux upon the emigrant trains along the Oregon Trail, and in an effort to restore peaceful relations a Peace Commission, appointed by President Johnson, convened another council in the summer of 1866.[12] As often in American history, the Government was swayed by antagonistic counsels. The Indian Depart-

[11]The Bozeman Road ran northerly from Julesburg, Colorado, on the Oregon Trail, through the Powder River country to the upper Yellowstone, and thence westward to Virginia City. It was first traversed by gold seekers following General Connor's Powder River expedition of 1865.

[12]An account of this situation by the present Editor has been presented in Mrs. Carrington's *Absaraka, Home of the Crows*, the Lakeside Classics volume for 1950, pp. XXII–XXV.

ment, bolstered by a curious alliance of pacifist idealists and crassly materialistic go-getters, followed a program of sweet reason in dealing with its red wards, permitting them to obtain, meanwhile, unlimited quantities of guns and ammunition, theoretically for use in hunting game but quite as readily employed in killing soldiers.[13] Upon the army, meanwhile, devolved the duty of punishing the very warriors whom the Indian Department was engaged in coddling.

The antagonistic governmental policies found characteristic expression at Fort Laramie in 1866. At the very moment the Peace Commission was exercising its blandishments upon the Sioux, General Carrington's army 700 strong appeared on the scene, en route to the Powder for the purpose of establishing a line of forts for the protection of travelers over the Bozeman Road. Upon this, Red Cloud and other chiefs in sympathy with him denounced the Council as a fraud and proclaimed their determination to kill every white man who should venture beyond the Powder River.

---

[13]Not the least remarkable aspect of the situation is the fact that the hostile warriors were commonly equipped with better arms and ammunition, obtained through the complaisance, if not the direct provision, of the Indian Department, than were the soldiers of the regular army. In particular, the carbines supplied to the cavalry had but a limited range, and the quality of the shells supplied for use in them was gravely defective.

The establishment of Forts Reno, Philip Kearny, and C. F. Smith followed, all inadequately defended by the Government. Highlight of the ensuing Red Cloud's War was the investment of Fort Philip Kearny and the slaughter there on December 21, 1866 of Captain Fetterman's detachment of 81 men. General Carrington was delivered to the public as a scapegoat for the sins of his superiors, and the foolish and disgraceful Fort Laramie treaty of 1868 was concluded.

For perhaps the only time in American history prior to 1953 the Government confessed its defeat in a war it had undertaken. The triumphant red men had contemptuously ignored another Peace Commission dispatched in 1867, and they consented to deal with the Government in 1868 only on terms dictated by themselves. By the treaty, all of the country north of the North Platte and east of the Big Horn Mountains was recognized as unceded Indian territory, from which the white man was excluded: the Bozeman Road was closed, and the three obnoxious forts so recently established to guard it were abandoned; and all of present-day South Dakota lying west of the Missouri was erected as a Sioux reservation.

If solemn treaties are not to be regarded as mere scraps of paper the possession by the Sioux of the country thus recognized by the Government as theirs would seem to have been assured

for all coming time. But public opinion and desires supersede mere paper promises. The westward thrust of white settlement paid slight heed
to the Fort Laramie treaty of 1868, which the
Government itself presently began to ignore.
Construction of the Northern Pacific Railroad
was begun in 1870 and in 1873 the road was
opened to Bismarck. Civil War and business difficulties halted its further progress for several
years. In 1873, however, surveyors for the road
selected a route for it up the south bank of the
Yellowstone. This was a clear violation of the
Fort Laramie Treaty, yet despite the protests of
the Sioux the Government provided military es-
corts to protect the surveyors, and established
several new forts to safeguard the line.[13] Numerous small-scale attacks upon the whites ensued
during 1871 and 1872, leading the Government
to order Colonel Custer and the Seventh Cavalry
from the South to the upper Missouri. In 1873
General D. S. Stanley led a formidable force
(which included the Seventh Cavalry) from Forts
Rice and Abraham Lincoln westward to the Yellowstone intent upon overawing the hostile Indians. It marched as far as Glendive Creek, near
whose junction with the Yellowstone a supply

[13]Fort McLean (soon renamed Fort Abraham Lincoln)
at the crossing of the Missouri, Fort Keogh on the Yellowstone, and Fort Ellis near Bozeman.

depot was established, and during the three-month excursion several encounters with the Indians occurred.

Following the conclusion of the Yellowstone Expedition, Custer was assigned to the command of Fort Abraham Lincoln. From here he was ordered by General Sheridan to conduct a reconnaissance of the Black Hills in the summer of 1874 with the objective, among others, of opening a military road between Fort Abraham Lincoln and Fort Laramie.

In the eyes of the Sioux the Black Hills were their most prized possession. In plain disregard of the Fort Laramie Treaty, which guaranteed their ownership of the Hills, the Government now dispatched a formidable military force to survey the area with a view to its ultimate occupation. Custer left Fort Abraham Lincoln at the head of 1200 soldiers on June 1 and having accomplished his mission returned there on August 22. His enthusiastic description of the natural beauty of the Hills, accompanied by the news that gold deposits in paying quantities had been found there, could not fail to stir the imagination of fortune seekers to a fevered pitch.[14]

[14]Ere now Custer had become an expert with the pen as well as the sword (see *My Life on the Plains*, the Lakeside Classics volume for 1952). "This valley," he wrote of the Belle Fourche "in one respect presented the most wonder-

Although the Government sought to protect the rights of the Indians until a treaty granting mining rights and the temporary occupation of the country could be negotiated, when the Indian spokesmen countered its proffers with extravagant demands of their own the embargo was raised and white adventurers flocked into the Hills unhindered. The winter of 1875–76 found more than 10,000 fortune-hunters congregated in Custer City, the earliest mining center. The discovery of gold in Deadwood Gulch early in 1876 caused a stampede to that center which became, almost in a day, "the most exciting and picturesque mining

ful as well as beautiful aspect. Its equal I have never seen and such, too, was the testimony of all who beheld it. In no private or public park have I ever seen such a profuse display of flowers. Every step of our march that day was amid flowers of the most exquisite color and perfume. So luxuriant in growth were they that men plucked them without dismounting from the saddle. . . . It was a strange sight to glance back at the advancing columns of cavalry and behold the men with beautiful bouquets in their hands, while the headgears of the horses were decorated with wreaths of flowers fit to crown a queen of the May." Little wonder, what with further descriptions of "rippling streams of clear, cold water," "grazing whose only fault was its too great luxuriance," "an abundance of timber, principally pine, poplar, and several varieties of oak," it was scarcely necessary for Custer to add that he had discovered gold in the Hills "to induce white men to determine that the Black Hills was too good a country for the Indians to possess." Doane Robinson in *South Dakota Hist. Colls.*, II, 408–13.

camp on the Continent." Perhaps the best contemporary description of it is the one supplied by our Author when Crook's bedraggled army arrived on the scene a few months later.

Such, briefly sketched, was the background for the Sioux War of 1876. Less than a decade earlier Red Cloud had fought the white government to a standstill and had triumphantly dictated his own terms of peace. Evidently it was now time for the Sioux to make another stand for their rights, if they were not to surrender their country altogether. As if to climax the story of governmental ineptitude and blundering, in the early winter of 1875–76 many Indians from the different Agencies departed to hunt buffaloes in the Powder River country. This the Agents had encouraged, since their supply of provisions for the Indians was inadequate. Yet on December 6, 1875 the Commissioner of Indian Affairs instructed the Agents to notify the Indians scattered over the unceded area that they must return to the agencies before the close of January, 1876, or they would be regarded as hostile. Difficulties arising from the distances involved and the season of winter weather rendered it practically certain that the Commissioner's deadline could not be met.[15] Yet on February 1 the Secretary of the

[15]None of the messengers sent to inform the Indians of the Commissioner's order were able to return to their

Interior notified the Secretary of War that since the hostile Indians had not complied with his order he was turning them over to the military department for such action as it might deem fitting to take.

The stage was now set for the greatest of all white-Indian wars. Action began promptly when on March 1 General Crook marched from Fort Fetterman at the head of 800 soldiers in search of the recalcitrant red men. In weather ranging to 26° below zero, on March 17 a portion of Crook's command led by General Joseph J. Reynolds struck and destroyed Chief Crazy Horse's winter encampment on the Powder. It proved to be a Pyrrhic victory, for Crazy Horse's warriors quickly followed the retiring soldiers and recaptured their pony herd, compelling Crook, short of provisions and encumbered with wounded, to abandon the campaign and return to Fort Fetterman.

Meanwhile, from his Chicago headquarters General Sheridan, Commander of the Department of the Missouri, was devising a comprehensive plan of operations designed to entrap the Sioux between three converging armies, when submission or annihilation would be their fate. From Fort

Agencies by January 31. With respect to the weather, General Sheridan reported that in late November the cold was such that even the army was compelled to suspend operations. Doane Robinson in *South Dakota Hist. Colls.,* II, 422–23.

Fetterman General Crook, adequately reinforced as it was thought, was to resume his northward invasion of the Powder River country which he had unsuccessfully attempted in March; another column, commanded by General Gibbon, was to advance southeastwardly from Fort Ellis in Montana; still another column led by General Terry, was to march westward from Fort Abraham Lincoln. The junction of the three armies in the Yellowstone-Powder River region, it was expected, would mark the end of Sioux resistance to the Government.

Sheridan and Crook, Gibbon and Terry and Custer were numbered among the most renowned generals of the Civil War, their reputation won on many a hard-fought field. Yet they totally failed to corner the Sioux, who inflicted two severe defeats upon the converging armies, and in the end succumbed only to superior resources and to paucity of food and other supplies.

On May 29 Crook with an army of 1050 men began his second advance upon the Powder River country. With him went our Author as special correspondent of the Chicago *Times*, and for the further story of the campaign the reader may be left to his competent pen. To the Editor remains the task of acquainting him with the manner of man Correspondent Finerty was, and of providing some evaluation of his narrative.

John F. Finerty was a gift to America of the Emerald Isle, where he was born in County Galway, September 10, 1846. He came to America in 1864 and soon after his arrival enlisted in the Ninety-fourth New York Regiment. Following the war he became a newspaper man in Chicago, serving the Chicago *Republican* as a reporter from 1868 to 1871 and City Editor in 1871–72. From the latter year until 1875 he was employed by the Chicago *Tribune*. Precisely when he transferred to the *Times* has not been learned. In the spring of 1876 he was assigned by Editor Storey to accompany General Crook's army in the Sioux campaign then about to open.

Finerty's own account discloses that he preferred to go with General Custer's command. Fortunately for our readers he was overruled by his employer. But for this he would probably have perished with Custer, and his subsequent narrative would never have been written.[16]

Even as it was, his employer had but scant reason to expect Finerty to return in safety from the war. He had all the typical Irishman's fondness for a fight, and throughout the campaign he repeatedly exposed himself beyond the call of prudence or of duty, winning the admiration of both officers and men by his daredevil conduct. Of this

[16]Such was the fate of Mark Kellogg, the only correspondent who followed Custer to the Little Big Horn.

fact, we have the convincing testimony of such professional soldiers as Captain John G. Bourke and General Charles King. In the desperate battle of the Rosebud General Crook ordered Colonel Mills to lead his cavalry battalion down the canon toward the Sioux encampment. As with the Six Hundred at Balaklava, it was a ride "into the jaws of death," whose almost certain outcome, but for the timely abandonment of the movement, was the annihilation of the entire battalion. "At the head of that column" wrote Captain Bourke, "rode two men who have since made their mark in far different spheres; John F. Finerty, who has since represented one of the Illinois districts in Congress, and Frederick Schwatka, noted as a bold and successful Arctic explorer."[17]

Opportunely the column was recalled by Crook in time to escape from the trap into which Crazy Horse had planned to lure it, and Finerty survived to join, as a volunteer, a few days later the reconnaissance of the country upon which Crook dispatched Lieutenant Sibley's small command. This was an undertaking of extreme hazard and only by an eyelash did the party escape complete destruction. At the moment of setting out, Captain Bourke inquired what kind of an epitaph Finerty wished to have written for him, while Captain Wells grimly directed his orderly: "Bring

[17]*On the Border with Crook,* 315.

Mr. Finerty a hundred rounds of Troop E ammunition."[18]

In reporting upon this affair to General Sheridan, General Crook expressed his grateful appreciation of the conduct of the guides and of the two citizen volunteers—Finerty and an old frontiersman and packer—who had participated in it. General Charles King, writing of the assault upon the Indians concealed in a den at the battle of Slim Buttes, stated: "A squad of newspaper correspondents, led by that reckless Hibernian, Finerty of the Chicago *Times,* came tearing over pencil in hand, all eagerness for items, just as a second volley came from the concealed foe and three more of their assailants dropped, bleeding, in their tracks."[19]

Toward nightfall, when the army was engaged in repelling Crazy Horse's attack, one of the soldiers had just succeeded in knocking a warrior from his saddle and capturing his party. "Even while his comrades are shouting their congratulations," King wrote, "up comes Jack Finerty, who seeks his items on the skirmish line, and uses pencil and carbine with equal facility. Finerty wants the name of the man who killed that Indian and learning from the eager voices of the men that it is

[18]Finerty's own narrative, *post,* Chap. XIII; Bourke, *On the Border with Crook,* 331–33.
[19]*Campaigning with Crook,* (New York, 1905), 116.

Paddy Nihil, he delightedly heads a new paragraph of his dispatch 'Nihil Fit,' shakes hands with his brother Patlander, and scurries off to take a hand in the uproar on the left."[20] And in summing up his characterization of the entire group of correspondents who accompanied the army, General King described Finerty as "the gem of the lot."[21]

Returned from the wars in safety, Finerty lived to become one of Chicago's best-known citizens. For several years he continued his employment on the *Times*, serving as special correspondent on General Mills' Sioux campaign of 1879, on General Merritt's Ute campaign the same year, and on General Carr's Apache campaign of 1881. Meantime, from 1879 to 1881 he was the *Times'* correspondent in Washington. In 1882 he married Sadie J. Hennessey and in the same year founded the *Citizen*, a weekly Chicago paper. Soon afterward he was elected to Congress as an Independent Democrat, serving from March, 1883 to March, 1885.[22]

[20]*Ibid*, 130.
[21]*Ibid*, 153.
[22]So stated in the official biography of members of Congress. But Finerty's sketch in *Who's Who in America*, which presumably was furnished by himself, states that he was a Republican until 1900. *The Book of Chicagoans*, 1905 ed., states that he was elected to Congress as an Independent, supported Blaine in 1884, and remained a Republican until 1900.

Throughout his career Finerty was an ardent Hibernian, and was known as a radical advocate of Irish independence. Down to 1905 he had served seven terms as President of the United Irish Societies of Chicago and at this time was serving as President of the United Irish League of America. Although his formal education closed when he left Ireland, his writings show that he possessed an extensive familiarity with history and general literature. He was an accomplished orator, and during his later years a popular lecturer on historical subjects. When, on July 4, 1905 the State of Montana dedicated an equestrian statue on the State Capitol Grounds at Helena to General Thomas F. Meagher, organizer of the New York Irish Brigade in the Civil War and subsequently Secretary and acting Governor of Montana Territory, Finerty was chosen to deliver the principal oration of the day. His portrait published in this connection by the State Historical Society of Montana shows him in military uniform and the current publication designates him as Colonel Finerty. How he acquired this military title is unknown to the present Editor. Of his oratorical performance on this occasion the contemporary newspaper report states: "He spoke for nearly an hour, and during the course of his address not a person left the audience, and so quiet did the people keep that those fartherest away could hear distinctly every word he said." The address, delivered without notes or written preparation, is further characterized as a magnificent effort, which was frequently interrupted by applause, and at its close the orator was accorded an ovation.[23]

Finerty died at his Chicago home June 10, 1908 and was accorded a funeral such as any man might covet. The services were in charge of the G.A.R. and several hundred veterans accompanied the body from the home to the Holy Angels Church where the funeral service was held. The mile-long procession to the Church was headed by a platoon of police followed in due order by the veterans, members of the family in carriages, and by members of the United Irish Society, the Irish Fellowship Club, and other organizations. Numbered among the honorary pallbearers were the Mayor of Chicago, no less than six judges, and many leading citizens of varied faiths and affiliations: Right Reverend Samuel Fallows, Rabbi E. G. Hirsch, Roger Sullivan and William Lorimer, leading Democratic politicians, famed surgeon, Dr. John B. Murphy, and other leading business and professional men.[24]

[23]Montana Historical Society, *Contributions*, VI, 121–25.
[24]Chicago *Record Herald*, June 11 and 13, 1908; Chicago *Tribune*, June 13, 1908.

War-Path and Bivouac, containing two parts, was published in 1890. Part I, reproduced in the present volume, narrates the story of Crook's campaign of 1876 and to some extent the allied campaigns of Generals Terry, Gibbon, and Custer. Part II, entitled "Campaign on the British Line," omitted from our present volume, tells the story of General Miles' campaign of 1879 against the Sioux, and the Nez Percés under Chief Joseph. Several chapters of "Addenda," devoted to such subjects as the careers of Crook and Custer, army life and discipline, etc., complete the volume, which apparently was privately printed by the Author. How large the edition may have been, or how rare are copies at the present time, is unknown to the Editor. For the purpose of reprinting, the copy belonging to the Newberry Library of Chicago has been used.

War-Path and Bivouac presents to the reader an excellent example of military reporting. Finerty was a seasoned journalist, acquainted with army life through his prior service in the Civil War. Still in the prime of his physical and intellectual power, he avoided no hardship and shirked no danger in the pursuit of his calling. Although the *Times* was sharply critical of the national Administration, I am unable to discover that Reporter Finerty permitted this to color his reports from the scene of action. Nor does General Crook seem to have resented the criticisms which the Author expressed of his conduct of the campaign.

Since this was waged in 1876 and *War-Path and Bivouac* was not published until 1890 one may reasonably ask whether, and to what extent, the book differs from the writer's contemporary reports of the campaign. Comparison of its contents with the file of the *Times* for 1876 preserved in the Newberry Library discloses that for much of the contents of the book the Author copied verbatim his contemporary letters to the *Times*. Much more of the book, however, seems not to have been published in the *Times*. For this fact there are obvious explanations. The *Times* had other correspondents besides Finerty with the armies, whose reports were being published. Newspapers were much smaller eighty years ago than they are now, and it is reasonable to presume that some of Finerty's reports were omitted from publication because of lack of space to print them. There were, also, frequent periods of days or weeks of time when he had no means of forwarding reports. This was particularly true of the long march of the army from the mouth of the Powder to the Black Hills, when for a period of several weeks it was wholly out of touch with the civilized world. When the reports which Finerty may have written during such periods of isolation finally reached his Chicago office, they may reasonably have been discarded in favor of more timely news.

However this may be, it seems certain that the Author preserved his note books of the campaign, and that he had them at hand when in 1890 he was engaged in organizing the copy for the book. It may be noted, however, that since Finerty was not a participant in the Custer and Dull Knife campaigns, Chapters XIV and XXIV, devoted respectively to these affairs, were necessarily based upon such information as he assembled at a subsequent date.

In editing the present reprint of *War-Path and Bivouac* I have exercised complete freedom to impose my own typographical style upon it. Editorial fashions with respect to typography change from decade to decade, and even currently there is no consensus with respect to them. In particular, I have broken up numerous excessively long paragraphs and have eliminated a really extraordinary quantity of commas, capital letters, and quotation marks which are found in the original edition. In a very few instances I have corrected a date or other obvious error of the Author (or his printer), where such corrections were necessary. In short, I have subjected the Author's copy to such editing as I would apply if he were currently submitting it for editorial approval.

As in former years, I am indebted to my wife, Letitia, for the performance of much essential editorial service. The staffs of the Newberry Library in Chicago and the Burton Historical Collection of the Detroit Public Library have placed the resources of these great historical collections at my service. To the latter in particular I am indebted for repeated and varied assistance. Registrar Eleanor Ferry of the Detroit Institute of Arts kindly supplied the photograph of the Custer Guidon owned by that Institution, together with all available information concerning its history. Mrs. Gertrude B. MacAhan, Curator of the St. Joseph County Historical Museum at Niles, Michigan generously placed that institution's unusual collection of Sitting Bull pictographs and other material at my disposal. To Miss Josephine Cobb of the Still Pictures Section, National Archives, and Mrs. Margaret C. Blaker, Archives Assistant, Bureau of American Ethnology, I am indebted for helpful guidance in the procural of illustrative material from their respective institutions. As in former years, the Publishers have afforded me unlimited freedom to edit the volume at my discretion, and Mrs. Lucille R. Wyant has prepared the maps designed to assist the reader in understanding the course of events described by the Author.   M. M. QUAIFE

Detroit, January 21, 1955

WAR-PATH AND BIVOUAC,

—— OR ——

THE CONQUEST OF THE SIOUX,

A NARRATIVE OF STIRRING PERSONAL EXPERIENCES AND ADVEN-
TURES IN THE BIG HORN AND YELLOWSTONE EXPEDITION
OF 1876, AND IN THE CAMPAIGN ON THE
BRITISH BORDER, IN 1879.

—— BY ——

JOHN F. FINERTY

WAR CORRESPONDENT FOR THE CHICAGO "TIMES."

—————————

PUBLICATION OFFICE:

UNITY BUILDING, 79 DEARBORN STREET

CHICAGO.

PREFACE AND DEDICATION

IT had long been my intention to publish the volume which I now submit to the public. The book is, as far as human fallibility will permit, a faithful narrative of stirring events the like of which can never again occur upon our continent.

Stories of Indian warfare, even when not founded entirely upon fact, have ever been popular with people of all nations, and more particularly with the American people, to whom such warfare is rendered familiar both by tradition and experience. These memoirs aim at laying before the public the adventures, privations, heroism and horrors of our last great Indian wars, exactly as they presented themselves to the writer in battle, on the march or in bivouac.

The valor of the American army has never been impugned, but millions of our own citizens do not know, even yet, what privations our brave soldiers endured and what noble sacrifices they made in advancing our banner in the wilderness of the West and in subduing the savage and sanguinary tribes that so long barred the path of progress in our Territories.

The soldier who falls wounded while battling against a civilized foe feels certain of receiving humane consideration if he should fall into hos-

tile hands, but our soldiers who were disabled in
the Indian campaigns had ever before them the
terrors of fiendish torture and mutilation in case
of capture by the savages. Buried for months at a
time in the very heart of the wilderness, excluded
from every solace of civilization, exposed to the
stealthy strategy of the most cunning and merciless of all existing human races, unsheltered, for
the most part, from the fury of the elements, deprived of the ordinary food of mankind and compelled to live, at times, on that against which the
civilized stomach revolts, the soldiers of the regular army seldom or never complained and always
went cheerfully into "the gap of danger."

In former years the Congress of our country
through a strange system of reasoning rewarded
the bravery and devotion of our regular troops
by assuming that their deeds of arms against
savages in revolt should not be ranked among
acts of warfare deserving of national recognition!
It is some satisfaction, even at this late day, to
know that the national legislature no longer looks
upon services rendered by the troops against
hostile savages with contemptuous eyes, and that
the bill granting brevet rank to the more distinguished among the Indian fighters of the regular army has now become a law.

If these frankly-written pages serve to place before the Congress and the people of the United

States the deeds and the sufferings of the national army while struggling in several most important campaigns for the extension of our peaceful borders, the safety of our hardy pioneers and the honor of our martial name, I will feel greatly recompensed for the labor of their production.

The gallant service in which Harney. Fremont. Sully, Stanley, Connors, Crook, Miles, Merritt, Terry, Mackenzie, Gibbon, Carr and other heroic chiefs distinguished themselves against the intrepid hostile Indians, and in which Custer, Canby, Fetterman, Kidder, Elliot, Brown, Grummond, Yates, McIntosh, Calhoun, Keogh, McKinney, and many more as brave as they were died fighting against overwhelming numbers deserves honor at the hands of the nation whose glory it has maintained and whose progress it has insured.[1]

Whether as regulars or volunteers, our soldiers, at all times and under all circumstances,

---

[1] For the deaths of Fetterman, Brown, and Grummond see Mrs. Margaret Carrington's *Absaraka, Home of the Crows,* the Lakeside Classics volume for 1950. For Kidder and Elliot see General Custer's *My Life on the Plains,* the Lakeside Classics volume for 1952. Lieutenant James Calhoun, Captain M. W. Keogh, and Captain G. W. Yates perished with Custer in the Battle of the Little Big Horn, June 28, 1876. General Edward S. Canby was murdered April 11, 1873, while engaged upon a peace mission to the Modocs of northern California. Lieutenant John A. McKinney was killed in the defeat of Dull Knife's band, November 25, 1876.

have deserved well of their country. From the day of Concord Bridge, when the citizen-soldiery of Massachusetts "fired the shot heard 'round the world," to that of the Little Big Horn, when Custer at the head of his three hundred died like Leonidas at Thermopylæ, the American army, whether in victory or disaster, has ever been worthy of the flag which it carries and of the nation which it defends. In this spirit I respectfully dedicate this book to the American army and the American nation.

JOHN F. FINERTY

Chicago, April, 1890.

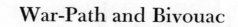

War-Path and Bivouac

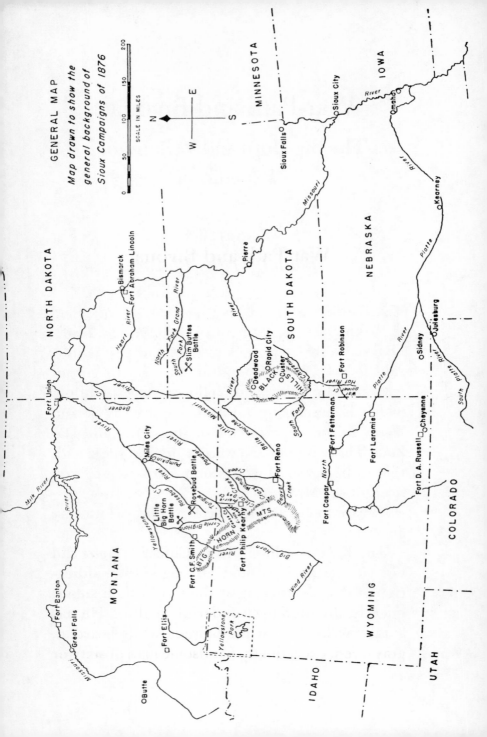

GENERAL MAP

Map drawn to show the
general background of
Sioux Campaigns of 1876

War-Path and Bivouac

The Big Horn and Yellowstone Expedition

CHAPTER I

Bound for the Plains

IN the beginning of May, 1876, I was attached to the city department of the Chicago *Times*. One day Mr. Clinton Snowden, the city editor, said to me, "Mr. Storey wants a man to go out with the Big Horn and Yellowstone expedition, which is organizing under Generals Crook and Terry in the departments of the Platte and Dakota. There is apt to be warm work out there with the Indians, so if you don't care to go, you needn't see Mr. Storey."

"I care to go, and I'll see Mr. Storey," was my answer.

The famous editor of the Chicago *Times* did not, at that period, show any significant indication of that "withering at the top" which subsequently obscured his wonderful faculties. He was a tall, well-built, white-haired, white-bearded, gray-eyed, exceedingly handsome man of sixty or thereabout, with a courteous, but somewhat cynical, manner.[2]

"You are the young man Mr. Snowden mentioned for the Plains?" he asked, as soon as I had made my presence known by the usual half-shy demonstrations, because everybody who did not know him well, and who had heard his reputation on the outside, approached the formidable Vermonter in somewhat gingerly fashion.

I replied in the affirmative. "Well, how soon can you be ready?" he inquired.

"At any time it may please you to name," was my prompt reply.

"You should have your outfit first. Better get some of it here—perhaps all. You are going with Crook's column," said Mr. Storey, with his customary decisiveness and rapidity.

"I understood I was to go with Custer," I rejoined. "I know General Custer, but am not acquainted with General Crook."

[2]Wilbur F. Storey, owner and editor of the Chicago *Times*, was one of the outstanding journalists of the mid-nineteenth century. A native of Salisbury, Vermont, he began his journalistic career at the age of twelve. After various engagements and residences, in 1853 he purchased an interest in the Detroit *Free Press,* of which he subsequently became sole owner, making it an outstanding Democratic organ. In 1861 he purchased the Chicago *Times*, with which his subsequent career was identified. An ardent Democrat, he vigorously opposed President Lincoln and the prosecution of the war, gaining for his

"That will make no difference, whatever," said he. "Terry commands over Custer, and Crook, who knows more about the Indians, is likely to do the hard work. Custer is a brave soldier—none braver—but he has been out there some years already and has not succeeded in bringing the Sioux to a decisive engagement. Crook did well in Arizona.[3] However, it is settled that you go with Crook. Go to Mr. Patterson (the manager) and get what funds you may need for your outfit and other expenses. Report to me when you are ready."

It did not take me long to get ready. I called first upon General Sheridan and asked him for a letter of introduction to General Crook, and also

paper the reputation of a Copperhead publication. Failing health terminated his active career in 1878. He died October 27, 1884. *Dictionary of American Biography.*

[3]On General Crook's notable subsequent operations against the Apaches in Arizona see Britton Davis; *The Truth About Geronimo,* the Lakeside Classics volume for 1951. Storey's allusion (in 1876), however, is to Crook's earlier Arizona Apache campaigns and administration, from 1871 to 1875. Eminently successful in terminating the current warfare, he was transferred to the Department of the Platte in 1875. Seven years later (1882) he was returned to Arizona to assume control of the renewed Indian warfare. Here he remained until almost the close of the final hostilities with the Apaches, resigning his command in the spring of 1886 over a criticism by General Sherman of his conduct of the Geronimo campaign. For a more comprehensive account of Crook's operations see John G. Bourke, *On the Border with Crook.*

for a general letter to such officers as I might meet on the frontier.[4]

The gallant General very promptly, and in a spirit of the most generous cordiality, acceded to my request. He gave me some advice, which I afterward found valuable, and wished me every success in my undertaking.

"I'll try and do your kindness no discredit, General," I ventured to remark, as I took my leave.

"I am fully confident of that, but let me warn you that you will find General Crook a hard campaigner," said he, laughingly.

My next care was to purchase arms and a riding outfit, and, having said farewell to friends and received the final instructions of Mr. Storey, who enjoined me to "spare no expense and use the wires freely, whenever practicable," I left Chicago to join General Crook's command on Saturday morning, May 6, 1876.

The rain fell in torrents, and the wind shrieked fiercely as the train on the Northwestern road,

[4]General Philip S. Sheridan, famous Union Commander in the Civil War, was promoted by President Grant to the rank of lieutenant-general, March 4, 1869. In 1884 he succeeded General Sherman as commander-in-chief of the U.S. Army. For many years following his promotion to lieutenant-general he commanded the Department of the Missouri, with his military headquarters at Chicago. *Dictionary of American Biography.*

well freighted with passengers, steamed out of the depot, bound for Omaha. I reached the latter city on Sunday morning and found General Crook at his headquarters, busily engaged in reading reports from officers stationed on the Indian frontier. He was then a spare but athletic man of about forty, with fair hair, clipped close, and a blond beard which seemed to part naturally at the point of the chin. His nose was long and aquiline, and his blue-gray eyes were bright and piercing. He looked, in fact, every inch a soldier, except that he wore no uniform.

The General saluted me curtly, and I handed him the letter of introduction which I had procured in Chicago from General Sheridan, who then commanded the Military Department of the Missouri. Having read it, Crook smiled and said: "You had better go to Fort Sidney or Fort Russell, where the expedition is now being formed.[5] You will need an animal, and can purchase one, perhaps, at Cheyenne. Can you ride and shoot well?"

"I can ride fairly, General. As for shooting, I don't know. I'd engage, however, to hit a haystack at two hundred yards."

[5]Fort D. A. Russell at Cheyenne, Wyoming, established in 1867, entedates the founding of Cheyenne. Over a long period of years it became one of the best-equipped military establishments in the country. Fort Sidney was

He laughed and said, "Very well. We'll have some tough times, I think. I am going with my aide, Mr. Bourke,[6] to the agencies to get some friendly Indians to go with us. I fear we'll have to rely upon the Crows and Snakes, because the Sioux, Cheyennes and Arapahoes are disaffected, and all may join the hostiles. However, I'll be at Fort Fetterman about the middle of the month. You can make messing arrangements with some officer going out from Fort Russell. You had better be with the cavalry."

I thanked the General, and proceeded to my hotel. Next morning found me en route over the Union Pacific Road to Cheyenne. The weather had greatly improved, but after passing the line of what may be called eastern Nebraska nothing

at Sidney, Cheyenne County, Nebraska, a town on the Union Pacific Railroad about 100 miles east of Cheyenne. In 1881 it had a population of 1069.

[6]John G. Bourke graduated from West Point in 1869. Assigned to service in New Mexico, he became General Crook's aide in August, 1871. His books, *On the Border with Crook,* published in 1891, and *An Apache Campaign,* published in 1886, supply vivid accounts of his long service under Crook. An observant and careful scholar, Bourke authored numerous valuable sketches of primitive life, based upon his observations of the life of the western and southwestern Indians. *Dictionary of American Biography.* Bourke's narrative of the Sioux campaign of 1876 and General Charles King's *Campaigning with Crook* provide valuable accounts which parallel our Author's narrative.

could beautify the landscape. Monotonous flats and equally monotonous swells, almost devoid of trees and covered only partially by short, sickly-looking grass made up the main body of the scenery. In those days herds of antelopes still roamed at will over the Plains of Nebraska and Wyoming, and even the buffaloes had not been driven entirely from the valley of the Platte; but there was about the country, even under the bright May sunshine, a look of savage desolation. It has improved somewhat since 1876, but not enough to make any person mistake the region between North Platte and Cheyenne for the Garden of Eden. The prairie dogs abounded by the million, and the mean-looking coyote made the dismal waste resonant, particularly at night, with his lugubrious howls.

That night I stood for a long time on the rear platform of the Pullman car and watched the moonbeams play upon the rippled surface of the shallow and eccentric Platte. I thought of all the labor and all the blood it had cost to build the railroad and to settle the country even as sparsely as it was then settled; for along that river, but a few years previously, the buffaloes grazed by myriads, and the wild Indians chased them on their fleet ponies, occasionally varying their amusement by raiding an imigrant train or attacking a small party of railroad builders. The very ground over which the train traveled slowly, on an upgrade toward the Rocky Mountains, had been soaked with the best blood of the innocent and the brave, the air around had rung with the shrieks of dishonored maids and matrons and with the death groans of victims tortured at the stake. Nathless the moonlight, the region appeared to me as a dark and bloody ground, once peopled by human demons, and then by pioneers, whose lives must have been as bleak and lonesome as the country which they inhabited. Filled with such thoughts, I retired to rest.

"We're nearing Sidney, sah," said the colored porter, as he pulled aside the curtain of my berth. I sprang up immediately and had barely dressed myself when the train came to a halt at the station. The platform was crowded with citizens and soldiers, the barracks of the latter being quite close to the town. Nearly all the military wore the yellow facings of the cavalry. I was particularly struck by the appearance of one officer a first lieutenant and evidently a foreigner. He wore his kepi low on his forehead, and beneath it his hooked nose overhung a blond mustache of generous proportions. His eyes were light blue, his cheeks yellow and rather sunken. He was about the middle stature and wore huge dragoon boots. Thick smoke from an enormous pipe rose upon the morning air, and he paced up and down like a caged tiger. I breakfasted at the railroad restaurant, and as the train was in no hurry to get away I had a chance to say a few words to the warrior already described.

"Has your regiment got the route for the front yet, Lieutenant?" I inquired.

"Some of it," he replied in a thick German accent, without removing his pipe. "Our battalion should have it already, but 'tis always the vay, Got tamn the luck! 'tis alvays the vay!"

"I guess 'twill be all right in a day or two, Lieutenant!" I remarked.

"Vell, may be so, but they're alvays slighting the Third Cavalry, at headquarters. Ve ought to have moved a veek ago."

"I saw General Crook at Omaha, and he said he would be at Fetterman by the 15th."

"You don't zay so? Then ve get off. Vell, dat is good. Are you in the army?"

"No; I am going out as correspondent for the Chicago *Times*."

"Vell, I am so glad to meet you. My name is Von Leuttwitz. The train is going. Good-bye. We shall meet again."

We did meet again, and, to anticipate somewhat, under circumstances the reverse of pleasant for the gallant, but unfortunate lieutenant, who, after having campaigned over Europe and America, and having fought in, perhaps, a hundred pitched battles, lost his leg at Slim Buttes fight on the following 9th of September.[7]

The train proceeded slowly, toiling laboriously up the ever-increasing grade toward Cheyenne, through a still bare and dismal landscape. Early in the afternoon we passed the long snow sheds, and, emerging from them, beheld toward the southwest the distant summits of Long's and Gray's peaks of the Rocky Mountains. Less than an hour brought us to Cheyenne, which is only three miles from Fort D. A. Russell, my immediate objective point. As at Sidney, the railroad platform was crowded with soldiers and citizens, many of the latter prospectors driven from the southern passes of the Black Hills of Dakota by the hostile Indians. I put up at an inviting hotel, and was greatly interested in the conversation around me. All spoke of "the Hills," of the Indian hostilities, and of the probable result of the contemplated military expedition.

As I was well acquainted in Cheyenne, I had little difficulty in making myself at home. No-

[7]Adolphus H. Von Leuttwitz, a native of Prussia, enlisted as a private soldier in the Union Army January 1, 1862. Before the close of the year he had risen to the rank of captain. In 1867 he was commissioned a second lieutenant in the regular service and assigned to the Third U.S. Cavalry Regiment. For his role and wounding in the battle of Slim Buttes, September 9, 1876, see *post*, Chap. 20.

body seemed to know when the expedition would start, but all felt confident that there would be music in the air before the June roses came into bloom. At a book store, with the proprietor of which I was on friendly terms, I was introduced to Col. Guy V. Henry of the Third Cavalry. He was, then, a very fine-looking, although slight and somewhat pale, officer, and, what was still better, he was well up in all things concerning the projected Indian campaign.[8]

"We will march from this railroad in two columns," said he. "One will form at Medicine Bow, ninety miles or so westward, and will cross the North Platte River at Fort Fetterman. The other will march from Fort Russell to Fort Laramie, cross the North Platte there, and march by the left bank, so as to join the other column in front of Fetterman. This I have heard, not officially, but on sufficiently good authority. From

[8]Guy V. Henry graduated from the U.S. Military Academy in 1861 in the same class with General George A. Custer. He was brevetted colonel in March, 1865 for gallant and meritorious service throughout the war, and returned to the regular service with his old regiment, the First U.S. Artillery, in December. On December 15, 1870 he was transferred to the Third Cavalry, eventually attaining the rank of colonel in 1897, major general of volunteers in 1898, and brigadier general in the regular army the same year. He received numerous brevets for service in the Civil War and in subsequent Indian wars, and was severely wounded in Crook's battle of the Rosebud on June 17, 1876. He died, October 27, 1899.

Fetterman we will march north until we strike the Indians. That is about the program."

I asked the Colonel's advice in regard to procuring a horse, and was soon in possession of a very fine animal, which subsequently met with a tragical fate in the wild recesses of the Big Horn Mountains. Colonel Henry's mess being full, a circumstance that he and I mutually regretted, I made arrangements with a captain of the Third Cavalry to join his, and having thus provided for the campaign I set about enjoying myself as best I could until the hour for marching should strike. Cheyenne, in 1876, still preserved most of the characteristics of a crude frontier town. Gambling was openly practiced, by day as well as by night, and the social evil, of the very lowest type, was offensively visible wherever the eye might turn. No respectable maid or matron ventured out unattended after nightfall, while occasional murders and suicides "streaked the pale air with blood."[9]

Notwithstanding these almost inevitable drawbacks, there were then, as there are now, level heads and loyal hearts in Cheyenne and I can never forget the many pleasant evenings I spent

[9]For a sketch of early-day Cheyenne, known for a time as "Hell-on-Wheels," see Mrs. Carrington's *Absaraka*, 22–23. For an interesting account of life at Fort D.A. Russell as experienced by an army bride in 1874, see Mrs. Martha Summerhayes' *Vanished Arizona*, the Lakeside Classics volume for 1937.

there in company with some officers of the Fort
Russell garrison and such distinguished citizens
as Editors Swan and Glascke. Col. Luke Murrin,
Dr. Whitehead, Sheriff O'Brien, Messrs. French,
Harrington, Dyer, MacNamara, Miller, Haas and
many other right good fellows, who will ever live
in my grateful remembrance. I believe that all of
the gentlemen mentioned, with the exception of
Mr. MacNamara, still survive. If I have omitted
the names of any of the friends of that period, the
omission, I can assure my readers, is entirely un-
intentional, for a manlier, more generous or hospitable group of men it has rarely been my good
fortune to encounter.

On the 12th or 13th of May it was known that
General Crook and his staff had arrived during
the night, but were off on the wings of the wind,
overland, to Fort Laramie in the morning. Captain Sutorius, with whom I had arranged to mess,
sent me word on the 14th that the command was
under orders, and that I had better take up my
residence at Fort Russell during the night.[10]
Messrs. Dyer and MacNamara insisted on taking
my traps to the Fort in a spring wagon, drawn by

[10]Captain Alexander Sutorius, who figures in the
Author's further narrative, was a native of Switzerland
who enlisted in the army as a private in 1854. During the
Civil War he became a lieutenant in the Third U.S.
Cavalry Regiment, and a captain in 1869. He was dis-
missed from the service on September, 25, 1876.

a spirited horse. I rode on horseback beside them. Just as we neared the entrance of the parade ground their beast took fright and ran away with great skill and energy. I attempted in vain to keep up with the procession. In front of the quarters of Captain Peale, of the Second Cavalry, an officer who has since suffered many misfortunes, the wagon was upset.[11] MacNamara, a pretty heavy man, described the arc of a circle in the air and fell upon the crown of his head. His high hat was crushed down upon his face, and he presented a ludicrous spectacle enough, but, most fortunately, he escaped serious injury, and relieved his feelings by thundering anathemas against the runaway animal and all concerned in the catastrophe. Dyer was thrown out also, and suffered a gash over the eye-brow, the scar of which still remains. My effects were strewn all over Fort Russell, and half a dozen orderlies were, by the courtesy of Captain Peale and other officers, engaged for some time in picking them up. I have since learned the wisdom and the beauty of moving in light marching order. Both Captains Peale and Sutorius treated us most kindly,

[11]James T. Peale served as a volunteer throughout the Civil War, winning a brevet as lieutenant colonel of volunteers for gallant and meritorious service during the war. Following the war he was commissioned a lieutenant in the Second U.S. Cavalry Regiment, and captain in 1875. On December 20, 1880 he was dismissed from the service.

and, in view of their subsequent misfortunes, I
feel bound to bear witness that on that occasion,
as on many others, they showed that their hearts
were in the right place, although their heads
might be sometimes weak.

Next day I called upon the commandant of the
fort, Gen. J. J. Reynolds, Colonel of the Third
Cavalry, who received me with that courteous
bearing so characteristic of the American regular
officer.[12] He spoke pleasantly of the approaching
campaign, but regretted that he personally could
have no part in it. He did not say why, but I understood perfectly that he and the Department
Commander, General Crook, were not on good
terms, owing to a disagreement relative to Reynolds' action during the short Crazy Horse Village campaign of the preceding March. Reynolds
stormed the village, but was unable to retain it,
and, in his retreat, the Indians attacked his rear

[12]General Joseph J. Reynolds graduated from the U.S.
Military Academy in 1843 in the same class as General
U. S. Grant. Apart from other duties, he served for several
years as an instructor in various branches of study at the
Academy. Resigning his commission in 1857, he was employed as Professor of Engineering in Washington University, Saint Louis until 1861. During the Civil War he
attained the rank of major general of volunteers, and in
July, 1866 was appointed Colonel of the 26th U.S. Infantry. He was transferred to the Third U.S. Cavalry in
1870, and retired from the service in 1877. For gallantry
at Chickamauga, he was brevetted a major general in
1867. He died, February 25, 1899.

guard and stampeded the pony herd of 800 horses he had captured. General Crook held that General Reynolds ought to have shot the ponies rather than allow them to fall again into the hands of their savage owners. A court martial grew out of the controversy, but nothing serious came of it, as far as I can remember, and General Reynolds was soon afterward, at his own request, placed upon the retired list of the army.[13]

As I was taking my leave, General Reynolds said: "As you have not been out after Indians previously, allow an old soldier to give you this piece of advice. Never stray far from the main column, and never trust a horse or an Indian."

I promised to follow the General's advice as closely as possible, and made my adieus. Orders had reached the Fort that the troops were to

[13]General Crook began the operations of 1876 by making a midwinter march northward from Fort Fetterman through the Tongue and Powder River country in search of the Sioux. The band led by Crazy Horse was discovered wintering on the Powder, and on March 17 a detachment of six companies of cavalry led by General Reynolds surprised and destroyed the village. His precipitate retreat, with victory already attained, still remains unexplained. Although Crook rejoined the detachment a day or two later, lack of supplies and the condition of the command compelled him to retire to Fort Reno and abandon the campaign, chief responsibility for whose failure rested with Reynolds. For this he, along with several other officers, was subjected to court martial. Record of the proceedings has not been found.

move to Fort Laramie on the morning of the 17th, and all felt grateful that the period of inaction was almost at an end. Before giving my account of the famous campaign, I must briefly relate the causes that led to the great Indian War of 1876.

CHAPTER II
The Black Hills Fever

THERE had raged for many years a war between the Sioux Nation, composed of about a dozen different tribes of the same race under various designations, and nearly all the other Indian tribes of the Northwest. The Northern Cheyennes were generally confederated with the Sioux in the field, and the common enemy would seem to have been the Crow, or Absaraka, nation. The Sioux and Cheyennes together were more than a match for all the other tribes combined, and even at this day the former peoples hold their numerical superiority unimpaired. There must be nearly 70,000 Sioux and their kindred tribes in existence, and they still possess at least 5,000 able-bodied warriors, more or less well armed.

But times have greatly changed since the spring of 1876. Then nearly all of Dakota, northern Nebraska, northern Wyoming, northern and eastern Montana lay at the mercy of the savages, who, since the completion of the treaty of 1868, which filled them with ungovernable pride, had been mainly successful in excluding all white men from the immense region, which may be roughly described as bounded on the east by the 104th meridian; on the west by the Big Horn Mountains; on the south by the North Platte, and on the north by the Yellowstone River. In fact, the northern boundary, in Montana, extended practically to the frontier of the British possessions. About 240,000 square miles were comprised in the lands ceded, or virtually surrendered, by the Government to the Indians, one-half for occupation and the establishment of agencies, farms, schools and other mediums of civilization, while the other half was devoted to hunting grounds, which no white man could enter without the special permission of the Indians themselves.

All this magnificent territory was turned over and guaranteed to the savages by solemn treaty with the United States Government. The latter made the treaty with what may be termed undignified haste. The country, at the time, was sick of war. Colonel Fetterman, with his command of nearly one hundred men and three officers, had been overwhelmed and massacred by the Sioux, near Fort Philip Kearny in December, 1866.[14]

Other small detachments of the army had been slaughtered here and there throughout the savage region. The old Montana emigrant road had

[14]The classic account of this affair is Mrs. Margaret Carrington's narrative in *Absaraka, Home of the Crows,* the Lakeside Classics volume for 1950. The number killed in the destruction of Fetterman's detachment, December

been paved with the bodies and reddened with the blood of countless victims of Indian hatred, and, indeed, twenty years ago, strange as it may now appear to American readers, nobody, least of all the authorities at Washington, thought that what was then a howling, if handsome, wilderness would be settled within so short a period by white people. Worse than all else, the Government weakly agreed to dismantle the military forts established along the Montana emigrant trail, running within a few miles of the base of the Big Horn Range, namely, Fort Reno, situated on Middle Fork of the Powder River; Fort Philip Kearny, situated on Clear Fork of the same stream, and Fort C. F. Smith, situated on the Big Horn River, all these being on the east side of the celebrated mountain chain.

The Sioux had no legitimate claim to the Big Horn region. A part of it belonged originally to the Crows, whom the stronger tribe constantly persecuted, and who, by the treaty of 1868, were placed at the mercy of their ruthless enemies. Other friendly tribes, such as the Snakes, or Shoshones, and the Bannocks bordered on the ancient Crow territory, and were treated as foemen

21, 1866, was 79 officers and men and 2 civilian volunteers. Although commonly called a massacre, more correctly speaking it was a battle between two armed forces, in which the white force was annihilated by the victors.

by the greedy Sioux and the haughty Cheyennes.
The abolition of the three forts named fairly in-
flated the Sioux. The finest hunting grounds in
the world had fallen into their possession, and
the American Government, instead of standing
by and strengthening the Crows, their ancient
friends and allies, unwisely abandoned the very
positions that would have held the more ferocious
tribes in check. The Crows had a most unhappy
time of it after the treaty was ratified. Their lands
were constantly raided by the Sioux. Several desperate battles were fought and, finally, the weak-
er tribe was compelled to seek safety beyond the
Big Horn River.

Had the Sioux and the Crows been left to settle the difficulty between themselves, few of the
latter tribe would be left on the face of the earth
today. The white man's government might
make what treaties it pleased with the Indians,
but it was quite a different matter to get the
white man himself to respect the official parch-
ment. Three-fourths of the Black Hills region
and all of the Big Horn were barred by the
Great Father and Sitting Bull against the enterprise of the daring, restless and acquisitive Caucasian race. The military expeditions under
Generals Sully, Connor, Stanley and Custer, all
of which were partially unsuccessful, had attracted the attention of the country to the great

region already specified.[15] The beauty and variety of the landscape; the immense quantities of the noblest species of American game; the serrated mountains and forest-covered hills; the fine grazing lands and rushing streams, born of the snows of the majestic Big Horn peaks; and, above all else, the rumor of great gold deposits, the dream of wealth which hurled Cortez on Mexico and Pizarro on Peru, fired the Caucasian heart with the spirit of adventure and exploration, to which the attendant and well-recognized danger lent an additional zest.

The expedition of General Custer, which entered the Black Hills proper—those of Dakota—in 1874, confirmed the reports of gold finds, and thereafter a wall of fire, not to mention a wall of

[15]Subsequent to the Sioux uprising in Minnesota in 1862, General Alfred Sully led three successive expeditions into the upper Missouri country, in 1863, 1864, and 1865. On the second of these he marched westward across North Dakota from the Missouri to the lower Yellowstone, defeating the Sioux in the battle of Killdeer Mountain, July 28, 1864. In the summer of 1865 General Patrick E. Connor led an expedition to the Powder River country, where on August 19 he established Fort Reno at the Powder River crossing of the Bozeman Trail. The fort was soon abandoned and was rebuilt and reoccupied by General Carrington in 1866. In 1873 General David S. Stanley led an expedition, which Custer and his Seventh Cavalry Regiment accompanied, into the Yellowstone area to guard the building of the Northern Pacific Railroad.

Indians, could not stop the encroachments of
that terrible white race before which all other
races of mankind, from Thibet to Hindostan and
from Algiers to Zululand, have gone down. At
the news of gold the grizzled '49er shook the dust
of California from his feet and started overland,
accompanied by daring comrades, for the far-
distant Hills; the Australian miner left his pick
half buried in the antipodean sands and started,
by ship and saddle, for the same goal; the dia-
mond hunter of Brazil and of the Cape; the veteran prospectors of Colorado and western Montana; the Tar Heels of the Carolina hills; the
reduced gentlemen of Europe; the worried and
worn city clerks of London, Liverpool, New York,
or Chicago; the stout English yeoman, tired of
high rents and poor returns; the sturdy Scotch-
man, tempted from stubborn plodding after
wealth to seek fortune under more rapid conditions; the light-hearted Irishman, who drinks in
the spirit of adventure with his mother's milk;
the daring mine delvers of Wales and of Cornwall;
the precarious gambler of Monte Carlo—in short,
every man who lacked fortune, and who would
rather be scalped than remain poor, saw in the
vision of the Black Hills, El Dorado; and to those
picturesquely somber eminences the adventurers
of the earth, some honest and some the opposite,
came trooping in masses, like clouds at eventide.

In vain did the Government issue its proclamations; in vain were our veteran regiments of cavalry and infantry, commanded by warriors true and tried, drawn up across the path of the daring invaders; in vain were arrests made, baggage seized, horses confiscated and wagons burned; no earthly power could hinder that bewildering swarm of human ants. They laughed at the proclamations, evaded the soldiers, broke jail, did without wagons or outfit of any kind, and, undaunted by the fierce war whoops of the exasperated Sioux, rushed on to the fight for gold with burning hearts and naked hands!

Our soldiers, whom no foe, white, red or black, could make recreant to their flag upon the field of honor, overcome by the moral epidemic, deserted by the squad to join the grand army of indomitable adventurers. And soon, from Buffalo Gap to Inyan Kara,[16] and from Bear Butte to Great Cañon the sound of the pick and spade made all the land resonant with the music of Midas. Thickly as the mushrooms grow in the

---

[16]Inyan Kara is a lone peak some 6400 feet high a few miles south of Sundance in Crook County, Wyoming, near the upper waters of Inyan Kara Creek. Of it, General Charles King wrote (in 1880) that the Sioux called it "Heengha Kahga." The earliest maps simplified this into Inyan Kara; this, in turn, the school children of Deadwood, were taught to call "Indian Carry," *Campaigning with Crook,* 17.

summer nights on the herbage-robbed sheep range, rose "cities" innumerable along the Spearfish and the Deadwood and Rapid creeks. Placer and quartz mines developed with marvelous rapidity, and following the first and boldest adventurers, the eager but timid and ease-loving capitalists, who saw Indians in every sage brush, came in swarms. Rough board shanties and hospital tents were the chief architectural features of the new "cities," which swarmed with gamblers, harlots and thieves, as well as with honest miners. By the fall of 1875 the northern segment of the irregular, warty geological formation known as the Black Hills was prospected, staked and, in fairly good proportion, settled, after the rough, frontier fashion. Pierre and Bismarck on the Missouri River, and Sidney and Cheyenne on the Union Pacific Railroad became the supply depots of the new mining regions, and at that period enjoyed a prosperity which they have not equaled since.

All the passes leading into the Hills from the points mentioned swarmed with hostile Indians, most of whom were well fed at the Agencies, and all of whom boasted of being better armed and better supplied with fixed ammunition than the soldiers of our regular army. The rocks of Buffalo Gap and Red Cañon, particularly, rang with the rifle shots of the savages and the return fire of the hardy immigrants, many of whom paid with their

lives the penalty of their ambition. The stages
that ran to the Hills from the towns on the Missouri and the Union Pacific rarely ever escaped
attack, sometimes by robbers, but oftenest by Indians. All passengers, even the women, who were
at that time chiefly composed of the rough, if not
absolutely immoral, class, traveled with arms in
their hands ready for immediate action. Border
ruffians infested all the cities, and very soon became almost as great a menace to life and property as the savages themselves. Murders and suicides occurred in abundance as the gambling dens
increased and the low class saloons multiplied.

Notwithstanding these discouragements, the
period of 1874, '75 and '76 was the Augustan era,
if the term be not too transcendental, of the Black
Hills. The placer mines were soon exhausted,
and as it required capital to work the quartz ledges
the poor miners or the impatient ones who hoped
to get rich in a day, quickly stampeded for more
promising regions and left the mushroom cities
to the capitalists, the wage workers, the gamblers,
the women in scarlet, and to these, in later days,
may be added the ranchers, or cattle men. Mo-
rality has greatly improved in the Hills since 1876,
and business has settled down to a steady, old-
fashioned gait, but the first settlers still remember,
with vague regret, the stirring times of old when
gold dust passed as currency; when whisky was

bad and fighting general; when claims were held dear and life cheap; when the bronzed hunter or long-haired scout strutted around in half savage pride, and when the renowned Wild Bill, who subsequently met a fate so sudden and so awful, was at once the glory and the terror of that active, but primitive, community.[17] But enough of historical retrospection. I will now resume my narrative of the long and weary march which began at Fort Russell in the ides of May, and terminated at Fort Laramie in the last days of September, 1876.

[17]James B. Hickok, commonly known as Wild Bill, was assassinated at Deadwood, on August 2, 1876. Although his character has been called in question by some writers, he was trusted and admired by numerous prominent contemporaries, among others, General and Mrs. Custer. For Custer's characterization of Wild Bill see *My Life on the Plains*, the Lakeside Classics volume for 1952, pp. 67–71.

CHAPTER III
The March on the Platte

THE final order to move out on the expedition reached Fort Russell, as I think I have already stated, on May 16th. On the morning of the 17th several troops of the Third Cavalry and, I think, one or two of the Second Cavalry, under the order of Col. W. B. Royall, marched northward toward the Platte. It was my desire to accompany this column, but Captain Sutorius, Company E of the Third Cavalry, had to wait, under orders, until the morning of the 19th. Captain Wells, Troop E of the Second Cavalry, had orders to march with Sutorius. As I messed with the latter I was compelled to wait also, and I occupied myself during the brief interval in visiting Cheyenne and taking final leave of my kind friends in that city. I met there Mr. T. C. McMillan, now a State senator, who was going out as correspondent for another Chicago newspaper. Mr. McMillan was in feeble health at the time, but he was determined not to be left behind. He was fortunate in making messing arrangements with Captain Sutorius, who was the soul of hospitality. As McMillan had to purchase a horse and some outfit, we determined to follow, rather than accompany, the two troops mentioned, who marched for Lodge

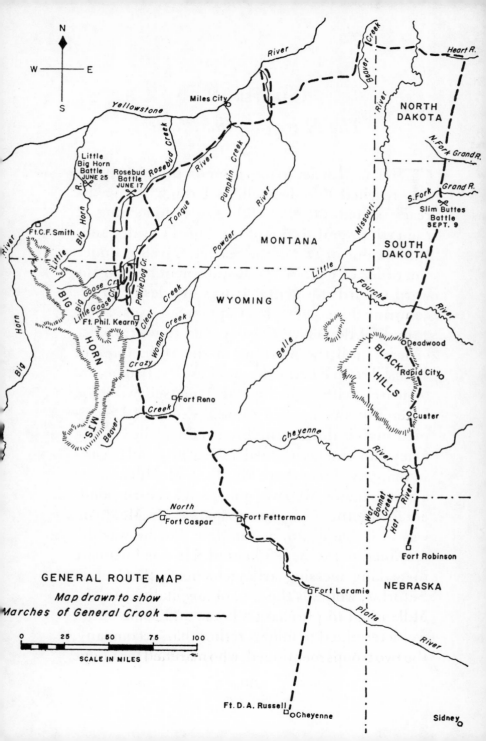

N

W ◆ E

S

River

Yellowstone

Miles City

Beaver Creek

Heart R.

NORTH DAKOTA

N. Fork Grand R.

Little Big Horn Battle JUNE 25

Rosebud Battle JUNE 17

Rosebud Creek

River

Pumpkin Creek

River

S. Fork *Grand R.*

Slim Buttes Battle SEPT. 9

Ft. C. F. Smith

Little Big Horn R.

Tongue

Powder River

MONTANA

Little

SOUTH DAKOTA

Missouri

River

Big Goose Cr.

Prairie Dog Cr.

River

Big Horn

BIG HORN MTS.

Little Goose Cr.

Ft. Phil. Kearny

Clear Creek

WYOMING

Belle

Fourche

River

Deadwood

Crazy Woman Creek

Rapid City

BLACK HILLS

Fort Reno

Beaver Creek

Cheyenne

River

Custer

Creek

GENERAL ROUTE MAP

Map drawn to show

Marches of General Crook ———

North

Fort Caspar

Fort Fetterman

War Bonnet Creek

Hat River

Fort Robinson

0   25   50   75   100

SCALE IN MILES

Fort Laramie

NEBRASKA

Platte

River

Ft. D. A. Russell

Cheyenne

Sidney

Pole Creek, eighteen miles distant from Fort Russell, at day break.

When McMillan had made his purchases we set out on horseback, accompanied for a few miles by the late George O'Brien, to overtake the command. Neither of us had been used to riding for some time, and as the day was fairly warm we did not over-exert ourselves in catching up with the column. There was a well-marked road to Lodge Pole Creek, through a country greatly devoid of beauty, so that we had no difficulty in keeping the trail. Mr. O'Brien bade us adieu on a little rising ground about five miles from the Fort, and then Mac and I urged our animals to a trot, as the afternoon was well advanced.

A little before sundown we came in sight of the shallow valley of Lodge Pole Creek and saw tents pitched along the banks of that stream, while hobbled or lariated horses were grazing around. Several canvas-covered army wagons and a number of soldiers engaged in attending to their horses completed the picture. Captain Sutorius welcomed us warmly, and explained that he had no lieutenant, one being on sick leave and the other detailed for other duty. He introduced us to the two officers of the Second Cavalry, Captain Wells and Lieutenant Sibley. The former was a veteran of the Civil War, covered with honorable scars, bluff, stern and heroic. Lieutenant Sibley, with whose career I was destined to be linked under circumstances which subsequently attracted the attention of the Continent, and which will live long in the tales and traditions of our regular army, was a young West Pointer who had distinguished himself under General Reynolds in the attack upon, and capture of, Crazy Horse's village on March 17th of that eventful year. He was about the middle height, well but slightly built, and with a handsome, expressive face.[18]

It does not take very long to become thoroughly at home with soldiers if they take a liking to you, and we were soon seated in Captain Sutorius' tent, partaking very industriously of plain military fare. The conversation turned chiefly on the campaign upon which we were entering. Captain Wells said that the Indians were in stronger force than most people imagined, and that General Crook, accustomed mostly to the southern In-

[18]Lieutenant Frederick W. Sibley graduated from the U.S. Military Academy in June, 1874 and was commissioned second lieutenant in the Second U.S. Cavalry. He attained the rank of captain in 1893 and major in July, 1902. In February, 1890 he was brevetted first lieutenant for gallant service in action against the Indians on the Little Big Horn, July 7, 1876.

Captain Elijah R. Wells enlisted as a private soldier in the Second Dragoon Regiment in April, 1858, rising to the rank of first sergeant in July, 1862, when he was commissioned second lieutenant and assigned to the second U.S. Cavalry Regiment. He became a captain in 1867, and retired from the army on April 23, 1879.

dians, hardly estimated at its real strength the powerful array of the savages. He joked in rough soldier fashion McMillan and myself on having had our hair cropped, as, he said, it would be a pity to cheat the Sioux out of our scalps. The bugle soon sounded, the horses were placed on the line—that is, tied by their halters to a strong rope stretched between wagons—curried and fed. The mules joined in their usual lugubrious evening chorus. We had a smoke, followed by a moderately strong toddy, and very soon, the sentinels having been posted, Sutorius, Mac and I lay down to rest on blankets and buffalo robes spread in the Captain's commodious wall tent.

I slept the sleep of the just, although I was occasionally conscious of McMillan's eternal cough and the Captain's profound snore, and thus opened, for me, the Big Horn and Yellowstone campaign. In the midst of a dream in which Indians, scalping-knives, warwhoops and tomahawks figured prominently, I was aroused by the shrill blast of the cavalry trumpets sounding the reveille. I sprang up instantly, as did my companions, made a very hasty and incomplete toilet, and, having swallowed a cup of coffee served in an army tin, was ready for the road. The little outfit moved like clockwork, and by six o'clock everything had pulled out of camp. The previous day's ride had rendered me quite stiff in the knee joints, as I had been riding with short stirrups. I soon learned that if a man wishes to avoid acute fatigue on a long march it is better to lengthen the stirrup leathers. I accordingly adopted the military plan, and found some relief. Indians, by the way, generally ride with short stirrups on long journeys. I suppose they get used to it, but I never could.

The country through which we were passing was monotonously ugly. In most places the ground was covered with sage-brush and cacti, and the clouds of alkaline dust raised by the hoofs of the troop horses were at once blinding and suffocating. I was tormented by thirst, and soon exhausted all the water in my canteen. The Captain, who was an old campaigner, advised me to place a small pebble in my mouth. I did so and saliva was produced, which greatly relieved my suffering. I found afterward, on many a hard, hot, dusty march, when water was scarce, that this simple remedy against thirst is very effective. The less water a soldier drinks on the march, the better it will be for his health.

The command was halted several times in order that the horses might have a chance to graze, and also to enable the inexperienced among the soldiers to get some of the soreness out of their bones. I was devoutly grateful for every halt. The shadows from the west were lengthening as we rode into camp at a place called Bear Springs, where wood and water abounded. The scenes and incidents of the preceding camp were duplicated here, but I learned that on the morrow we were to catch up with the column in advance, which was under the orders of Col. William B. Royall of the Third Cavalry, since colonel of the Fourth Cavalry, and now retired.[19]

We were in the saddle at daybreak, and marched with greater rapidity than usual. There were no halts of any great duration. About noon we encountered a stout young officer, attended by an orderly, riding at break-neck pace toward us. He halted, saluted the Captain, and said "Colonel Royall's compliments, and he requests that you march without halting until you join him. The other battalion is halted about a dozen miles farther on. I am going to the rear with orders, and will rejoin to-morrow or the day after."

The Captain introduced me to Lieut. Frederick Schwatka, whom I was to meet often afterward in that campaign, and whose name has since become

[19]Colonel William B. Royall was commissioned lieutenant in the Second Missouri Mounted Volunteers, July 31, 1846. Mustered out of the service in October, 1848, he became first lieutenant in the Second U.S. Cavalry Regiment in March, 1856, serving thereafter as an officer until his retirement, October 19, 1887. He was several times brevetted for gallant and meritorious conduct in the Civil War, and in 1890 was awarded the brevet of brigadier general for gallant service in Crook's battle on the Rosebud, June 17, 1876. He died December 13, 1895.

familiar to all the reading world as the intrepid
discoverer of the fate of Sir John Franklin, amid
the eternal snows and unspeakable perils of the
polar regions. Schwatka briefly but courteously
acknowledged the Captain's introduction, and,
having drained a little elixir of life from his superior's canteen, set out like a whirlwind to fulfill
his mission.[20]

[20]Frederick Schwatka was a native of Galena, Illinois,
who was taken to Oregon in early boyhood by his parents.
He graduated from the U.S. Military Academy in 1871
and for half a dozen years thereafter was chiefly engaged
in frontier service. However, his restlessly inquiring mind
won distinction for him in circles far removed from Indian
campaigns and western posts. In 1875 he was admitted to
the Nebraska bar, and a year later obtained a medical degree from Bellevue Hospital Medical College in New York.
   Intrigued by geographical curiosity, he persuaded the
American Geographical Society to finance an expedition,
of which he was joint commander, to solve the 30-year-old
mystery of the fate of Sir John Franklin's Arctic exploring
expedition. The party left New York City in June, 1878
and returned, brilliantly successful, over two years later,
having among other things made a sledge-journey of over
3200 miles, the largest such journey then known. More
significant, perhaps, was Schwatka's demonstration of the
fact that white men could exist in the Arctic regions by
adopting the native way of life. Schwatka resigned from
the army in 1885. He engaged in several other explora-
tions, and authored several books concerning them. His
useful life ended prematurely in 1892 through an over-
dose of poison, taken to relieve a painful stomach disorder.
G. W. Cullum, *Biographical Register of the Officials and
Graduates of the U.S. Academy, and Dictionary of American
Biography.*

"Close up there! Trot!" shouted Captain Sutorius, who was in advance. "Trot!" repeated Captain Wells, in stentorian tones; and away we went, up hill and down dale, leaving the wagon train to the care of its ordinary escort. After going at a trot for what seemed to me, galled and somewhat jaded as I was, an interminable time, we finally reached an elevation in the road from which we beheld, although at a considerable distance, what seemed to be a force of cavalry, apparently going into camp. We continued advancing, but at a slower pace, and within an hour came upon the rearmost wagons of Royall's train, guarded by a troop of horse. We soon reached the main body, and I had then the pleasure of meeting Colonel Royall, a tall, handsome Virginian of about fifty, with a full gray mustache, dark eyebrows overhanging a pair of bright blue eyes, and a high forehead, on the apex of which, through the cropped hair, as he raised his cap in salute, appeared one of several scars inflicted by a rebel saber in front of Richmond during the Civil War. Among the other officers to whom I was introduced I remember Col. Anson Mills, then in his prime, Lieutenant Lemley, Captain Andrews, Lieutenant Foster, Lieutenant Joseph Lawson and Lieutenant Charles Morton, all of the Third Cavalry; and Captain Rawolle, Lieutenant Huntington, and others of the Second Cavalry.

As it was still early in the day, and as our halting place was not desirable for the horses, Colonel Royall, after our wagon train had closed up, changed his mind about going into camp and the march was continued to a place called Huntoon's Ranch in the Chugwater Valley, where, having ridden over thirty miles since morning, I was rendered exceedingly happy by the order to halt and pitch our tents.[21] These latter did not come up for some time, and being as hungry as a bear I was glad to satisfy my craving with raw army bacon, hard tack and a tin full of abominably bad water. Then I lay down on my horse-blanket under a tree and fell fast asleep.

Supper was being served in Captain Sutorius' tent before I thought of waking up, and it took a good, honest poke in the ribs from the hardy Captain to recall me from the land of dreams. In spite of my long nap I slept soundly throughout the night and awoke early in the morning to hear the rain falling in torrents and pattering on our canvas shelter like a thousand drumsticks. An orderly came with the compliments of the commanding officer, to instruct the Captain not to strike tents, as, if the rain did not cease before 8 o'clock the

[21]Captain Bourke records that the rancher, Huntoon, had been killed by Indians, his body when found disclosing eleven wounds. The marauders were believed to have come from the Red Cloud Agency. *On the Border with Crook*, 285.

battalion would remain in camp, as the wagons could not be moved in the dense mud. This was welcome news to Mr. McMillan and myself, as we were both exceedingly fatigued. The rain did not cease to fall for twenty-four hours longer, and it was well on toward noon on the morning of May 23d when we dragged ourselves painfully out of the Chugwater mud and took up our march to Fort Laramie.

This march was brief and uneventful, and we were in camp on the prairie surrounding the Fort shortly after 1 o'clock. We picked up a few more troops at this point, and as Colonel Royall was fearful of being late at the rendezvous of still distant Fort Fetterman no time was lost in getting the command ready for the hard road before it. The entire column crossed the Laramie and North Platte rivers early on the morning of the 24th. The sky was cloudy, and a raw wind blew from the east. All of us hoped that the cool weather would continue, but we were doomed to sore disappointment in that, as in other, respects.

The men of the command were, for the most part, young, but well seasoned, and in their blue shirts, broad felt hats, cavalry boots and blue, or buckskin, pantaloons, for on an Indian campaign little attention is paid to uniform, looked both athletic and warlike. Their arms were as bright as hard rubbing could make them, and around the

waist of every stalwart trooper was a belt filled
with sixty rounds of fixed ammunition for the
Springfield carbine. Each man carried also a supply of revolver cartridges. The sabers had been
left behind at the different posts as useless en-
cumbrances. I well remember the martial bearing
of Guy V. Henry's fine troop of the Third, as with
arms clanking and harness jingling it trotted
rapidly along our whole flank in the dawn twi-
light to take its place at the head of the column.
"There goes Henry!" said our Captain, as the
troopers trotted by. They were fine fellows that
morning, and proved themselves to be as brave
and enduring as they were imposing in appearance, throughout the campaign.

Chapter IV
On to Fort Fetterman

OUR route was over an unfrequented path, known as the Old Utah route, through the Indian reservation on the left bank of the North Platte. This road was selected in order that the delay and expense of crossing the rapid river at Fetterman might be avoided.[22] The portion of the territory through which we moved had not been described, at least by the newspapers, for the reason that very few people cared to roam at that time through so dangerous and desolate a region in small parties.

Our first day's march from Fort Laramie was begun at 6 o'clock A. M., and by 12:30, including two halts, we went into camp on a bend of the Platte, twenty-four miles from our starting point. The first part of our route lay through an undulating grass country, lying within easy distance of the river. Ten miles through this kind of land

[22]The route followed by General Carrington from Fort Laramie to Fort Fetterman in 1866 (shown on the map prefixed to Mrs. Carrington's *Absaraka, Home of the Crows*), ran up the right or southerly side of the North Platte. By crossing the North Platte at Fort Laramie, Colonel Royall's detachment ascended the left, or northerly side of the river. Mrs. Carrington alludes to this "northern Mormon road." See *Absaraka, Home of the Crows*, 98.

brought us to an immense park, situated in the midst of five dotted bluffs, where we halted for some minutes. This "park" was simply the portal to one of the longest, darkest and most tortuous passes that can well be imagined.

It was a perfect labyrinth. Bluffs rose on each side to an immense altitude, and the turns were so abrupt that our advancing column frequently expected to bring up in a cul-de-sac. It was up hill and down dale for eight long miles, and had Colonel Royall been opposed by a capable foe, his part of Crook's expedition would never have reached the rendezvous. A couple of hundred resolute men there could have prevented the march of a vast army. In fact, the larger the latter the less chance would there be for successful battle. But we passed on unharmed through this Killecrankie of Wyoming.[23]

The sun shone magnificently and it was a splendid sight to see our seven companies of cavalry, their arms glittering and their equipment rattling as they 'wound like a monstrous serpent around that gloomy vale.' In some places the ascents and descents were so steep and rugged that

[23]Which General Carrington's party in 1866 had named Camp Phisterer Canon. For Mrs. Carrington's description, see *Absaraka, Home of the Crows*, 92–94. At the Pass of Killiecrankie in Perthshire, Scotland, a royalist army 4000 strong was crushed by a smaller Jacobite army, July 27, 1689.

the command had to dismount from front to rear and lead their horses. Sitting Bull lost a fine opportunity for clipping Crook's wings, and nearly all the officers recognized the fact. But we neither saw, heard, nor felt any Indians. Our troops moved on unmolested.

> Where's the embattled foe they seek?
> The cap or watch-fires, where?
> For save the eagle screaming high
> No sign of life is there.

A solitary elk standing on the edge of a cliff far above our pathway was the only living thing that, to all appearances, beheld our column.

After more than two hours of unceasing travel through the gorge, we finally unwound ourselves therefrom and struck a red-clay country where we could not find enough grass to give our weary horses a decent lunch; we did not, therefore, halt, but pushed on to a camp on the river bend, when we thankfully left the saddle and stretched our limbs upon the parched earth. Owing to the roughness of the road, the wagon-train and rear guard were more than five hours behind. Yet, in that lone camping ground we found the graves of two Mormon emigrants, killed, it was supposed, by Indians. One grave had over it a rude slab with the name, "Sarah Gibbons, July, 1854," cut upon it. The other inscription was absolutely indecipherable. Reveille sounded at dawn on

Thursday, May 25th, and the march was resumed one hour later. Prepared as we were to encounter a desert country, the scene that met our view was far beyond all expectation.

Our line of march was through what appeared to be a succession of brick-yards and extinct lime-kilns. In order to secure a good wagon-road we were compelled to avoid the Platte, and, with the exception of one stagnant pool, during that weary ride of thirty-five miles we saw no water until we struck the river again. The sun burned us almost to the bone and every man's complexion was scarlet. Despite all injunctions to the contrary, the tired and thirsty troops made a general raid upon the Platte when we reached that stream, and drank to satiety. The cheekiest of land speculators or the most conscienceless of newspaper correspondents could not say a word in behalf of that infernal region, which it would be the acme of exaggeration to term land. But some of our old Indian scouts said it was Arabia Felix compared with what lay between us and the Powder River. Why the government of the United States should keep an army for the purpose of robbing the Indians of such a territory is an unsolvable puzzle. It is a solemn mockery to call the place a reservation, unless dust, ashes and rocks be accounted of value to mankind. Not even one Indian could manage to exist on the desert tract over which we rode. Trees, there were absolutely none, unless down by the river, where some scrub timber occasionally appeared.

Some of the scenery was striking and savage. In the early morning we had the huge peak of Laramie, snow-covered, on our left. At 10 o'clock it was behind us, and at 2 o'clock, when we went into camp, it was almost in our front. This will give some idea of the zig-zag course we had to follow. Laramie Peak is a gigantic landmark, a fit sentinel over that portion of the great American desert.

"Boots and saddles" put us once more on the road, Friday morning. Instead of growing better, the country increased in worthlessness as we proceeded. We struck what are significantly termed the "Bad Lands," a succession of sand-pits and hills, with neither cacti nor sage-weed, which are almost universal there, nor blade of grass to relieve the wearied eye. Persons afflicted with weak vision are compelled to wear goggles while riding through those sands, which are white as chalk and dazzling as quicksilver. After making over twenty miles we again went to sleep upon the Platte, and our Colonel said we were just twenty miles from Fort Fetterman.

Daybreak on Saturday, May 27th, found us once more en route. The company of the Third Cavalry with which I messed, having been in ad-

vance on the previous day, formed the rear guard
and, consequently, marched at will. It was pretty
tedious, as the unfortunate mules of the wagon
train were nearly worn out, their backs galled by
heavy loads, and their legs swollen by a long
march.

We again struck a hilly country, full of red
sandstone and cut up by countless ravines, some
of which were of incredible depth. The Captain
determined to take a short cut from the wagon
road in order to explore the nature of the ground.
Mounting a high hill some ten miles from where
we had camped, we beheld a long, low, white
building on a bold, bare bluff, to the northwest.
This was our first glimpse of Fort Fetterman,
called after the gallant and unfortunate Captain
Fetterman, who perished only a few years previously in the Fort Philip Kearny massacre. Taking
the short cut, we found ourselves in a regular
trap, and were obliged to ride up and down places
that would make some of our city riders feel like
making their wills. Our Captain had, however, a
sure-footed horse, and did not dismount. Neither
did any of his men, and I, for the honor of my
calling, was compelled to follow their example.
Our horses nearly stood upon their heads, but
they did not go over. They were all bred in that
country and were sure-footed as mules. Try to
hold them up with the rein and down they go.

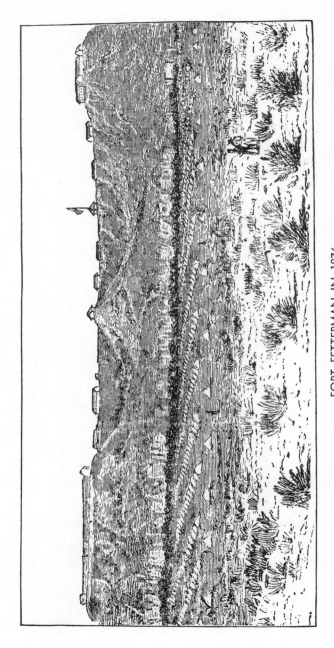

FORT FETTERMAN IN 1876

Reproduced from General Charles King's *Campaigning with Crook.*

Give them their own way and they'll carry you in safety over a glacier.

Having traversed about fifty ravines, we again reached the upper trail, much to my delight, for I had grown tired of steeple-chasing. Our experiment revealed nothing new in the character of the soil—if sand can be designated by that name. If neither flat nor stale, it certainly was unprofitable. By the time we regained the road the place of rendezvous lay right beneath us, and long lines of tents and clouds of cavalry horses and pack mules grazing in the valley informed us that Colonel Evans' column from Medicine Bow, the shorter route by one-half, had already gone into camp. At the same moment a long cloud of dust through which carbine-barrels and bridle-bits occasionally flashed, four miles ahead, showed us our main body entering the lines. The march was then down hill. Our teamsters lashed up their beasts until they cantered. The rear guard put spurs to their horses and trotted after. Half an hour later we were on the camping ground, and saw the desolate fort grinning at us from the bleak hill on the other side of the Platte. And thus we completed the ride from Russell to Fetterman.

Some officers informed us that the ferry between the camp and Fort Fetterman had broken down, and that we could not get our mail or send dispatches. The river at that point is so rapid and so full of whirlpools that few men care to swim it, and most horses refuse to do so. A wagon driver, together with a sergeant and two private soldiers of the Second Cavalry, tried the experiment of swimming their horses over a few days before and all were drowned. It was absolutely necessary for me to cross the river, and some other correspondents were in the same position. When we reached the ferry we found that it had been patched up in a temporary manner, and concluded to go across. When near the Fetterman bank the rope broke and we should have been swept down stream, at the imminent risk of drowning, but for the heroism of Lieutenant and Commissary Bubb, who plunged into the stream on horseback, caught a cable which somebody threw toward him, and towed us in safety to shore amid the plaudits of the spectators. We proceeded to the fort immediately and found General Crook at the commandant's quarters, busily engaged in forwarding the organization of his troops. He appeared to be in high spirits, and laughed grimly at our rough and miserably tanned appearance, stubble beards, dirty clothes and peeled noses.

"Oh," said he, "this is only the prelude. Wait until the play proper begins. After that you can say you were through the mill."

"We came over a pretty rough road, General," said one of our party.

"Yes," he answered, "that is a bad road, but there are worse in Wyoming. We've got to go over many of them."

He kindly invited us to dinner, but we preferred the sutler's establishment and he directed an orderly to show us there. Fort Fetterman is now abandoned. It was a hateful post—in summer, hell, and in winter, Spitzbergen. The whole army dreaded being quartered there, but all had to take their turn. Its abandonment was a wise proceeding on the part of the Government.[24]

[24]Fort Fetterman was situated on the south bank of the North Platte at the mouth of La Prele Creek. Near here the Bozeman Road leading northward to Montana and the Mormon and Oregon trails leading westward to Fort Caspar and the Sweetwater, diverged. The fort was established on July 19, 1867 and named in honor of Captain W. J. Fetterman who had been killed in the Fetterman Defeat, December 21, 1866. By 1872 the fort had become a well-equipped four-company post. In 1878 the garrison was withdrawn and almost all of the military reservation of sixty square miles was transferred to the Interior Department.

CHAPTER V

Marching on Powder River

GENERAL Crook, impatient for action, hardly gave us time to have our soiled clothing properly washed and dried, when, everything being ready, he marched us northward at noon on the 29th of May. Two companies of the Third Cavalry, commanded by Captain Van Vliet and Lieutenant Emmet Crawford had preceded us on the road to Fort Reno to look out for the expected contingent of Crow Indians from Montana. The remainder, a formidable cavalcade, cemented, as it were, by a few companies of stalwart infantry who furnished escort for the long wagon-train, streamed away from the Platte at a brisk pace and came to a halt at Sage Creek, thirteen miles north of Fetterman, in the afternoon. We were then fairly on the road to the Indian country proper— the lands secured to the Sioux, so far as that intangible instrument called a treaty could secure them anything. By the precautions taken in posting pickets and keeping the command well closed up on the march, even the most inexperienced could understand that we were in a region where active hostilities might begin at any moment.

At the Sage Creek camp, I was introduced by General Crook to Mr. Robert A. Strahorn, a distinguished western newspaper correspondent, who had made a reputation over the nom de plume of Alter Ego, and who in every situation proved himself as fearless as he was talented. The General also introduced me to Mr. Davenport of the New York *Herald,* and to Mr. Wasson of the California *Alta,* who had had extensive experience in many Indian campaigns. Mr. Davenport was entirely unused to frontier life and some of the young officers and his brother correspondents used to banter him a good deal with regard to the horrors of Indian warfare. He took it all in good part at the time, but he found means, before the campaign closed, to get more than even with some of the jokers. As a rule, all the correspondents got along well together, but one or two of them did not succeed in making themselves liked by several of the officers. Of all earthly experiences, none so tests the strength and weakness of human nature as an Indian campaign, especially when attended by hardship and hunger.

As we advanced, the commanding officers of the outfit increased and multiplied exceedingly. First, as a matter of course, came General Crook. Then Colonel Royall, frank and direct of speech, and often very emphatic in his observations to his subordinates. Then came Major Evans, a melancholy, philosophically inclined officer, devoted to literature, suffering from an old wound, and having, to all appearance, registered a vow never to smile, in any sense. Maj. H. E. Noyes, commanding a company, was appointed commander of the five troops of the Second Cavalry; while the ten troops of the Third Cavalry were divided into three battalions under the three senior company commanders, Col. Guy V. Henry, Maj. Anson Mills and Capt. Fred Van Vliet. Maj. Alexander Chambers commanded the five companies of the Fourth and Ninth Infantry, a very efficient body of men. Major John V. Furey looked after the wagon train, as he was quartermaster of the expedition, and Chief Packer, Tom Moore, an old follower of General Crooks, looked after the pack mule train and all that appertained thereto.

Nearly all of the officers mentioned had aides and adjutants, all of whom had orderlies, who blew their bugles with startling frequency and rode from one end of the line to the other as if the devil himself was after them. It is astonishing how much our bold dragoons can swear on proper provocation. The sentimental fair ones who so much admire our shoulder-strapped and be-frogged cavalry officers in a brilliant ball room ought to see and hear them when out on a rough campaign. They are then innocent of boiled shirts, their beards become a stubble, and only for the inevitable yellow stripe, which the weather turns muddy in color, on their pantaloons, they could hardly be distinguished from the private soldiers of their respective commands. The same is also true of the infantry officers. In contrast, however, with the professional mule packers and whackers, the officers were models of the early Christian type of mankind.

We had along a trifle over 1,000 mules, all immensely loaded with ammunition and other supplies. They were unamiable and unattractive animals, awkward, yet handy with their feet, and vilely discordant. The General, however, knew their value on a campaign, and had great respect for their eccentricities of manner and habit. Notwithstanding, I consider that the average mule is obstinate and even morose, in manner, and filthy, not to say immodest, in habit. But the animal has his fine points also. He is surer, if slower, than the horse, and can live where the latter would surely starve. Ears polite would be immeasurably shocked by the sounds and observations that accompany the starting of a pack train from camp in the early morning. The hybrids are cinched or girthed so tight by the packers that they are almost cut in two. Naturally the beasts don't want to move under such circumstances. They therefore stand stock still. This irritates the packers, who swear in a most artistic and perfectly inexhaustible fashion. They welt the animals with their rawhides most unmercifully, and the brutes

reply with their heels and the batteries of nature
in a most effective, if somewhat obscene, manner.
Suddenly, and generally simultaneously, they
dash forward, and matters run more tranquilly
during the rest of the day. Such is a part of the
romance of war. The mule-drivers used to have
an excellent time of it, and lived far better than
the soldiers. The latter were expected to do all
the fighting, while the mule-whackers had the
better part of the feasting.[25]

Although the country through which Colonel
Royall's column moved along the left bank of the

[25]With the wagon train on the northward march from
Fort Fetterman went the notorious Calamity Jane, disguised as a teamster. Near Fort Reno her disguise was discovered and she was placed under arrest to be returned to
Fort Fetterman. Much to the embarrassment, then and
subsequently, of General Mills, she proclaimed her familiarity with him, to the great glee of the soldiers. She had,
in fact, served as cook for one of his next-door neighbors
at Camp Sheridan. Calamity Jane was an unfortunate
child of the frontier whose father was killed and her
mother desperately wounded by the Sioux when she was
a mere infant. Brought in to Fort Laramie, she was adopted
by Sergeant Bassett and his wife and soon became the pet
of the garrison. Most of her adult career is associated with
the Black Hills area, where she was buried at Deadwood
in 1903. At the time of her Powder River exploit she may
have been about sixteen years old. Sentimental fiction
aside, she led an abandoned life, summed up by Doane
Robinson, the South Dakota historian, in the statement
that the best that can be said of her is that "there is some
good in the worst of us." Mills, *My Story,* 401, and Robinson, *Encyclopaedia of South Dakota.*

Platte to Fetterman was practically a wilderness, the section between that fort and Crazy Woman's Fork is not particularly bad; but there are enough Bad Lands here and there to about counterbalance the more fertile portions. The grass ranges along a few small streams in spring time and the early summer are fairly good, but the soil is, as a rule, poor and sandy, and the winter tarries long on the old Bozeman Trail, which General Crook's brigade traveled over for several hundred miles.[26] In fact, the whole country had a kind of arid, half-starved look in the beginning of June, 1876, and I fancy it has hardly improved much in appearance since that period. The grass seemed to be exceedingly coarse in most places, and was disfigured, wherever the eye turned, by the omnipresent sage brush and cruel cacti.

I wrote at the time to the paper I represented that ranchmen who cared little or nothing for the

[26]John M. Bozeman was a Georgian who joined the gold rush to Montana in 1862. Gold seekers then had great difficulty in reaching the Montana mines and Bozeman conceived the project of opening a direct route through the Indian country from Virginia City to the Oregon Trail at Julesburg, Colorado. To this effort he devoted his remaining years, being killed by Indians on April 20, 1867. The opening of the Bozeman Road and the subsequent establishment of forts along it precipitated the Red Cloud War of 1866–68, described in part by Mrs. Carrington in *Absaraka, Home of the Crows*. Crook's army in 1876 was following the Bozeman Road, as General Carrington had done two years before.

comforts of civilization could raise large herds of cattle in that region if the Sioux were subdued or friendly, but that for purposes of tillage the soil was unavailable. My candid judgment was that during a march of about 300 miles I had not seen a twenty-acre tract that could approach even the medium agricultural lands of Illinois or Iowa in productive power. I had not seen a single acre that could compare with the prime farming lands of the old States. The wealth of the soil must have been very deep down, for it certainly was not visible on the surface, except in the form of alkaline deposits, which resembled hoar frost. It lacked then, and I suppose it lacks still, several essentials toward making it reasonably habitable: first, water; second, timber; third, climate. In rocks, hills, ants, snakes, weeds and alkali that portion of Wyoming is rich indeed. If there should happen to be any gold in the heart of the Big Horn Mountains God must have placed it there to make up for the comparative worthlessness of a large portion of the Territory. I observed, also, that it needed neither a professor nor a philosopher to predict that that particular range of country could never become a part of that great agricultural Northwest, which is justly called the granary of the world; and that its highest destiny was to become a mammoth cattle range. My humble prediction has been fulfilled. Myriads of domestic

cattle have taken the place of the picturesque
buffaloes, and where the red Indian used to ride
on his wild forays the enterprising cowboy now
cracks his horse-whip and rounds up his herds.

Colonel Royall, at the outset of our march,
used to have us on the road at 5 o'clock in the
morning, but General Crook, on assuming command, fixed the hour at 6 o'clock for the infantry
and at 7:30 o'clock for the cavalry, in order that
the horses might have sufficient rest, as he intended to make night marches in pursuit of the
hostiles, accompanied by his pack train only, after
the campaign had been fully developed.

He detached from Sage Creek two companies of
the Third Cavalry under Captains Meinhold and
Vroom to patrol the country to the westward and
report the presence of fresh Indian trails, if any
such existed. The detachment took along four
days' rations, and was ordered to rejoin us at old
Fort Reno, on the Powder River. On the 30th of
May we marched from Sage Creek to what is called
the South Fork of the Cheyenne River, a puny,
muddy-looking rivulet, the rotten banks of which
were fringed with cottonwood trees and tangled,
rich undergrowth. The water was shockingly bad
and made many of the men quite sick. It was at
this point, during the scout of the preceding
March, that the Indians shot and killed the chief
herder of the expedition, the very first day out

from Fort Fetterman. We all felt that we were on
hostile and dangerous ground, but we were allowed to sleep in peace. The pickets, however,
were doubled, and every precaution against a
surprise was taken.

On the 31st of May the weather, which had
been rather mild and pleasant for several days,
suddenly changed. The thermometer fell to zero
and the wind rose to the proportions of a hurri-
cane. The sky became deeply overcast with omi-
nous-looking clouds, and whirlwinds raised columns of alkaline dust, which scalded our eyes and
gave to every object a hazy and filthy appearance.
Many of the tents were blown down, and the men
shivered around their watchfires as if it were midwinter. It was a relief to everybody when morning
came and "the general" was sounded. We marched
on Wind Creek, a very poor apology for a stream,
about twenty miles northward. Our course lay
over a somewhat bare, but undulating country.
About noon the clouds partially lifted and the
sun of the last day of May shone out fitfully to
cheer our weary road.

We soon gained the summit of an unusually
high swell in the prairie, called in frontier parlance a "divide," and beheld, with some degree
of joy, to our left and front, distant perhaps one
hundred miles, the chilly, white summits of the
mighty Big Horn Mountains. From this same di-

vide we had an exceptionally fine view of that portion of Wyoming which we had marched over. Looking backward, we could see the faint blue outline of Laramie Peak, almost dipping below the horizon. On our right, and almost due east, the dark group of the Black Hills of Dakota could be descried through a fieldglass. On our right front, northeastward, the Pumpkin Buttes, four long, somewhat irregular, but mountain-like, formations several hundred feet in height arose abruptly from the very bosom of the Bad Lands. Those buttes run very nearly north and south, the northernmost being nearly abreast of Fort Reno. But soon the lurking storm came back upon us with renewed fury and there was an end, for that day at least, of our enjoyment of savage scenery.

Wind Creek did not belie its name. A more comfortless bivouac rarely fell to a soldier's lot. Every inch of ground was covered with some species of cacti, each seemingly more full of thorns than its neighbor. The water was simply execrable, the wood scarce and the weather bitterly cold. By order of General Crook, who did not desire to be hampered with too many impediments, we had left our tent stoves at Fort Fetterman, and as the thermometer continued to fall we began to think that we had accidentally marched into Alaska. The storm, as night advanced, increased in fury, and came near playing us the shabby

trick which it inflicted on the English army in
1854, when nearly all the tents of the Crimean
expeditionary force were swept into the bay of
Balaklava. When the grim morning of Thursday,
June 1, 1876, broke upon Wind River, snow was
falling as thickly as it does in Chicago about
New Year's.

The shower did not continue very long, and
when it ceased we found the temperature much
more comfortable. We marched on that day to a
dreary place known as the Dry Fork of the Powder River, something over twenty miles. As every
officer and soldier wore a service overcoat, the
brigade looked much better, because more uniform, than usual. The first half of our journey
lay through and over a mountainous region, but
when we reached the highest crest of the divide,
and the valley of Powder River lay stretched out
before and beneath us, mile on mile, we concluded
that we had at last struck a portion of Wyoming
which we could praise with a fairly good con-
science.

Although the soil was marred by the brush-
wood and weeds which disfigure, more or less,
most portions of the Territory, the valley showed
evidences of fertility. It is inundated periodically
by copious mountain torrents, which follow the
"snow melts" and the rain storms. The vegetation
is comparatively good and a belt of cottonwood

timber follows the whole course of the river, from its source among the Big Horn Mountains to where it falls into the Yellowstone, opposite Sheridan Buttes, in Montana. We found many traces of Indian villages near our encampment, which indicated that the valley was a favorite haunt of the savages in the days, not so long removed, when the buffaloes covered the range as far as the eye could reach. Antelopes were the largest game we found in the locality because the buffaloes had chosen, temporarily, to graze on the then great ranges of the Yellowstone and Tongue rivers.

As we approached the river a young staff officer raised his field-glass to his eyes and looked steadily to the westward for some minutes. He soon rode up to General Crook and informed him that he had observed what he believed to be a cloud of Indians hovering on our left. The distance was too great to allow any of us to make out the precise character of the rapidly moving objects. Colonel Henry's company of the Third Cavalry was at once ordered to reconnoiter, and set out at a fast trot over the prairie. Our column had begun to straggle somewhat, owing to the uneven character of the road, and an aide-de-camp came riding rapidly from front to rear, shouting "Close up, close up!" which we did with great alacrity. Judging by the amount of bustle, the uninitiated among us began to believe that Sitting Bull and all his warriors must be close upon our heels.

A fight was expected, muskets were examined and carbines unslung. The saddle girths were tightened, and nearly every man in the outfit assumed a proper look of martial ferocity. Very soon we observed Henry's command approaching the rapidly-moving enemy, who seemed to be coming on with great fearlessness. The troop came to a halt, while the other party continued their movement in advance. Through our field-glasses we could then see that those dreaded Indians wore blue uniforms, rode American horses, and had a small pack train with them. They were, in fact, the two troops of cavalry detached under Meinhold and Vroom at Sage Creek by the General, returning from their scout. "What a fuss about nothing!" observed Crook, as he closed his telescope and resumed his place at the head of the column.

We rode almost immediately into camp on the Dry Fork of Powder River, and then we learned that the scouting party had seen no Indians or traces of Indians during their long ride. Captain Meinhold, a very fine-looking German officer with a romantic history, told me smilingly that the party had found no water since leaving the Platte, but that they had shot some deer, and in order to quench their thirst had emptied their brandy flasks with true military promptitude. Captain Vroom was then a magnificent specimen of the human race, tall, well-built and good-looking. He has since grown much stouter, the result, doubtless, of the absence of Indian campaigns, which would now seem to be almost at an end. One of Meinhold's men had wounded himself mortally by the accidental discharge of his pistol, and the poor fellow had suffered intensely on the subsequent march. He was placed in an ambulance, and made as comfortable as possible.

The absence of Indians surprised the men who had been over the road previously. Around the camp-fires, that evening, both officers and rank and file asked: "Where are the Sioux?" This interrogation was addressed by Captain Sutorius to Captain Wells at a bivouac fire of the Third Cavalry.

"Don't be alarmed," said Wells, in his grim, abrupt way. "If they want to find us, we will hear from them when we least expect. If they don't want to find us, we won't hear from them at all, but I think they will."

"They have neglected us strangely up to date," remarked Lieutenant Lemley. "Last time they serenaded us with rifle-shots every evening after we crossed the Platte. You have heard, I suppose, the joke on Lieutenant Bourke of Crook's staff?"

"No, let's hear it," shouted half a dozen future generals.

"Very well. We were camped on Crazy Woman's—a d—d mean place—and no Indians had been disturbing us for some nights. The thing was growing stale and we were all impatient for some kind of excitement, as it was awfully cold and we were slowly freezing to death. 'Let us go up to Bourke's tent,' some one suggested that night, and there all of us went. The Lieutenant was engaged in scanning a military map by the light of a candle. 'Hello, Bourke,' said one of the party, 'ain't you afraid the Indians will ventilate your tent if you keep that light burning?'

" 'Oh, no,' said Bourke. 'The Indians that have been firing into us are a small flying party. You may rely on it that you won't hear anything more from them this side of Tongue River. The distance is too great from their villages, and the weather is too cold. Mr. Indian doesn't care to be frozen. Now, I'll show you on this map the point where they will, most likely, make their first real at—'

"Whizz! pop! bang! zip! came a regular volley from the bluffs above our camp. A bullet struck the candle and put it out. Another made a large-sized hole in the map. The group scattered quicker than a line of skirmishers, and Bourke was left alone to meditate on the instability of Indian character."

It doesn't take much to make men laugh around a camp fire, and there was general hilarity at the expense of the gallant and genial staff-officer, who was one of the most efficient men connected with the expedition, and who has since been so much distinguished in successive Indian campaigns.

"Now, Lieutenant Schwatka, tell us about that Pawnee Indian picket you had on Powder River last March," said Captain Sutorius to a young officer, already introduced to my readers.

"You mean about the watch?" inquired Schwatka. "It happened in this way: We were ordered to make a detail for picket duty, and as the Pawnees were doing nothing in particular we thought we would give them a turn. My sergeant took half a dozen of them with the regular guard, and, having placed the picket post, explained to the chief Indian, as well as he could, that he and his men would have two hours on and four hours off duty until the guard was relieved. He said to the Pawnee: 'I will lend you my watch.' He struck a match and pointed to the dial. 'It is now 6 o'clock,' said he. 'When the shorter hand moves two points your first watch will be relieved. Do you understand me?'

" 'Hey—hey—good!' said the Indian, and stalked away upon his rounds. The sergeant, who was greatly fatigued, dropped into a fitful sleep by the low watch-fire of the main guard, and was

suddenly aroused by a hand laid heavily upon
his shoulder. He started up in some affright and
saw the Pawnee standing over him, with the
watch he had lent him in his hand. 'Well what
the deuce do you want?' asked the startled sergeant. 'Injun heap cold—much heap stiff,' replied the warrior. 'Ugh! that thing (indicating
the watch) much lie. Long finger (the minute
hand) him all right. Short finger (the hour hand)
him heap d——d tired!'

"The sergeant laughed and tried to enlighten
the chief as to his mistake, for he had really been
but a short time on guard. 'Ugh!' was all the disgusted brave would say, and thereafter he would
have nothing more to do with picket duty."

"By the way," said Lieutenant Reynolds, "you
all remember how on the night Bourke's tent was
fired into at Crazy Woman, a soldier got out of
his tent and in the frosty air of midnight shouted
loudly enough for all the command to hear him,
'I want to go ho-o-o-me!' "

A roar of laughter rewarded the Lieutenant's
anecdote, and we all, soon afterward, turned in
for the night.

Next morning, June 2d, we marched for old
Fort Reno, sixteen miles distant.[27] It was one of

---

[27]Fort Reno, formerly called Fort Connor, was renamed
by General Carrington in 1866 in honor of General Jesse
L. Reno, who was killed in the Civil War. The city of

the three forts abandoned by the Government, under treaty with the Sioux, in 1868. We approached the dismantled post through Dry Fork Cañon, which extended about three-fourths of the way. The bottom lands were covered thickly with cottonwood and showed very many remains of Indian villages. Emerging, at last, from the cañon, we mounted a bluff and saw, about two miles ahead of us, a small line of what appeared to be shelter tents, with animals grazing in the foreground. We soon discovered that they belonged to the two troops of the Third Cavalry, sent forward under Captain Van Vliet and Lieutenant Emmet Crawford to meet the expected Crow Indian allies, who were, however, not yet visible. Above their little camp, on the left bank of the Powder River, we observed the ruins of Fort Reno—nothing left but bare walls, scorched timbers and rusty pieces of iron.

We forded the stream, which was at low water, and speedily reached the camping ground. We were very kindly received by the officers who had preceded us. Captain Van Vliet, now Major, was tall, thin and good looking. He introduced his second in command of the company, Lieutenant Von Leuttwitz, whom I had already seen at Sidney. Lieutenant, since Captain, Emmet Crawford

Reno, Nevada, was also named in his honor. *Dictionary of American Biography.*

was over six feet high, with a genuine military face and a spare but athletic form. He and I formed a friendship then and there which was only terminated by his unfortunate death on Mexican soil, and by Mexican hands, several years later, while he was leading a scouting party in search of the murderous Apaches. The scout was made under what may be called a treaty, and I have always looked upon the shooting of gallant Crawford as a deliberate and cruel murder, which ought to have been promptly avenged on the dastardly perpetrators. Crawford treated several officers and myself to a most welcome stimulant. He was one of the most abstemious of men, but the virtue of hospitality had a large place in his noble nature. Van Vliet also did much for our comfort, and Von Leuttwitz made us all laugh heartily at a ballad of lamentation he had written because of the non-appearance of the Crow Indians, and the refrain of which was, "Crows, dear Crows, vere the d—l you are?"

Powder River is narrow, but rather rapid. In the rainy season it rises above its banks and inundates the country for miles on both sides of its course. Then it is both difficult and dangerous to attempt a crossing. The clay that composes its banks is generally of a black, brittle, gunpowdery appearance, and hence, it is commonly believed, the peculiar name of the river. The water is, at most seasons, exceedingly muddy, and is thoroughly impregnated with alkali, as many soldiers discovered to their sorrow before and after we left the place. The fort was beautifully situated, commanded a view of the country far and near, and to surprise it would have been impossible, with even ordinary vigilance. The low lands along the river were plentifully wooded, a circumstance that caused the death of many a brave fellow of the former garrisons, as the Indians used to lie in wait for the small wood parties sent out to cut timber and massacre them in detail. The grazing was about the best we had seen in Wyoming Territory up to that period. The entire mountain barrier of the Big Horn, softened and beautified by distance, is visible to the westward. Fort Reno had been the main defense of the old Montana Road, and since its abandonment, up to within about ten years, few white people, even in large parties, were venturous enough to travel that route. The fort had a strong stockade and must have been quite a fortress. Loads of old metal, wheels, stoves, parts of gun carriages, axles and other iron debris sufficient to make a Chicago junk dealer rich were lying there, then, uncared for. I suppose most of the stuff has since passed into nothingness.

Two hundred yards north of the abandoned site is the cemetery, where thirty-five soldiers and one officer, all victims of the Sioux Indians, sleep their last sleep. A small monument of brick and stone had been erected above their resting place, but this the Indians did not respect. The moment the garrison that had erected it crossed the river, it had been set upon and almost razed to the ground. The slab on which were distinguishable the words: "Erected as a memorial of respect to our comrades in arms, killed in defense," was broken. The stones placed to mark the graves were uprooted by the vengeful savages and many of the mounds were either leveled or scooped out. Even the rough headboards which proclaimed the names of the gallant dead were shivered into fragments, but the patronymics of Privates Murphy, Holt, Slagle, Riley and Laggin, nearly all of the 18th Infantry, killed May 27, 1867, could be distinguished by putting the pieces together.[28]

The most stoical of mortals could hardly fail to look with some degree of emotion at the lonely and dishonored resting places of those hapless

[28]Following the Fetterman Defeat, Dec. 21, 1866, Red Cloud continued to harass Forts Reno, Philip Kearny, and C. F. Smith, climaxing the war in the celebrated Wagon Box Battle, August 2, 1867 near Fort Philip Kearny, in which the Sioux suffered a severe defeat. Although no record has been found of an attack upon Fort Reno on May 27, 1867, the Author's report concerning the soldiers' tombstones indicates that a fight must have been waged at or near the fort on this date.

young men, so untimely and even ingloriously butchered by a lurking foe. They sleep far away from home and civilization, for even yet the place is only visited by the hardy ranchers and cowboys, who are little given to sentiment of any kind. For the poor soldiers lying out there Decoration Day never dawns, and neither mother, wife, sister nor sweetheart can brighten the sod above their bones with the floral tributes of fond remembrance. The Indian knows their place of rest, and follows them with his implacable hatred beyond the eternal river.

While the column was en route from Dry Fork to Reno we came upon the trail of a party of Montana miners bound for the Black Hills. We found several rifle pits thrown up in good military fashion, which showed that some among them were old soldiers and up to every species of Indian deviltry. Captain Van Vliet, while in advance, had picked up the following, written on a piece of board:

DRY FORK OF POWDER RIVER, May 27, 1876.

Captain St. John's party of Montana miners, sixty-five strong, leave here this morning for Whitewood. No Indian trouble yet. Don't know exactly how far it is to water. Filled nose-bags and gum boots with the liquid and rode off singing, "There's Room Enough in Paradise!"

The names signed to this peculiar, and rather devil-may-care document were Daniels, Silliman, Clark, Barrett, Morrill, Woods, Merrill, Buchanan, Wyman, Busse, Snyder, A. Daley, E. Jackson, J. Daley and others.

As the Crows, who had promised their alliance, still failed to appear, General Crook resolved to send his three reliable half-breed scouts, Frank Gruard, Louis Richard and Baptiste Pourier, to the Crow Agency, some three hundred miles away, in Montana, to bring the friendly Indians into camp. Each man was provided with an extra horse, and all were advised to travel as much as possible by night so as to avoid any bodies of hostiles that might be scouring the plains. It was a risky journey, and, as will be seen later on, was successfully performed. The General was particularly anxious to secure the Crows because of their well-known enmity to the Sioux, and also because it was a matter of boast with all the members of the tribe that they had never killed a white man. The latter statement is, however, open to doubt.

CHAPTER VI

Glimpses of the Big Horn Range

THAN the morning of Sunday, June 3, 1876, a lovelier never dawned in any clime. It was 6 o'clock when our entire command—no company or troop being detached—struck their tents and prepared for their day's march. An hour later we had turned our backs on Powder River with its gloomy associations and its three infernal forks, facetiously christened by Lieutenant Schwatka, Charcoal, Sulphur and Spitfire. We had to make nearly thirty miles in order to reach Crazy Woman's Fork, so called on account of some obscure Indian tradition. Very little water lay between the two streams, but the bunch grass was plentiful, and we found some fresh buffalo wallows—holes made in the ground by the humps of the animals when they refresh themselves by an earth bath—but none of the noble bisons, now, alas, all but extinct, showed themselves that day.

Our column, including cavalry, infantry, wagon train, pack train and ambulances, stretched out a distance of perhaps four miles. The infantry generally accompanied the wagon train, and acted as a most efficient escort. On June 3d the ten companies of the Third Cavalry under Major

Evans formed the van of the horse brigade, while
five companies of the Second Cavalry under
Major Noyes formed the rear. Crook, with his
staff, was away in advance of everything, as was
his custom. Colonel Royall, commanding the
whole of the horse and mounted on a fast-going
charger, regulated the time of the column, and
we marched like greased lightning. Were I to live
to the age of the biblical patriarchs I can never
forget the beauty of that scene. A friend and
myself allowed the soldiers to file somewhat
ahead in order that we might enjoy a complete
view. The cavalry rode by twos, the intervals
between the companies, except those which
formed the rear guard behind the pack mules,
being just sufficient to define the respective
commands. The wagons, 120 in all, with their
white awnings and massive wheels, each drawn
by six mules, covered the rising ground in advance of the horsemen, while the dark column of
infantry was dimly discernible in the van, because Crook always marched out his foot, for
obvious reasons, an hour or two ahead of his
horse. We used to joke about the infantry and
call them by their Indian nickname of "walk-a-
heaps," but before the campaign was over we
recognized that man is a hardier animal than the
horse, and that shank's mare is the very best
kind of a charger.

Our course lay over a gently swelling or
billowy plain, nearly bare of trees, but sufficiently
carpeted with young grass to render it fresh and
vernally verdant. A slight white frost of the previous night, just beginning to evaporate, laid the
dust and seemed to cover the prairie with countless diamonds. The sun beamed with a radiance
rarely seen in the denser atmosphere of the East.
Fifty miles in our front—we were marching
almost due westward—rose the mighty wall of
the Big Horn Mountains, Cloud Peak, the loftiest
point of the range, seeming to touch the cerulean-
hued canopy of the sky, its white apex standing
in bold and broad relief against the firmamental
blue. The base of the mountains, timber-covered,
as we discovered on nearer approach, had that
purple beauty of coloring which we sometimes
see in the masterpieces of the great landscape
painters. The snow line under the influence of
the solar rays gleamed like molten silver, and
all this, taken in conjunction with the green fore
and the dark middle ground, produced an effect
of dazzling grandeur. Even the rudest among the
hardy soldiery appeared to be impressed by the
spectacle. It was like a glimpse of the promised
land, albeit not from the mountains of Moab, but
from the Plains of Wyoming. Perhaps never
again did the splendid panorama of the sierra of
the Big Horn appear so magnificent to the eyes

that gazed upon the fullness of its glory on that brilliant morning of leafy June.

We observed on this march, along toward noon, supposed Indian signal fires. Our pickets had been much strengthened already, but now the General sent forward a strong cavalry detachment to feel for the expected enemy, who might attack us at any moment. We then suspected, what we afterwards knew to be correct, that the main body of the Indians was in Montana, keeping watch on the columns under Terry, and particularly the command of General Gibbon, who had under him the infantry of the expedition. It was well known that General Custer with the Seventh Cavalry had left Fort Abraham Lincoln in the middle of May, and was liable to be heard from before many days.[29] Now, however, that they knew of the presence of Crook's brigade in their country, we all knew that the Indians would not leave us unmolested much longer. Bugle calls were abolished and all orders were transmitted through the officers of the respective staffs.

Crazy Woman's Fork, like all of its sister streams, is fed from the snows of the Big Horn

[29]General Terry, whose command comprised some 600 men of the Seventh Cavalry under command of Custer and about 400 infantry, left Fort Abraham Lincoln on the Missouri on May 17. Following the general course of the

and its water is icy cold even in summer. But it was a treacherous spot in which to camp and had been the theater of many a direful tragedy. Scrubwood and gullies abound at the crossing of the Montana Trail, and these always induce Indians to form ambuscades. The Montana miners had evidently preceded us, for we saw their well-devised fortifications. The wagons had also moved on two tracks, which showed that in passing ravines and other dangerous places the practiced frontiersmen had marched between their teams, so as to be ready for instant defense. Our pickets were soon posted, supper served, and we fell off to sleep as tranquilly as if there were no Indians to disturb our happiness or no gory imaginings to tinge our dreams.

Our next march was a short one, Clear Fork being only a little over twenty miles from Crazy Woman. The water of Clear Fork is absolutely translucent, and in the days of which I am writing there was not in America a more prolific haunt of the exquisite brook trout. This stream is also a tributary of the Powder, but flows independently, thus escaping contamination, through very many miles of as charming

Northern Pacific Railroad, the army arrived at the mouth of Powder River on June 9. On June 21 he advanced to the mouth of the Rosebud, where he effected a junction with General Gibbon's force which had marched from Fort Ellis (near Bozeman).

a game country as ever the eye of man rested upon.

On that day, for the first time I saw an Indian grave. It was situated on a little bluff above the creek. After dismounting I went up to observe it. The Sioux never put their dead under ground. This grave was a buffalo hide supported by willow slips and leather thongs, strapped upon four cotton-wood poles about six feet high. The corpse had been removed either by the Indians themselves or by the miners who had passed through a few days before. Around lay two blue blankets with red trimmings, a piece of a jacket all covered with beads, a moccasin, a fragment of Highland tartan, a brilliant shawl and a quantity of horse hair. Scarcely had I noted these objects when a squad of young fellows from the Ninth Infantry walked up the hill after firewood. They evidently were lacking in the bump of veneration, as the following remarks will show:

"Hello, Sam, what in h—— is that?"

"That—oh, that is the lay-out of some d—d dead Indian. Let's pull it down. Here, boys, each of you grab a pole and we'll tear it up by the roots."

They did tear it up by the roots, and within ten minutes the Indian tomb was helping to boil the dinners of the Ninth Infantry. Thus the relationship of all men to each other in point of savagery was established. The Sioux defaced the white graves at Reno. The whites converted the Sioux funeral pedestal into kindling-wood. It was all the same to the dead on both sides.

In the evening two rough-looking fellows came into camp and reported that they belonged to a party which was coming from the Black Hills to the Big Horn. The main body, they said, was a day's march behind us. It was their fires we saw the day before. The men went away like Arabs and only when they had gone did it strike our officers that they were squaw men from the Sioux camp, who visited us in the capacity of spies in behalf of their Indian people-in-law. It seemed stupid not to have detained the rascals as prisoners.

June 5th was one of our shortest marches, only sixteen miles. We got into camp at old Fort Philip Kearny about noon, and were located in a most delightful valley at the foothills of the Big Horn Mountains. This is a celebrated spot. Here it was that Colonel Carrington founded the fort made bloodily famous by the slaughter of Fetterman, Brown, Grummond and eighty-three soldiers on December 22, 1866. The world has heard the story how the wood party was attacked down Piney Creek, half a mile from the post. How Fetterman and the rest, being signaled, went to their relief. How a party of Indians decoyed them beyond the bluffs and then fell upon them like an avalanche, killing every man and mutilating every body except that of Metzker, a bugler, who fought with such desperate valor that the Indians covered the remains with a buffalo robe as a token of their savage respect. They attempted to take this brave bugler alive, but he killed so many of the warriors that he had to be finished. This much Red Cloud's people subsequently told our soldiers.[30]

From our camp we could plainly see the fatal ravine on the old Fort Smith Road where those brave but hapless soldiers fell. They call the place surrounding it Massacre Hill. Alas, for glory! I visited the cemetery near the site of the fort that afternoon. The humble railing around it was torn down by the Sioux. The brick monument above

[30]The official return of those killed in the Fort Fetterman battle, December 21, 1866 lists Adolph Metzlers, a bugler of Company C, Second U.S. Cavalry. Mrs. Carrington's detailed account of the battle affords no mention of any circumstance attending his death or the Sioux story of the sparing of his body. She describes, however, the killing on December 6 of Sergeant Bowers, who killed three Sioux before being overpowered, and who had previously distinguished himself by his intrepidity in defending the hay parties. Conceivably the subsequent Sioux stories confused the two men, although their forbearance to Bowers was limited to splitting his head with a hatchet. See *Absaraka, Home of the Crows,* 225–26 and 315. The number killed in Fetterman's Defeat was 79 soldiers and 2 civilians.

the bodies of the officers was half demolished, and a long, low mound, upon which the grass grew damp, rank and dismal, indicated the last resting-place of the unfortunate men who met their dreadful fate at the hands of the very Indians who were then being fed on government rations at the Red Cloud Agency.[31] Red Cloud, now old and half paralytic, was a prime mover in that butchery. The event closed Colonel Carrington's career, although the court of inquiry acquitted him, chiefly on the ground that he positively ordered Col. Fetterman not to pursue the Indians beyond the bluffs.[32]

We passed, on our road to Philip Kearny, Lake De Smet, called after the famed Jesuit, a sheet of salt water without visible outlet, about two and one-half miles long by about half a mile average width.[33]

[31]Mrs. Carrington, who was an eye-witness of the burial ceremony, does not mention any separation of the bodies of the officers from those of the private soldiers. The burial pit, over which the "long, low mound" seen by our Author was raised, was 50 feet long and 7 feet deep. Before interment, the bodies were placed in pine cases duly numbered, with names of the occupants, for future identification. *Absaraka, Home of the Crows,* 240–41.

[32]For the smearing of Colonel Carrington and the twenty-year suppression of his defense before the Committee of Investigation of the disaster in 1867, see the present Editor's Introduction to Mrs. Carrington's *Absaraka, Home of the Crows,* XXXII–XXXVIII.

[33]Lake De Smet was named for Father Pierre Jean De Smet, who is reputed to have been its white discoverer. A

Somebody came into camp in the afternoon and told General Crook that there were buffaloes grazing beyond Massacre Hill. Acting on the information, he, with Captain Nickerson of his staff and Major Chambers of the infantry mounted his horse and rode out in pursuit. They went far beyond our lines, saw a dozen deer and one grizzly bear, but no buffaloes. Crook, however, shot a cow elk.

Whoever selected the site of Fort Philip Kearny did not do so with an eye to the safety of its garrison. It was commanded by high wooded bluffs within easy range on every side. Indians could have easily approached within a couple of hundred yards of the stockade without much fear of discovery. A dozen better sites could have been selected in the immediate neighborhood.

It was said that the officer who made the selection, Colonel ———, was influenced thereto by his wife, a lady of some will. He used to delight in sounding the bugle calls himself. One morning, it is related, he was proceeding to sound reveille, when his wife asked him: "Where are

native of Belgium, he came to America in 1823, where he entered the Jesuit Order. In 1838 he began his career as missionary to the western Indians, for which he is chiefly remembered. In the course of his missionary labors he is reputed to have traveled 180,000 miles, crossing the Atlantic sixteen times. *Dictionary of American Biography*, and Mrs. Carrington's *Absaraka, Home of the Crows*, 165–67.

you going with that bugle?" He explained
briefly.

"You may march all you please," said she,
"but here *I* will remain. This is as good a place
for your fort as any other."

The Colonel, who desired domestic happiness,
gave in right away, and so Fort Philip Kearny, of
bloody memory, came to be built.[34]

Crook wanted to establish his permanent camp
at a place called Goose Creek, reported to be only
eight miles from Philip Kearny. The whole command, wagons and all, started out to find it early
on the morning of June 6th. We crossed the
Great Piney, a rapid mountain torrent, and
marched through the fatal ravine in which Fetterman's column got cut to pieces. So perfect a
trap was never seen. There was no way out of it.
A small party had no more chance of escaping
those 1,500 Sioux, in such a position, than an
exhausted fly has to break away from the strong
spider who has it fast in the web. Fetterman, it is
said, was in bad humor with his commanding
officer when he left the fort, and hence his rashness and the tragic result thereof. Not unavenged

[34]This is a characteristic specimen of the yarns, founded
upon campfire gossip, which tradition spins. The site selected for Fort Philip Kearny was chosen by Colonel Carrington with utmost care following a personal reconnaissance of the entire vicinity. See Mrs. Carrington's *Absaraka, Home of the Crows,* Chapter II.

he died, however, for 180 Indians, by their own acknowledgment, were killed or wounded. Every man of the expedition looked with interest at a spot scarcely second to Fort William Henry as a gloomy memorial of Indian warfare.[35]

Our road lay through one of the richest grass ranges that I have ever seen. It is capable of high cultivation. The air was laden with perfume, the ravines being filled with wild flowers of many species. We marched on for hours, but no Goose Creek appeared. Crook had evidently changed his mind, for we diverged to the northeast somewhat abruptly, following the course of a stream called Beaver Creek. It ran at the base of a range of red hills, scraggy and wild, and we were not long in leaving the beauteous scenery of the morning far behind us. We found out that we were on the old Bridger Trail, and marched five and twenty miles before halting at the desired point. En route we

[35]Figures concerning Indian losses in battle are difficult to obtain and commonly much exaggerated. There is reasonable doubt that Red Cloud's loss in Fetterman's defeat was as great as our Author states.

At Fort William Henry August 10, 1759, Lieutenant Colonel Munro surrendered his force of 2500 men to French General Montcalm under a promise of safe conduct to Fort Edward. Ignoring this, and despite the efforts of Montcalm, the latter's Indian allies fell upon the helpless English soldiers, slaughtering some fifty or more and maltreating or carrying several hundred into captivity. The affair remained, as the present mention indicates, for more than a century a well-remembered atrocity story.

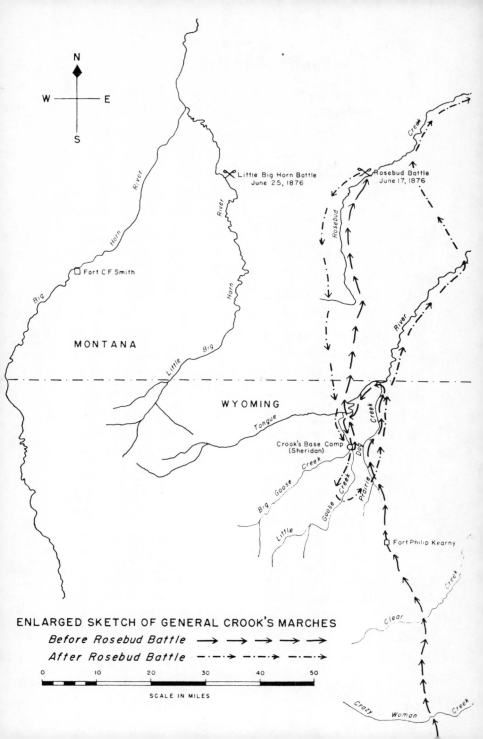

N

W   E

S

Horn   River

River

Little Big Horn Battle
June 25, 1876

Rosebud Battle
June 17, 1876

Rosebud

Creek

☐ Fort C.F.Smith

Big   Horn

MONTANA

Little   Big   Horn

River

— —

WYOMING

Tongue

Dog   Creek

Crook's Base Camp
(Sheridan)

Big   Goose   Creek

Goose   Creek

Prairie

Little

☐ Fort Philip Kearny

Creek

ENLARGED SKETCH OF GENERAL CROOK'S MARCHES

Before Rosebud Battle → → → → →

After Rosebud Battle -·→ -·→ -·→ -·→

Clear

0   10   20   30   40   50

SCALE IN MILES

Crazy   Woman   Creek

struck a buffalo herd and our men killed six of the animals, all in prime condition. We saw a number of deer, and wild fowl sprang up at almost every step. The plain was indented with buffalo tracks, showing that we had struck a belt of the hunting grounds. The veterans said where you find the buffaloes there you find the Indians too. But we saw no red-skins that day. A heavy thunder-storm, accompanied by fierce rain, made our camp rather dreary. At the camp-fires an adjutant told us that Crook was marching on Tongue River.

The continuous marching over rough roads told severely on our stock. Many of the pack mules were half-flayed alive, their loads having galled them dreadfully. Several cavalry horses looked worn out and not a few of the men were suffering from inflammatory rheumatism, a disease quite prevalent in Wyoming. We had only one cavalry and four infantry ambulances, and three doctors looked after the whole command. "Put the sick in the wagons," was the order, the ambulances being full. A sick man might as well be stretched upon the rack as in an army wagon. But a man has no business to be wounded or taken ill while engaged in that kind of enterprise. In the words of Marshal Massena before Torres Vedras, the soldier on an Indian campaign must have the heart of a lion and the stomach of a mouse.

We reached the Prairie Dog branch of Beaver Creek early on the morning of the 7th of June, and we followed that creek over hills and rocks for about eighteen miles. It was an execrable road, the stream being of a winding character, and we had to cross and re-cross it several times, drawing our knees up on our saddles and shouldering our carbines to save them from being wet. The wagons also had a hard time in keeping up, and it was quite late when they and the rear guard finally reached camp at the junction of Prairie Dog Creek with Tongue River[36]. It was a point where few white men had been previously, and was situated about half a dozen miles from the Montana line, in the very heart of the hostile country. Tongue River wound around the neck of land on which our tents were pitched, like a horse shoe. Prairie Dog Creek bounded us on the south; a low ridge rose to our left, and in front, beyond Tongue River and commanding it and

[36]The Author's description of the route the army was following cannot be harmonized with the actual geography of the area. Beaver Creek is a tributary of Big Goose, and Prairie Dog is a stream distinct from both. It runs almost due north a short distance east of Little Goose Creek to its junction with the Tongue near the Montana-Wyoming border. To the Editor it seems probable that from the site of Fort Philip Kearny the army marched to the headwaters of Prairie Dog Creek and thence down that stream to the Tongue, where it went into camp at the junction of the two streams.

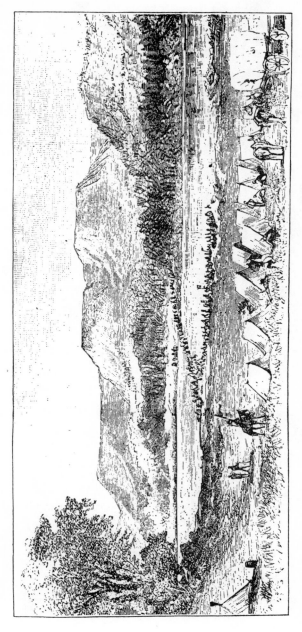

GENERAL CROOK'S ARMY ON TONGUE RIVER

Reproduced from General Charles King's Campaigning with Crook.

our camp, there stood a bold, steep bluff. The bottom lands were well covered with timber. Some of the officers found fault with the position, on account of its rather exposed situation, but others treated the matter lightly and said there was nothing to be apprehended.

At that period General Crook seemed to be a man of iron. He endured heat, cold, marching and every species of discomfort with Indian-like stolidity. If he felt weariness, he never made anybody the wiser. While apparently frank to all who approached him, he was very uncommunicative except to his aides. He was also a born Nimrod, and always rode far in advance of the column, attended by a few officers and an orderly or two, chasing whatever species of game he might happen to find. Looking back at his conduct of that time I cannot help thinking that luck was greatly on his side, because, as we very soon found out, the General might have run into a strong war party of the Sioux any day, and then nothing could have saved him and his few attendants. He was frequently warned of the risk he ran, but paid no attention to the advice.

At this camp Private Francis Tierney, alias Doyle, born in Albany, N. Y., and a member of Company B of the Third Cavalry, who had accidentally shot himself in the bivouac on the dry branch of the South Cheyenne River on the eve-

ning of May 30th, died. He was buried during
the afternoon with military honors. Every officer
and soldier not on duty attended the funeral, and
the burial service was impressively read by Col.
Guy V Henry over the grave, which was dug in
a lonely spot among the low hills surrounding
the place. The body was wrapped in an overcoat
and blanket, and Captain Meinhold shoveled the
first spadeful of clay on the cold remains. A rough
granite boulder was rolled upon the grave and
the young soldier was shut out forever from the
living world. Three volleys, the warrior's requi-
em, pealed above his tomb, and we left him to his
ever-enduring sleep. Except, perhaps, the burial
of a human being in mid-ocean, the interment of
a soldier in the great American wilderness of that
epoch was about the gloomiest of funeral experiences. It was, indeed, a sad destiny that led this
young man to die, accidentally, it is true, by his
own hand, the first of Crook's brigade to lay his
bones in the terra incognita of Wyoming.

CHAPTER VII

The First Fusillade

AT about 11 o'clock on the night of June 8th I was aroused from sleep by the loud and persistent howling of what seemed to be a band of coyotes, animals that the Indians often imitate when approaching a camp. Soon afterward a deep voice was heard shouting down by the river to the men encamped there. Captain Sutorius, who was also aroused, said: "That sounds like the voice of an Indian." The sound appeared to come from the tall bluff above Tongue River. General Crook's attention was called to the matter and he sent Arnold, a half-breed scout, to interview the mysterious visitor. Arnold recognized the Crow dialect, but, thinking it rather imperfect, had his suspicions aroused. The savage was invisible, being concealed among the rocks and brush on the opposite bank.

"Any half-breeds there, any Crows?" he asked, as Arnold challenged him. The scout made some reply which was not understood by the party of the first part, for the Indian asked in louder tones than previously "Have the Crows come yet?"

The Scout, unfortunately, replied in one of the Sioux idioms, whereupon the savage became silent and was not heard from again that night. General Crook was very angry, because he believed that the nocturnal visitor was a runner from the expected Crow Indians, whose arrival had been so long delayed. And we were not very long in finding out that the General had made a correct guess.

It is rather singular that in 1876 most of the people skilled in mining seemed certain that gold would be found in the Big Horn Mountains and the streams that had their sources among them. A few stray miners had attached themselves to Crook's column, in the hope of prospecting for the precious metal. A man named Wyatt was particularly enthusiastic on the subject. He was a strange genius, and had explored most of the out-of-the-way places on the frontier. Wyatt told me in Tongue River camp that the two miners suspected of being squaw men who followed us to Clear Creek said to him that they were from Montana, and four of them had left there for the Black Hills early in the spring. Being a small party, they were afraid to keep the lower road and therefore footed it through the mountains, living on game. When they reached Crazy Woman's Fork they saw a bar in the middle of the river and determined to prospect it. Having no pan, they extemporized one out of a blanket and a willow hoop. In two days, they told Wyatt, $70 in gold was panned out. Then they left for the Black Hills, where one of the party died.

Matters not being prosperous there, they organized a party of sixty men and started for Crazy Woman, which they reached one day after we left. They had followed Crook's command to buy sugar and coffee, of which they obtained a small quantity. They did not show Wyatt any gold specimens. It was their intention, they said, to keep track of the expedition and to let General Crook know what success they might meet with. Wyatt gave their story for what it was worth, but was not prepared to vouch for the truth of all they said. In view of the fact that no gold has been discovered in that locality since, the story of the two tramps must have been a fabrication.

On the morning of the 9th some cavalry soldiers who had been out hunting buffaloes reported having found a fresh Indian trail, and during the night Captain Dewees' company of the Second Cavalry had been disturbed by something, and the firing of their pickets had aroused the whole camp so that expectation and excitement began to run pretty high. Some of the veterans swore that a recruit had been alarmed by the swaying of a bunch of sage brush in the night breeze, and it remained for Indians in the flesh to appear before many of them would believe that there were any hostiles in the country.

At about 6:30 o'clock on the evening of the 9th, just as the soldiers were currying their horses on the picket line, a shot was heard on the right of the camp and it was quickly followed by a volley which appeared to come from the commanding bluff beyond the river. This opinion was soon confirmed by the whistling and singing of bullets around our ears, and some of us did lively jumping around to get our arms. The Indians had come at last, and were ventilating our tents, by riddling the canvas, in a masterly manner. We were taken by surprise, and the men stood by their horses waiting for orders. Meanwhile Sheol appeared to have broken loose down by the river and all around the north line of our camp. If the casualties had borne any proportion to the sound of the firing, the mortality must have been immense. On our extreme left the pickets of the Second Cavalry kept up an incessant fire, which was very spiritedly responded to by the Sioux. The higher bluff, which commanded the entire camp, situated almost directly north, seemed alive with redskins, judging by the number of shots, although only two Indians, mounted on fleet ponies, were visible on the crest. They rode up and down in front of us repeatedly, and appeared to act in the double capacity of chiefs and lookouts.

Although a great number of soldiers fired upon them they appeared to bear charmed lives.

But the savages were rapidly getting the range of our camp and making things uncomfortably warm. Crook's headquarters and the infantry lines were immediately below them, while our tents on the southern slope offered a very attractive target. Their guns carried admirably, and made loungers, who thought themselves comparatively safe, hop around in a very lively, if not over-graceful, manner. The firing had lasted ten minutes when a brilliant flash of inspiration came upon the officer in command. The men had instinctively fallen in line, the worst thing they could have done under the circumstances. All at once a young staff-officer, excited and breathless, rode into the camp of the First Battalion of the Third Cavalry.

"Colonel Mills! Colonel Mills!" he shouted.

"Here, sir," replied the commander of the battalion.

"General Crook desires that you mount your men instantly, Colonel, cross the river and clear those bluffs of the Indians."

"All right," said Colonel Mills, and he gave the order.

All at once the four companies of our battalion —A, Lieutenant Lawson; E, Captain Sutorius; I, Captain Andrews and Lieutenant Foster, and M, Lieutenants Paul and Schwatka, were in the saddle.

"Forward!" shouted the Colonel, and forward we went.

A company of the Second Cavalry was extended among the timber on the left to cover the attack upon the bluffs. In a minute our charging companies were half wading, half swimming, through Tongue River, which is swift and broad at that point. The musketry continued to rattle and the balls to whiz as we crossed. Partially screened by cottonwood trees in the bottom-land, we escaped unhurt. In another minute we had gained the base of the bluffs, when we were ordered to halt and dismount, every eighth man holding the horses of the rest. Then we commenced to climb the rocks under a scattering fire from our friends, the Sioux. The bluffs were steep and slippery, and took quite a time to surmount. Company A had the extreme right; M, the right center; E, the left center, and I, the extreme left. We reached the plateau almost simultaneously. The plain extended about 1,000 yards north and east, at which distance there arose a ridge, and behind that, at perhaps the same distance, another ridge. We could see our late assailants scampering like deer, their fleet ponies carrying them as fast as the wind up the first ascent, where they turned and fired.

Our whole line replied and the boys rushed forward with a yell. The Sioux gave us another salute, the balls going about 100 feet above our heads, and skedaddled to the bluff farther back. There, nothing less than a long-range cannon could reach them, and we could pursue them no farther as the place was all rocks and ravines, in which the advantage lay with the red warriors. The latter showed themselves, at that safe distance, on the east of the ridge, and appeared to take delight in displaying their equestrian accomplishments. I borrowed a field-glass and had a look at them. Not more than a dozen were in view, although at least fifty must have fired upon us in the first place. Those that I saw were dressed in a variety of costumes. One fellow wore what seemed to be a tin helmet, with a horse-hair plume. Another chap wore a war bonnet, but most of them had the usual eagle feathers. To say the truth, they did not seem very badly scared, although they got out of the way with much celerity when they saw us coming in force. Our firing having completely ceased, we could hear other firing on the south side of the river, far to the left, where the Second Cavalry had their pickets. This, we subsequently learned, was caused by a daring attempt made by the Indians to cross a ford at that point and take the camp in rear, with the object of driving off the herd. They failed signally, and lost one man killed and some wounded. Whether our party killed any of the

Sioux I don't know. They did their best, which is all that could be asked of them.

Our casualties were comparatively few, owing to the prompt action of Mills' battalion, but quite sufficient to cure skeptics of the idea that there were no hostiles in the neighborhood. After the Indians retired, Mills' men were withdrawn to camp and the bluff was garrisoned by Captain Rawolle's company of the Second Cavalry, who had a most miserable experience, as they did not bring their tents to the other side and had to endure in the open a pitiless rainfall all through the night. The evident object of the savages was to set us on foot by stampeding our herd.

Many ludicrous stories grew out of this skirmish and one in particular deserves to be recorded. During the firing the pipe of Colonel Mills' tent stove had been perforated, greatly to the horror of his colored servant, who was by no means in love with grim-visaged war. The correspondent of a southern paper, an officer by the way, recorded the fact, and his paper, taking a practical view of the statement, came out in a wise editorial and condemned the Colonel's rashness in wearing a stove-pipe hat in the field! When the paper finally reached us everybody laughed immoderately, and Mills didn't hear the last of that "stove pipe" for a long time.

General Crook began to grow restive under the

continued absence of the friendly Indians, and, not liking his position on Tongue River, moved his command through a fairly fertile country to Goose, or Wildgoose, Creek, about fourteen miles from the scene of the Indian attack and repulse. The creek which bears a name so undignified is really a fine mountain stream, having two branches, known as Big and Little Goose Creek, which, diverging near the foothills of the Big Horn, finally come together and empty themselves into the copious waters of Tongue River. This was a thoroughly delightful camping ground, well wooded, watered and supplied with game, while the scenery was all that could be asked for. That fine region, then terrorized by the war parties of the Sioux and shunned by the Caucasian race, is now thickly settled, and several thriving hamlets have been built on the sites of our old encampments. Herds innumerable now feed where only the buffaloes roamed as late as 1876. We got into camp in a pelting rain, which, however, speedily ceased, and the weather became delightful.

CHAPTER VIII
Indians in War Paint

JUST as we began to give up all hope of ever again seeing our scouts or hearing from our Indian allies, Frank Gruard and Louis Richard, accompanied by a gigantic Crow chief, came into camp at noon on the 14th and amid the cheers of the soldiers rode direct to the General's headquarters. I proceeded there at once and had an interview with the celebrated scout, Gruard, who is half a Frenchman and half a Sandwich Islander. He was brought to this country from Honolulu when a mere boy; ran the mail for the Government on the Pacific Coast for some years, and, when only nineteen years old, was captured by Crazy Horse's band of Sioux. The Chief spared the young man's life, and he lived in the Indian village, having espoused a handsome squaw, for some years.

A misunderstanding with his wife's relatives made the village too hot for him, and being allowed comparative liberty he took the very earliest opportunity of taking French leave. He was then about twenty-eight years of age, was familiar with every inch of the country, could speak nearly every Indian dialect, and was invaluable to General Crook, who would rather have lost a third of his command, it is said, than be deprived of Frank Gruard.[37]

The Scout told the writer that he and his companions had had a hard time of it since they left Fort Reno to search for the Crows. A band of Sioux got sight of them the second day out and chased them into the mountains. They eluded their pursuers, and after four days' hard riding reached the Big Horn River, which they had to swim with their horses. A few miles from that stream they saw an Indian village, full of women and warriors. The latter to the number of about 300 charged down upon them, mounted on ponies. The scouts had a river between them and the Indians—a small river, but sufficient to insure their safe retreat.

The red men fired upon them without effect, and then Gruard, by their large, bushy heads, entirely different from the trimmer Sioux, recognized the Crows. He immediately shouted to them in their own language and very soon the three scouts were in their midst, saluted by a storm of

[37] John G. Bourke characterized Gruard as "one of the most remarkable woodsmen I have ever met; no Indian could surpass him in his intimate acquaintance with all that pertained to the topography, animal life, and other particulars [of the region]. His bravery and fidelity were never questioned. He never flinched under fire, and never growled at privation." Louis Richard, Baptiste Pourier, Baptiste Garnier and the other scouts were also highly commended by Bourke. *On the Border with Crook,* 255.

"Hows!" Then they learned that five Crow scouts had started to find our camp.

It was this party that attempted to speak to us from Tongue River bluffs previously, but when Arnold spoke Sioux they became alarmed, suspecting a trap, and retreated. They would have come in, only that Gruard told them we were going to camp on Goose Creek. They saw us leave Fort Philip Kearny, but when we took the Tongue River road they concluded we were not the party they were looking for, and turned back. Gruard soon set matters right, and before many hours had nearly 200 warriors ready for the road.

They were, he said, within ten miles of our camp, but with true Indian caution declined to come in until perfectly assured that it would be a safe proceeding. Baptiste Pourier had remained behind with the Indians to give them confidence. Five Snake, or Shoshone, scouts, sent from their tribe at Sweetwater Valley to notify the Crows that they were coming to help us and should be treated as friends, were with the party. Louis Richard, the Indian scout, and Major Burt went back for the Crows. We waited impatiently for their arrival. At six o'clock a picket galloped into camp to notify Crook that his allies were in sight.

Then we saw a grove of spears and a crowd of ponies upon the northern heights, and there broke upon the air a fierce, savage whoop. The Crows had come in sight of our camp, and this was their mode of announcing their satisfaction. We went down to the creek to meet them, and a picturesque tribe they were. Their horses—nearly every man had an extra pony—were little beauties, and neighed shrilly at their American brethren, who unused to Indians, kicked, plunged and reared in a manner that threatened a general stampede. "How! How!" the Crows shouted to us, one by one, as they filed past. When near enough, they extended their hands and gave ours a hearty shaking. Most of them were young men, many of whom were handsomer than some white people I have met. Three squaws were there on horseback, wives of the chiefs.

The head sachems were Old Crow, Medicine Crow, Feather Head, and Good Heart, all deadly enemies of the Sioux. Each man wore a gaily colored mantle, handsome leggings, eagle feathers, and elaborately worked moccasins. In addition to their carbines and spears, they carried the primeval bow and arrow. Their hair was long, but gracefully tied up and gorgeously plumed. Their features as a rule were aquiline, and the Crows have the least prominent cheek bones of any Indians that I have yet encountered. The squaws wore a kind of half-petticoat and parted their hair in the middle, the only means of guessing at their sex. Quick as lightning they gained the center of our camp, dismounted, watered and lariated their ponies, constructed their tepees or lodges, and like magic the Indian village arose in our midst. Fires were lighted without delay and the Crows were soon devouring their evening meal of dried bear's meat and black-tailed deer.

In the middle of this repast we saw several warriors raise their heads and say "Ugh, ugh! Shoshone." They pointed southward, and, coming down the bluffs in that direction, we saw a line of horsemen, brilliantly attired, riding at whirlwind speed. Crook sent a scout to meet them. Hardly had he time to start forward when the new-comers crossed the creek and in column of twos, like a company of regular cavalry, rode in among us. They carried two beautiful American flags and each warrior bore a pennon. They looked like Cossacks of the Don, but were splendidly armed with government rifles and revolvers. Nearly all wore magnificent war bonnets and scarlet mantles. They were not as large as the Crow Indians, nor as good-looking, but they appeared to be hardy and resolute. The meeting between them and the Crows was boisterous and exciting. Demoniacal yells rang through the camp, and then this wild cavalry galloped down to headquarters, rode around Crook and his staff, saluted, and, following the example of the Crows, were soon bivouacked and deep in their rough and ready suppers. Tom Cosgrove,

ENCAMPMENT OF CHIEF WASHAKIE IN WIND RIVER MOUNTAINS

From photograph by William H. Jackson.
Reproduced by courtesy of the Smithsonian Institution.

chief of scouts in the Wind River Valley, accompanied them. His lieutenant was Nelson Yurnell, and his interpreter a young half-breed called Ulah Clair. The Indian chiefs of the Snakes present were Wesha and Nawkee, with the two sons of old Washakie.[38]

That night an immense fire was kindled near Crook's tent, and there all the chiefs of both tribes, together with our commanding officers, held a "big talk." Louis Richard acted as interpreter and had a hard time of it, having to translate in three or four languages. A quarter of an hour intervened between each sentence. The chiefs squatted on their heels according to their ancient custom, and passed the long pipe from man to man. Crook stood in the circle with his hands in his pockets, looking half-bored, half-happy. Major Randall, chief of scouts, and other members of the staff were with him. The Indians were quite jolly, and laughed heartily whenever the interpreter made any kind of blunder.

[38]Washakie, chief of the eastern or Green River band of the Shoshones, was born probably about 1804 and died February 15, 1900. Throughout his long life he was notable for his unfailing friendship for the whites, one evidence of which was afforded by a paper signed by over 9000 overland emigrants testifying to the aid given them by Washakie's followers when crossing the Plains. Fort Washakie near Lander, Wyoming, formerly known as Camp Brown, was renamed in his honor in 1878. *Dictionary of American Biography* and Grace R. Hebard, *Washakie.*

The Snakes retired from the council first. They said very little. Old Crow, the greatest chief of the Crow nation, made the only consecutive speech of the night, and it was a short one. Translated, it was as follows: "The great white chief will hear his Indian brother. These are our lands by inheritance. The Great Spirit gave them to our fathers, but the Sioux stole them from us. They hunt upon our mountains. They fish in our streams. They have stolen our horses. They have murdered our squaws, our children. What white man has done these things to us? The face of the Sioux is red, but his heart is black. But the heart of the pale face has ever been red to the Crow. ['Ugh!' 'Ugh!' 'Hey!'] The scalp of no white man hangs in our lodges. They are thick as grass in the wigwams of the Sioux. ['Ugh!'] The great white chief will lead us against no other tribe of red men. Our war is with the Sioux and only them. We want back our lands. We want their women for our slaves, to work for us as our women have had to work for them. We want their horses for our young men, and their mules for our squaws. The Sioux have trampled upon our hearts. We shall spit upon their scalps. ['Ugh!' 'Hey!' and terrific yelling.] The great white chief sees that my young men have come to fight. No Sioux shall see their backs. Where the white warrior goes there shall we be also. It is good. Is my brother content?"

The Chief and Crook shook hands amid a storm of "Ughs" and yells. All the red men then left the council fire and went to their villages, where they put on their war-paint and made night hideous with a war-dance and barbarous music. They imitated in succession every beast and bird of the North American forests. Now they roared like a bison bull. Then they mimicked a wildcat. All at once they broke out with the near, fierce howling of a pack of wolves; gradually the sound would die away until you might imagine that the animals were miles off, when all of a sudden the howling would rise within a few yards, and in the darkness you would try to discern the foul coyotes—next to the Indians the pest of the Plains.

All night long, despite the incredible fatigue they must have endured in coming to join us, the savages continued their infernal orgies. Their music is fitter for hell than for earth. And yet these were not the worst red men existing. These were the truly "good" Indians. Our young soldiers appeared to relish the yelling business immensely, and made abortive attempts to imitate the Indians, greatly to the amusement of those grotesque savages. I fell asleep dreaming of roistering devils and lakes of brimstone.

Crook was bristling for a fight. The Sioux were said to be encamped on the Rosebud, near the Yellowstone River, holding Gibbon at bay.

"They are numerous as grass," was the definite Crow manner of stating the strength of the enemy.

Some of the officers who had had charge of different tribes of Indians at their respective agencies were fond of discussing at the evening camp-fires the characteristics of the various Indian bands or nations. From what may be termed the consensus of military opinion I learned what follows:

Nearly every Indian of any note whatever possessed at that time two equines—one, a pony for pack work, the other, a horse for war and the chase. The latter can go like a meteor and has wonderful endurance. Mounted upon him, the Indian warrior could secure a retreat from the *Chasseurs d'Afrique* of Macmahon, with all their Arab horses.

The Indian war-horse is not as beautiful a beast as the Arabian, but he has more toughness than an ordinary mule. These combined qualities of strength, speed and "endurance" made him the main stay of the red man of the Plains, whether he was Sioux, Cheyenne or Snake. Where the breed came from, or of what blood compounded, nobody seems to know. It is not a mustang, neither is it an Arabian—perhaps a combination of both. It may be for aught we know indigenous to this continent, a theory sustained by the fact that the

Indians can get more work out of such a horse than any other race of men, white, black or yellow.[39]

When Indians kill game on the hunt they cut out the tongue, liver and heart, and unless very hungry leave the carcass to rot upon the prairie. They don't want to load their horses much unless when near their villages, where the squaws can dry the meat, for the average Indian is still unchanged—still the same mysterious, untamable, barbaric, unreasonable, childish, superstitious, treacherous, thievish, murderous creature, with rare exceptions, that he has been since first Co-

---

[39]Horses were brought to the West Indies by the Spaniards before the close of the fifteenth century. Their introduction to the continental mainland and their subsequent acquisition by the Indians followed as a matter of course. Although our Author was misinformed on the subject, there is no mystery about the origin of the horses owned by the western Indians. Nor is the suggestion of Arabian inheritance fanciful, for the Spaniards derived their horses from the Moors, whose final expulsion from the Spanish Peninsula was contemporaneous with the Columbian discovery of America. For a more adequate discussion of the subject see article on "The Spanish Horse in America," in James T. Adams (Editor), *Dictionary of American History*. For descriptions of the employment of horses, particularly in warfare, by the western Indians see Mrs. Carrington's *Absaraka, Home of the Crows,* 208–11, General Custer's *My Life on the Plains,* 251–54, and General James' *Three Years Among the Indians and Mexicans,* 240–42 and 256, the Lakeside Classics volumes respectively for 1950, 1952, and 1953.

lumbus set eyes upon him at San Salvador.
Whether friendly or hostile, the average Indian
is a plunderer. He will first steal from his enemy.
If he cannot get enough that way, he steals from
his friends. While the warriors are fat, tall and
good-looking, except in a few cases, the squaws
are squatty, yellow, ugly and greasy looking.
Hard work disfigures them, for their lazy brutes of
sons, husbands and brothers will do no work, and
the unfortunate women are used as so many pack
mules. Treated with common fairness, the squaws
might grow tolerably comely, their figures being
generally worse than their faces. It is acknowledged
by all that the Sioux women are better treated
and handsomer than those of all other tribes. Also
they are more virtuous, and the gayest white
Adonises confess that the girls of that race seldom yield to the seducer. [40]

The Sioux abhor harlots, and treat them in a
most inhuman manner—even as they treat white

[40]The subject of "virtue" among the Sioux deserves a
far longer commentary than our available space permits.
Nor can it be approached without some understanding of
the widely differing mores of the white and the red races.
As in ancient Rome, the Indian man was lord of the
family, who might loan his wife or daughter to the white
visitor for a price or as an act of simple hospitality. For
the latter to take her without such permission was a different matter. For a concrete illustration of the western
Indian attitude in the Seventies see *"Yellowstone Kelly"*
(New Haven, 1926), 34–36.

captive women—when they are detected. If they
do not kill them outright, they injure them for life
and then drive them from the tribe. Among the
married, such as their marriage is—for polygamy
is a recognized institution in the tribe—adultery
generally means death to the female concerned if
she is discovered, while among the interested
braves it begets a feud that only blood can extinguish. The Sioux hold it a sin against nature—according to their ideas of sin and nature—for a
woman to remain unmarried, and they sometimes
punish her, if she continues obstinate, in a very
cruel and indelicate fashion. Fortunately for the
Sioux women, they, for the most part, believe in
matrimony and are spared all trouble on the score
of their prolonged virginity.

Imagine all the old maids in America being
punished because the men of their generation did
not have the good taste to woo and marry them!
The Sioux will not have any old maids hanging
around their wigwams. This is a truly patriarchal
way of providing husbands for the fair sex. The
other Indian tribes are more lax in their ideas of
female propriety, and care much less whether a
woman is married or the reverse. Taken all in all,
the Sioux must be descendants of Cain, and are
veritable children of the devil. The rest are a very
little behind them, except in point of personal appearance and daring, in which the Sioux excel

nearly all other Indians. Most of them are greedy, greasy, gassy, lazy and knavish.

In connection with the subject of female Sioux virtue, I am reminded of a story which caused great amusement in military circles several years ago. A certain handsome and dashing cavalry officer, now deceased, was badly smitten with the really pretty daughter of a leading Sioux chief, whose village was situated quite close to the post. Lieutenant ———— paid some attentions to the girl, in order to while away the tedious summer hours, and one day remarked casually to a half-breed interpreter that he would like to own the savage princess and take her East as a living curiosity. The half-breed, taking the matter seriously, informed the maiden's warlike sire. The latter took the matter in good faith also, and resolved to make the giving away of his daughter in marriage, for that was how he understood it, memorable. The gay lieutenant was then acting adjutant of his battalion, and at the evening parade, just as he had "set his battle in array," heard a most infernal tumult in the direction of the Indian village. The major in command looked both annoyed and astonished, and asked for an explanation. The adjutant could give none, but, by order of his superior rode in the direction of the disturbance to find out, if possible, its meaning. As he approached the village he saw a great cavalcade moving toward him at full speed, with the old chief and his daughter heading the procession. A horrible suspicion dawned upon the mind of the unlucky adjutant, and this was confirmed a moment later when the half-breed interpreter, and author of all the mischief, rode forward to inform the officer that Spotted Elk was coming up to the post in due order to surrender his daughter into the keeping of Lieutenant ———— as his wife, or one of his wives. Uttering a most heart-felt malediction on the Chief, the girl, the interpreter, and the whole Indian generation, Lieutenant ———— spurred back to the parade, requested to be relieved on the ground of sudden illness, wrote a note of explanation to his commanding officer, obtained temporary leave of absence, which was afterwards extended, and bade an eternal farewell to the post and the village and the Indian princess.

Long afterwards I met the hero of the foregoing adventure, and found him one of the most winning and gifted officers of the army, who, although an American, had all of an Irishman's heart for the ladies, and all the Hibernian's fondness for getting into love scrapes. Poor ————! He died in the flower of his years—died, too, plainly and unromantically in his bed, and not, as he would wish to have died, on the broad field and at the head of charging squadrons.

CHAPTER IX
Scout and Buffalo Hunt

OUR Indian allies kept up their terrible racket during the whole night after their arrival in our camp, but next morning, June 15th, they were up bright and early to receive rations, ammunition and, such as needed them, new government guns. They were an exceedingly picturesque assemblage, painted and befeathered in all the barbaric splendor of the Indian tribes of that day. They sat in a huge semicircle around the tents and wagons of the quartermaster's department, and received their supplies with aboriginal solemnity; often, however, betraying their satisfaction by the inevitable Indian grunt, which has the sound of "ugh!"

The General had determined to mount his infantry on mules in order to expedite their movements when marching against the Sioux. Accordingly the mules destined for this duty, to the number of 200, most of them entirely unbroken to the saddle, were taken to a flat space down by the creek and a few hundred yards from camp. The unhappy infantry men who were to mount the animals were brought there also, while Colonel Chambers, Major Burt, Captain Luhn, and the officers of Crook's staff, aided by several veteran sergeants who had seen mounted service, proceeded to break in the unwilling riders. I subsequently saw those foot soldiers do their duty most heroically, but I am bound in truth to confess that their bearing on the morning of June 15, 1876, was anything but awe-inspiring.

The mules, first of all, were forced to take the regulation cavalry bridle into their unwilling jaws, and then the rather clumsy McClellan saddle, universally used in our service at that period, was placed upon their backs, doubly secured by girth and surcingle. Then the fun began. A cloud of mule-heels shod in iron would rise simultaneously in the air, while the shrill neighing and squealing of the brutes displayed the great indignation that possessed them. They were then allowed to quiet down somewhat, and the unused infantry were ordered to mount their rebellious steeds. Immediately some of the mules ran off, bucking fiercely, and every minute a score of foot soldiers would either stand on their heads or measure their length in the deep, soft grass, which alone prevented their bones being broken. Other mules would buck right where they stood, and then a soldier might be seen shooting up in the air like a rocket, and his very dull thud would soon after be heard as his body struck mother earth in his fall from among the clouds.

The Indians, attracted by the noise and full of native devilment, rushed down from the quartermaster's to see the sport, and their deep laughter at every mishap denoted the satisfaction they felt at the discomfiture of the battered and disgusted infantry. Some of the young warriors would seize the runaway mules, jump upon their backs and demonstrate to the whole command what a natural-born equestrian the North American Indian is. The officers persevered in the experiment, and by noon most of the foot troops had acquired sufficient mastery over their mounts to enable them to keep their saddles with a doubtful degree of adhesiveness.

All day of the 15th was devoted to active preparations for the approaching movement against the hostiles. Arms were cleaned, horses re-shod, haversacks and saddle-bags filled, and ammunition stowed wherever it could be carried. The General determined to move out on the following morning with his pack train only. The wagons were to be left behind under command of Major and Quartermaster John V. Furey with one hundred men to guard them, besides the mule-drivers. An island near the junction of Big and Little Goose Creek was picked out as a good defensive position, and arrangements were made to occupy it accordingly. The soldiers detailed for wagon guard were greatly disgusted—all but one

man, whose face expressed unlimited satisfaction.
I had previously noticed his disposition on the
day the Sioux attacked our Tongue River camp.
He was, I think, about the only constitutional
coward in the whole command. I told him that
with such feelings he had no business to enlist at
all, and he replied, most fervently: "They'll never
catch me in this fix again, if I have to desert when
I get back to the railroad, if I ever do." The unhappy man's delight at escaping the chances of
the coming battle was ludicrous to behold.

The great mass of the soldiers were young men,
careless, courageous and eminently light-hearted.
The rank and file, as a majority, were of either
Irish or German birth or parentage, but there
was also a fair-sized contingent of what may be
called Anglo-Americans, particularly among the
non-commissioned officers. Taken as a whole,
Crook's command was a fine organization, and its
officers, four-fifths of whom were native Americans and West Pointers, were fully in sympathy
with the ardor of their men.

General Crook was particular to see that everything was in perfect order before giving the word
to march. The wagon train was parked in the position already selected. Every man carried four
days' rations and as much ammunition as animal
and rider could stand up under. All the tents
were left with the wagon train, and then each

man knew that he had to sleep under the star-spangled canopy of heaven when his day's march would be over.

Two hours before daylight on June 16, 1876, the whole encampment was aroused by the loud exhortations—sermons, perhaps—addressed by the medicine men and head soldiers of the Crow and Snake Indians to the eager warriors of their respective bands. The harangues lasted for nearly an hour, and then the Indians breakfasted to satiety on the government rations issued the previous day, because it is a rule with the savages never to miss a good opportunity of making a meal, especially when on the war-path. The bugles of our command were silent, but, notwithstanding, everything worked like magic. Tents were abandoned to the quartermaster and every man of the expedition except the hundred detached was in the saddle, having barely swallowed a tin full of black coffee and a hard tack, as the sun rose redly on the eastern horizon.

Our course was north by west, and lay through a fine buffalo grass region, on which signs of the bison were recent. The cavalry, fifteen companies of the Second and Third under Royall, Evans, Noyes, Henry, Mills and Van Vliet, led the van. Then followed the splendid mule pack train, commanded by Chief Packer Tom Moore, as bold a frontiersman as ever looked at an enemy through the sight of his rifle; and, in rear, galled but gallant, rode, on muleback, the 200 hardy infantry under Col. Alex. Chambers and the brave Major Andy Burt. The Indians, with war bonnets nodding and lances brilliant with steel and feathers, headed by their favorite chiefs, rode tumultuously, in careless order, filled with barbaric pride of arms, on our flanks. I felt a respect for the American Indian that day.

We nearly turned our backs upon the Big Horn Range, but its prolonged flank, so to speak, still showed itself through the corners of our left eyes, toward the northwest. We were marching over the finest game country in the world and soon our advance under Major Randall of the 23d Infantry, chief of scouts, came upon a small group of buffaloes, which ran like the wind at the sight of our column. "There will be music in the air now, sure," remarked the veteran Captain Andrews to Sutorius. "Wherever you see buffaloes there, too, you will find Indians," and he lifted his glass to view the retreat of the affrighted bisons.

Just then we halted, and at the remount the muzzle of my carbine struck the hammer of my revolver, which by some oversight was left down upon the cartridge. An explosion followed. I felt as if somebody had hit me a vigorous blow with a stick on the right rear of my pantaloons, and my horse, a neat little charger, lent me for the occa-

sion in order to spare my own mount, reeled under the shock. The column halted, thinking I was
done for, but at the word "Forward!" shouted
impatiently by the commanding officer, it began
to move. I dismounted quietly and found that a
portion of the cantle of the saddle had been
blown off, but the bullet must have lodged in the
earth. Lloyd, Captain Sutorius' servant, said
"You were not made to be killed by bullets, or
that would have fixed you," and I was congratu-
lated heartily by the soldiers as I remounted and
galloped to the head of the column. Just then
Colonel Henry, who was in advance, rode back
along the line and said he had heard I was hurt.
"Is the bullet in your person?" he asked. "I don't
know, Colonel," I answered. "Then by Jove it is
about time you found out," said he, and rode
away laughing heartily at my state of indecision,
which speedily found the rounds of the whole
brigade, from the General to the youngest mule
packer.

We were moving over an undulating surface,
covered with rich grasses and watered by many
small, but limpid streams. The atmosphere was
delightful and the perfume caused by the tram-
pling of the myriad prairie flowers under the
horses' hoofs delicious. Our cavalcade extended,
or seemed to extend, for miles, and all marched
in that profound silence peculiar to the regular

army of the United States, and particularly to the mounted service. We had begun to enter the great northern hunting grounds par excellence, the country dear to the heart of the doomed savage, and for which he was willing to shed his life blood to the very last drop.

All at once we ascended to the crest of a grassy slope, and then a sight burst upon us calculated to thrill the coldest heart in the command. Far as the eye could reach on both sides of our route the somber, superb buffaloes were grazing in thousands! The earth was brown with them. "Steady men, keep your ranks," was the command of the officers from front to rear as many of the younger soldiers, rendered frantic by the sight of the noble game, made a movement as if to break from the column in wild pursuit. Then arose on our right and left such a storm of discordant shouts as can come only from savage throats. The Crow warriors on the west and the Shoshones on the east, throwing off all that might impede them and leaving the abandoned traps to the care of their docile squaws, dashed off like mounted maniacs, and made for the gigantic herd of bisons. Then rang out the crack of the rifle, the whoop and the yell of triumph, as buffalo after buffalo went down before the fire of those matchless horsemen and superb shots! The bisons, for great, lumbering, hump-backed, short-headed creatures, ran like the wind, but the fleet Indian ponies soon brought their wild riders within range and the work of destruction proceeded apace.

The iron discipline of the army kept the soldiers in their ranks, but their glowing cheeks and kindling eyes proclaimed the feverish excitement, the Nimrod passion that consumed them. For at least five and twenty miles this strange scene was continued, our dark mass of regulars and mules moving at quick time through a country green as emerald, their flanks fringed by painted savages and the motionless, or fast-flying forms of the monster monarchs of the western wilds. I don't think that a buffalo hunt surrounded by such martial and picturesque features had previously occurred upon the American Plains, and I am certain nothing like it has been seen since. In fact it would be impossible in these days, because the buffalo—that truest brute representative of the America of Columbus—is almost as extinct as the dodo, the result of the paltry greed of hide hunters and of the gross carelessness of Congress in regard to necessary game laws. That wild, romantic, incomparable hunt will never be forgotten by those who witnessed it.

General Crook, who desired to surprise the village of the Sioux, supposed to be situated in the cañon of the Rosebud, at the point near its northern debouch called the Indian Paradise, was an-

noyed by the conduct of his savage allies, which
could not help alarming the wary foe with whom
he had to contend; but nothing could check the
Indians, so long as a buffalo remained in sight
and daylight lasted. Contrary to their general
custom the savages killed the animals in sheer
wantonness, and when reproached by the officers
said: "better kill buffalo than have him feed the
Sioux!"

The sun was low when we approached the
Rosebud Valley, but still in the distance, right,
left and in front, we could hear the rapid crack-
ling of the Indian guns as they literally strewed
the plain with the carcasses of the unfortunate
bisons. Quiet reigned only when the sun had set
and we went into camp in an amphitheatrical valley, commanded on all sides by steep, but not
lofty, bluffs. Pickets were posted along the eleva-
tions and the command proceeded to bivouac in a
great circle with the horses and pack mules in the
center, for fear of a sudden attack and possible
stampede.

The General gave orders that no fires should
be lit, for fear of alarming the Sioux, but the Indian allies paid no attention to them. They lit
what fires they listed, and proceeded to gorge
themselves with fresh buffalo meat, roasted on
the cinders. They also, when they had feasted
sufficiently, set up one of their weird, indescrib-

able war chants, of which they never seemed to tire. General Crook called upon the Crows and Snakes to furnish men to scout ahead of our camp during the night, but he could induce a few only of the latter tribe to go forward under Tom Cosgrove and Frank Gruard. The General was angry enough to punish the recalcitrant savages severely, but it would never have done to make them enemies at that stage of the game. He, therefore, submitted with characteristic philosophy to the inevitable.

In that northern climate the nights are about as cold in June as those of Illinois in late October, and the single blanket which we were allowed to carry barely kept off the chill of the falling dew. The whole command sank early to repose, except those whose duty it was to watch over our slumbers and the boastful, howling Indians, who kept up their war songs throughout most of the night. Captain Sutorius, lying on the ground next to me, with saddle for pillow and wrapped in his blanket, said: "We will have a fight to-morrow, mark my words—I feel it in the air." These were the last words I heard as I sank to sleep.

Let me say by way of preface to the succeeding chapter, and what I wrote in '76 remains just as true to-day, if there are any hostile red-skins left on the continent, that the position of a newspaper correspondent in an Indian expedition forces him to go in with the rest. There is virtually no such thing as rear, unless with the reserve, which is generally called into action before the fight is over. Besides, if the journalist does not share the toil and the danger his mouth is shut, for if he presumed to criticise any movement some officer would say to him: "What the deuce have you to say about it? You were skulking in the rear, and got everything by hearsay. We don't care what you think." Let no easy-going journalist suppose that an Indian campaign is a picnic. If he goes out on such business he must go prepared to ride his forty or fifty miles a day, go sometimes on half rations, sleep on the ground with small covering, roast, sweat, freeze, and make the acquaintance of such vermin or reptiles as may flourish in the vicinity of his couch; and, finally, be ready to fight Sitting Bull or Satan when the trouble begins, for God and the United States hate noncombatants. Thus was I, who am peaceably disposed, placed in the position of an eye-witness, my mess being with the Third Cavalry, which was about to get most of the hard knocks at Rosebud fight.

CHAPTER X
Battle of the Rosebud

DAWN had not yet begun to tinge the horizon above the eastern bluffs when every man of the expedition was astir. How it came about I know not, but I suppose each company commander was quietly notified by the headquarters' orderlies to get under arms. Low cooking fires were allowed to be kindled so that the men might have coffee before moving farther down the cañon, and every horse and mule was saddled and loaded with military dispatch. The Indians, having digested their buffalo hump banquet of the previous night, were quite alert, but prepared to go on with another feast. The General, however, sent his half-breed scouts to inform them that they must hurry up and go forward. The Snakes, to their credit be it recorded, obeyed with some degree of martial alacrity, but the Crows seemed to act very reluctantly. It was evident that both tribes had a very wholesome respect for Sioux prowess. I noticed, among other things, that the singing had ceased, and it was quite apparent that the gentle savages began to view the coming conflict with feelings the reverse of hilarious.

They got their war horses ready, looked to their arms, and at last in the dim morning light

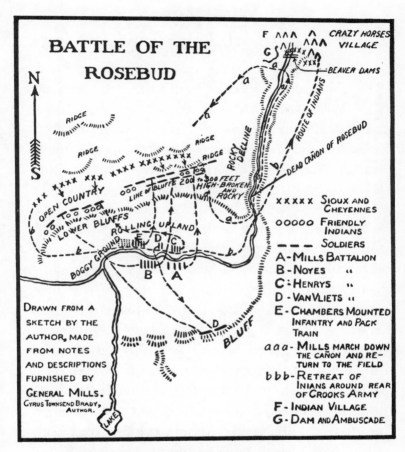

THE BATTLE OF THE ROSEBUD, JUNE 17, 1876

Map drawn by Cyrus Townsend Brady
from information supplied by General Anson Mills.

a large party left camp and speedily disappeared over the crests of the northern bluffs. The soldiers, with their horses and mules saddled up and bridled, awaited the order to move forward with that warlike impatience peculiar to men who prefer to face danger at once rather than be on the lookout for it everlastingly. They were as cheerful as ever, joked with each other in low tones, and occasionally borrowed, or lent, a chew of tobacco in order to kill time. A few of the younger men, grasping the pommels of their saddles and leaning their heads against their horses, dropped off into a cat nap.

Presently we saw the infantry move out on their mules, and within a few minutes the several cavalry battalions were properly marshaled and all were moving down the valley in the gray dawn with the regularity of a machine, complicated, but under perfect control. We marched on in this fashion, the cavalry finally outstripping the infantry, halting occasionally, until the sun was well above the horizon. At about 8 o'clock we halted in a valley, very similar in formation to the one in which we had pitched our camp the preceding night. Rosebud stream, indicated by the thick growth of wild roses or sweet brier, from which its name is derived, flowed sluggishly through it, dividing it from south to north into two almost equal parts. The hills seemed to rise on every side, and we were within easy musket shot of those most remote.

Our horses were rather tired from the long march of the 16th and orders came to unsaddle and let them graze. Our battalion (Mills') occupied the right bank of the creek with the Second Cavalry, while on the left bank were the infantry and Henry's and Van Vliet's battalions of the Third Cavalry. The pack train was also on that side of the stream, together with such of the Indians as did not move out before daybreak to look for the Sioux, whom they were by no means anxious to find. The young warriors of the two tribes were running races with their ponies, and the soldiers in their vicinity were enjoying the sport hugely.

The sun became intensely hot in that close valley, so I threw myself upon the ground, resting my head upon my saddle. Captain Sutorius, with Lieutenant Von Leuttwitz, who had been transferred to Company E, sat near me smoking. At 8:30 o'clock, without any warning, we heard a few shots from behind the bluffs to the north. "They are shooting buffaloes over there," said the Captain. Very soon we began to know, by the alternate rise and fall of the reports, that the shots were not all fired in one direction. Hardly had we reached this conclusion when a score or two of our Indian scouts appeared upon the northern crest and rode down the slopes with incredible speed. "Saddle up, there—saddle up, there, quick!" shouted Colonel Mills, and immediately all the cavalry within sight, without waiting for formal orders, were mounted and ready for action. General Crook, who appreciated the situation, had already ordered the companies of the Fourth and Ninth Infantry, posted at the foot of the northern slopes, to deploy as skirmishers, leaving their mules with the holders.

Hardly had this precaution been taken when the flying Crow and Snake scouts, utterly panic stricken, came into camp shouting at the top of their voices: "Heap Sioux! heap Sioux!" gesticulating wildly in the direction of the bluffs which they had abandoned in such haste. All looked in that direction, and there, sure enough, were the Sioux in goodly numbers and in loose, but formidable, array. The singing of the bullets above our heads speedily convinced us that they had called on business. I looked along the rugged, stalwart line of our company and saw no cowardly blanching in any of the bronzed faces there. "Why the d——l don't they order us to charge?" asked the brave Von Leuttwitz. "Here comes Lemley (the regimental adjutant) now," answered Sutorius. "How do you feel about it, eh?" he inquired, turning to me. "It is the anniversary of Bunker Hill," was my answer. "The day is of

good omen." "By Jove, I never thought of that,"
cried Sutorius, and (loud enough for the soldiers
to hear) "It is the anniversary of Bunker Hill,
we're in luck." The men waved their carbines,
which were right shouldered, but, true to the
parade etiquette of the American army, did not
cheer, although they forgot all about etiquette
later on. Up, meanwhile, bound on bound,
his gallant horse covered with foam, came Lemley.

"The commanding officer's compliments, Colonel Mills!" he yelled. "Your battalion will charge
those bluffs on the center."

Mills immediately swung his fine battalion, consisting of Troops A, E, I and M, by the right into
line, and rising in his stirrups shouted "Charge!"
Forward we went at our best pace to reach the
crest occupied by the enemy, who, meanwhile,
were not idle, for men and horses rolled over
pretty rapidly as we began the ascent. Many
horses, owing to the rugged nature of the ground,
fell upon their riders without receiving a wound.
We went like a storm, and the Indians waited for
us until we were within fifty paces. We were
going too rapidly to use our carbines, but several
of the men fired their revolvers, with what effect
I could neither then, nor afterward, determine,
for all passed like a flash of lightning, or a dream.
I remember, though, that our men broke into a

mad cheer as the Sioux, unable to face that impetuous line of warriors of the superior race, broke and fled with what white men would consider undignified speed. Out of the dust of the tumult, at this distance of time, I remember how well our troops kept their formation and how gallantly they sat their horses as they galloped fiercely up the rough ascent.

We got that line of heights and were immediately dismounted and formed in open order as skirmishers along the rocky crest. While Mills' battalion was executing the movement described, General Crook ordered the Second Battalion of the Third Cavalry under Col. Guy V. Henry, consisting of Troops B, D, F and L, to charge the right of the Sioux array, which was hotly pressing our steady infantry. Henry executed the order with characteristic dash and promptitude and the Indians were compelled to fall back in great confusion all along the line.[41]

General Crook kept the five troops of the Second Cavalry under Noyes in reserve, and ordered

[41]For General Mills' own account of the battle, written in old age, see *My Story*, 404–410. In various details it differs from the Author's account. General Mills believed that he was the first to discover the approaching Sioux, of which he warned General Crook, who was engaged in a game of cards with some of the officers. Mills also characterized Crook's red allies as entirely worthless, affirming that Crook would have been better off without them.

Troops C and G of the Third Cavalry under
Captain Van Vliet and Lieutenant Crawford to
occupy the bluffs on our left rear, so as to check
any movement that might be made by the wily
enemy from that direction. Those bluffs were
somewhat loftier than the eminences occupied by
the rest of our forces, and Crawford told me, subsequently, that a splendid view of the fight was
obtained from them.

General Crook divined that the Indian force
before him was a strong body—not less, perhaps,
than 2,500 warriors—sent out to make a rear
guard fight so as to cover the retreat of their
village, which was situated at the other end of
the cañon. He detached Troop I of the Third
Cavalry, Captain Andrews and Lieutenant Foster,
from Mills to Henry after the former had taken
the first line of heights. He reinforced our line
with the friendly Indians, who seemed to be
partially stampeded, and brought up the whole
of the Second Cavalry within supporting distance.
The Sioux, having rallied on the second line of
heights, became bold and impudent again. They
rode up and down rapidly, sometimes wheeling
in circles, slapping an indelicate portion of their
persons at us and beckoning us to come on. One
chief, probably the late lamented Crazy Horse,
directed their movements by signals made with a
pocket mirror or some other reflector.

Under Crook's orders our whole line remounted, and after another rapid charge we became masters of the second crest. When we got there, another just like it rose on the other side of the valley. There, too, were the savages, as fresh, apparently, as ever. We dismounted, accordingly, and the firing began again. It was now evident that the weight of the fighting was shifting from our front, of which Major Evans had general command, to our left, where Royall and Henry cheered on their men. Still the enemy were thick enough on the third crest, and Colonel Mills, who had active charge of our operations, wished to dislodge them. The volume of fire, rapid and ever increasing, came from our left. The wind freshened from the west and we could hear the uproar distinctly.

Soon, however, the restless foe came back upon us, apparently reinforced. He made a vigorous push for our center down some rocky ravines, which gave him good cover. Just then a tremendous yell arose behind us, and along through the intervals of our battalions came the tumultuous array of the Crow and Shoshone Indians, rallied and led back to action by Major George M. Randall and Lieutenant John G. Bourke of General Crook's staff. Orderly Sergeant John Van Moll of Troop A, Mills' battalion, a brave and gigantic soldier, who was subsequently basely murdered by a drunken mutineer of his company, dashed forward on foot with them. The two bodies of savages, all stripped to the breech-clout, moccasins and war bonnet, came together in the trough of the valley, the Sioux having descended to meet our allies with right good will.

All, except Sergeant Van Moll, were mounted. Then began a most exciting encounter. The wild foemen, covering themselves with their horses while going at full speed, blazed away rapidly. Our regulars did not fire because it would have been sure death to some of the friendly Indians, who were barely distinguishable by a red badge which they carried. Horses fell dead by the score (they were heaped there when the fight closed) but, strange to relate, the casualties among the warriors, including both sides, did not certainly exceed five and twenty. The whooping was persistent, but the Indian voice is less hoarse than that of the Caucasian and has a sort of wolfish bark to it, doubtless the result of heredity, because the Indians for untold ages have been imitators of the vocal characteristics of the prairie wolf. The absence of very heavy losses in this combat goes far to prove the wisdom of the Indian method of fighting.

Finally the Sioux on the right, hearing the yelping and firing of the rival tribes, came up in great numbers and our Indians, carefully picking up their wounded and making their uninjured horses carry double, began to draw off in good order. Sergeant Van Moll was left alone on foot. A dozen Sioux dashed at him. Major Randall and Lieutenant Bourke, who had probably not noticed him in the general melee, but who, in the crisis, recognized his stature and his danger, turned their horses to rush to his rescue. They called on the Indians to follow them. One small, misshapen Crow warrior mounted on a fleet pony outstripped all others. He dashed boldly in among the Sioux against whom Van Moll was dauntlessly defending himself, seized the big Sergeant by the shoulder and motioned him to jump up behind. The Sioux were too astonished to realize what had been done until they saw the long-legged Sergeant, mounted behind the little Crow, known as Humpy, dash toward our lines like the wind. Then they opened fire, but we opened also and compelled them to seek higher ground. The whole line of our battalion cheered Humpy and Van Moll as they passed us on the home stretch. There were no insects on them, either.

In order to check the insolence of the Sioux we were compelled to drive them from the third ridge. Our ground was more favorable for quick movements than that occupied by Royall, who found much difficulty in forcing the savages in his front, mostly the flower of the brave Cheyenne tribe, to retire. One portion of his line under Captain Vroom pushed out beyond its supports, deceived by the rugged character of the ground, and suffered quite severely. In fact, the Indians got between it and the main body and nothing but the coolness of its commander and the skillful management of Colonels Royall and Henry saved Troop L of the Third Cavalry from annihilation on that day. Lieutenant Morton, one of Colonel Royall's aids, Captain Andrews and Lieutenant Foster of Troop I, since dead, particularly distinguished themselves in extricating Vroom from his perilous position.

In repelling the audacious charge of the Cheyennes upon his battalion the undaunted Colonel Henry, one of the most accomplished officers in the army, was struck by a bullet which passed through both cheek bones, broke the bridge of his nose and destroyed the optic nerve in one eye. His orderly, in attempting to assist him, was also wounded, but, temporarily blinded as he was and throwing blood from his mouth by the handful, Henry sat his horse for several minutes in front of the enemy. He finally fell to the ground, and as that portion of our line, discouraged by the fall of so brave a chief, gave ground a little, the Sioux charged over his prostrate body, but were speedily repelled, and he was happily rescued by some soldiers of his command.

Several hours later, when returning from the pursuit of the hostiles, I saw Colonel Henry lying on a blanket, his face covered with a bloody cloth, around which the summer flies were buzzing fiercely, and a soldier keeping the wounded man's horse in such a position as to throw the animal's shadow upon the gallant sufferer. There was absolutely no other shade in that neighborhood. When I ventured to condole with the Colonel he merely said, in a low but firm voice: "It is nothing. For this are we soldiers!" and forthwith he did me the honor of advising me to join the army! Colonel Henry's sufferings when our retrograde movement began, and, in fact, until—after a jolting journey of several hundred miles by mule litter and wagon—he reached Fort Russell, were horrible, as were, indeed, those of all the wounded.

As the day advanced, General Crook became tired of the indecisiveness of the action and resolved to bring matters to a crisis. He rode up to where the officers of Mills' battalion were standing or sitting behind their men, who were prone on the skirmish line, and said, in effect: "It is time to stop this skirmishing, Colonel. You must take your battalion and go for their village away down the cañon." "All right, sir," replied Mills, and the order to retire and remount was given. The Indians, thinking we were retreating, became audacious and fairly hailed bullets after us, wounding several soldiers. One man, named Harold, received a singular wound. He was in the act of firing when a bullet from the Indians passed along the barrel of his carbine, glanced around his left shoulder, traversed the neck under the skin, and finally lodged in the point of his lower jaw. The shock laid him low for a moment, but, picking himself up, he had the nerve to reach for his weapon, which had fallen from his hand, and bore it with him off the ground. Our men, under the eyes of the officers, retired in orderly time, and the whistling of the bullets could not induce them to forget that they were American soldiers. Under such conditions it was easy to understand how steady discipline can conquer mere numbers.

Troops A, E and M of Mills' battalion, having remounted, guided by the scout Gruard plunged immediately into what is called, on what authority I know not, the Dead Cañon of Rosebud Valley. It is a dark, narrow and winding defile over a dozen miles in length, and the main Indian village was supposed to be situated in the north end of it. Lieutenant Bourke of Crook's staff accompanied the column. A body of Sioux posted on a bluff which commanded the west side of the mouth of the cañon was brilliantly dislodged by a bold charge of Troop E under Captain Sutorius and

Lieutenant Von Leuttwitz. After this our march began in earnest.

The bluffs on both sides of the ravine were thickly covered with rocks and fir trees, thus affording ample protection to an enemy and making it impossible for our cavalry to act as flankers. Colonel Mills ordered the section of the battalion moving on the east side of the cañon to cover their comrades on the west side, if fired upon, and vice versa. This was good advice and good strategy in the position in which we were placed. We began to think our force rather weak for so venturous an enterprise, but Lieutenant Bourke informed the Colonel that the five troops of the Second Cavalry under Major Noyes were marching behind us. A slight rise in the valley enabled us to see the dust stirred up by the supporting column some distance in the rear.

The day had become absolutely perfect and we all felt elated, exhilarated as we were by our morning's experience. Nevertheless, some of the more thoughtful officers had their misgivings, because the cañon was certainly a most dangerous defile, where all the advantage would be on the side of the savages. General Custer, although not marching in a position so dangerous and with a force nearly equal to ours, suffered annihilation at the hands of the same enemy about eighteen miles farther westward only eight days afterward.

Noyes, marching his battalion rapidly, soon overtook our rear guard and the whole column increased its pace. Fresh signs of Indians began to appear in all directions, and we began to feel that the sighting of their village must be only a question of a few miles farther on. We came to a halt in a kind of cross cañon, which had an opening toward the west, and there tightened up our horse girths and got ready for what we believed must be a desperate fight. The keen-eared Gruard pointed toward the occident, and said to Colonel Mills: "I hear firing in that direction, sir." Just then there was a sound of fierce galloping behind us and a horseman dressed in buckskin and wearing a long beard, originally black, but turned temporarily gray by the dust, shot by the halted command and dashed up to where Colonel Mills and the other officers were standing.

In was Major A. H. Nickerson of the General's staff. He has been unfortunate since, but he showed himself a hero on that day at least. He had ridden, with a single orderly, through the cañon to overtake us, at the imminent peril of his life.[42]

"Mills," he said, "Royall is hard pressed and

[42]Azor H. Nickerson served throughout the Civil War, attaining the rank of captain of infantry, and of brevet major of volunteers for gallant conduct at Antietam and Gettysburg. He was appointed lieutenant in the regular

must be relieved. Henry is badly wounded, and Vroom's troop is all cut up. The General orders that you and Noyes defile by your left flank out of this cañon and fall on the rear of the Indians who are pressing Royall." This, then, was the firing that Gruard had heard.

Crook's order was instantly obeyed, and we were fortunate enough to find a comparatively easy way out of the elongated trap into which duty had led us. We defiled as nearly as possible by the heads of companies in parallel columns, so as to carry out the order with greater celerity. We were soon clear of Dead Cañon, although we had to lead our horses carefully over and among the boulders and fallen timber. The crest of the side of the ravine proved to be a sort of plateau, and there we could hear quite plainly the noise of the attack on Royall's front. We got out from among the loose rocks and scraggy trees that fringed the rim of the gulf and found ourselves in quite an open country. "Prepare to mount— mount!" shouted the officers, and we were again in the saddle. Then we urged our animals to their best pace and speedily came in view of the contending parties.

army in February, 1866, and from July, 1868 to June 25, 1878 held the rank of captain. He resigned with the rank of major in November, 1883. Nothing has been found concerning the misfortune alluded to by the Author.

The Indians had their ponies, guarded mostly by mere boys, in rear of the low, rocky crest which they occupied. The position held by Royall rose somewhat higher, and both lines could be seen at a glance. There was very heavy firing and the Sioux were evidently preparing to make an attack in force, as they were riding in by the score, especially from the point abandoned by Mills' battalion in its movement down the cañon, and which was partially held thereafter by the friendly Indians, a few infantry and a body of sturdy mule packers commanded by the brave Tom Moore, who fought on that day as if he had been a private soldier. Suddenly the Sioux lookouts observed our unexpected approach and gave the alarm to their friends.

We dashed forward at a wild gallop, cheering as we went, and I am sure we were all anxious at that moment to avenge our comrades of Henry's battalion. But the cunning savages did not wait for us. They picked up their wounded, all but thirteen of their dead, and broke away to the northwest on their fleet ponies, leaving us only the thirteen scalps, 150 dead horses and ponies and a few old blankets and war bonnets as trophies of the fray. Our losses, including the friendly Indians, amounted to about fifty, most of the casualties being in the Third Cavalry, which bore the brunt of the fight on the Rosebud. Thus ended the engagement which was the prelude to the great tragedy that occurred eight days later in the neighboring valley of the Little Big Horn.

The General was dissatisfied with the result of the encounter, because the Indians had clearly accomplished the main object of their offensive movement, the safe retreat of their village. Yet he could not justly blame the troops who, both officers and men, did all that could be done under the circumstances. We had driven the Indians about five miles from the point where the fight began and the General decided to return there in order that we might be nearer water. The troops had nearly used up their rations and had fired about 25,000 rounds of ammunition. It often takes an immense amount of lead to send even one Indian to the happy hunting grounds.

The obstinacy, or timidity, of the Crow scouts in the morning spoiled General Crook's plans. It was originally his intention to fling his whole force on the Indian village, and win or lose all by a single blow. The fall of Guy V. Henry early in the fight on the left had a bad effect upon the soldiers, and Captain Vroom's company became entangled so badly that a temporary success raised the spirits of the Indians and enabled them to keep our left wing in check sufficiently long to allow the savages to effect the safe retreat of their village to the valley of the Little Big Horn. Had

Crook's original plan been carried out to the letter, our whole force—about 1,100 men— would have been in the hostile village at noon, and in the light of after events it is not improbable that all of us would have settled there permanently. Five thousand able-bodied warriors, well armed, would have given Crook all the trouble he wanted, if he had struck their village.[43]

I am bound to add, for the honor of the jour-

[43]Excuses apart, Crazy Horse administered a smashing defeat to General Crook. That the Indians retreated several miles during the battle signifies little. Crazy Horse's own subsequent explanation was that he was seeking to lure Crook within reach of his main force of warriors under Gall and Sitting Bull. General Mills relates that upon meeting Crook upon the conclusion of the battle he "never saw a man more dejected." The Sioux, upon withdrawing from Mills on the right, had swung around to the extreme left, where they had charged through the squadrons of Van Vliet and Henry, stationed upon open ground, "knocking [the soldiers] from their horses with lances and knives, dismounting and killing them, cutting the arms of several off at the elbows in the midst of the fight and carrying them away. . . . We then all realized for the first time that while we were lucky not to have been entirely vanquished, we had been most humiliatingly defeated. . . ." Crook's official report of the battle, made to General Sheridan on June 19 is noticeably reticent concerning his losses and his intended resumption of hostilities. Concerning it, General Mills states: "The next day we returned to our camp on Goose Creek, where General Crook and all of us made very brief reports of the battle, having little pride in our achievement," *My Story*, 409.

That Crazy Horse, by calling up his reserves who had taken no part in the battle, could have annihilated Crook's

nalistic profession, that Mr. McMillan, who accompanied our battalion, showed marked gallantry throughout the affair, which lasted from 8 in the morning until 2 in the afternoon, and the officers with the other commands spoke warmly that evening of the courage displayed by Messrs. Strahorn, Wasson, and Davenport.[44]

army seems probable. But the Indian conception of how wars should be waged differed radically from that of the white man. To take the foe by surprise, strike a blow, and retire to fight another day was the Indian's ideal procedure. Only the stupid white man voluntarily incurred heavy loss in the hope of inflicting a greater loss upon his foe. To the mind of the Indian the prospect of wiping out Crook's army at the cost of probable heavy loss to himself made no appeal. This conception, difficult for civilized minds to grasp, may perhaps help to explain why, in the long struggle between the white and the red races, the latter went down to defeat. On the subject of the Indian conception of warfare General Nelson A. Miles wrote:

"The Indian is a most dangerous warrior within 200 yards, the range within which he is accustomed to kill game. . . . The Indian also is very brave—when he is successful. War is entirely voluntary with him. If he thinks it is a good day for scalps and plunder he is very daring, but if he thinks the signs are not favorable and he and his companions are receiving serious injury he can withdraw, with no loss of caste or reputation with his fellows. There is no such thing as order, positive authority, or discipline among them." Nelson A. Miles *Serving the Republic* (N.Y., 1911), p. 163.

[44]Modesty prevented the Author from mentioning his own role in the battle. He was a recklessly brave daredevil Irishman whose conduct in the campaign evoked the admiration of the soldiers. See *Ante*, xxxiv–xxxvii.

Our wounded were placed on extemporized travois or mule litters and our dead were carried on the backs of horses to our camp of the morning, where they received honorable burial. Nearly all had turned black from the heat, and one soldier, named Potts, had not less than a dozen Indian arrows sticking in his body. This resulted from the fact that he was killed nearest to the Indian position and the young warriors had time to indulge their barbarity before the corpse was rescued.

One young Shoshone Indian, left in the rear to herd the horses of his tribe, was killed by a small party of daring Cheyennes, who, during the heat of Royall's fight, rode in between that officer's left and the right of Van Vliet. The latter supposed that the adventurous savages were some of our redskins, so natural and unconcerned were all their actions. The Cheyennes slew the poor boy with their tomahawks, took his scalp, "leaving not a wrack behind," and drove away a part of his herd. Van Vliet, as the marauders were returning, had his suspicions aroused and ordered Crawford's men to fire upon them. This they did with such good effect that the raiders were glad to drop the captured ponies and make off in a hurry, having lost one man killed (we found the body next day) and several wounded.

During the severest portion of the conflict General Crook's black charger was wounded under him. Lieutenant Lemley's horse was also hurt and rendered unfit for further service. Lieutenants Morton and Chase of the Third Cavalry did good service throughout the conflict, and narrowly escaped death while riding from one point of the line to the other. Lieutenant Lemley came near losing his scalp by riding close up to a party of hostile Indians whom he supposed were Crows. His escape was simply miraculous. In fact, in most cases it was difficult to tell our redskins from those of Sitting Bull. There is a strong family resemblance between all of them.

We went into camp at about 4 o'clock and were formed in a circle around our horses and pack train, as on the previous night. The hospital was established under the trees down by the sluggish creek, and there the surgeons exercised their skill with marvelous rapidity. Most of the injured men bore their sufferings stoically enough, but an occasional groan or half-smothered shriek would tell where the knife, or the probe, had struck an exposed nerve. The Indian wounded, some of them desperate cases, gave no indication of feeling, but submitted to be operated upon with the grim stolidity of their race.

General Crook decided that evening to retire on his base of supplies—the wagon train—with his wounded, in view of the fact that his rations were almost used up and that his ammunition had run pretty low. He was also convinced that all chance of surprising the Sioux camp was over for the present, and perhaps he felt that even if it could be surprised his small force would be unequal to the task of carrying it by storm. The Indians had shown themselves good fighters, and he shrewdly calculated that his men had been opposed to only a part of the well-armed warriors actually in the field.

During the night a melancholy wailing arose from the Snake camp down by the creek. They were "waking" the young warrior killed by the Cheyennes that morning, and calling upon the Great Spirit for vengeance. I never heard anything equal to the despairing cadence of that wail, so savage and so dismal. It annoyed some of the soldiers, but it had to be endured. The bodies of our slain were quietly buried within the limits of the camp, and every precaution was taken to obliterate the traces of sepulture. The Sioux did not disturb us that night.

There was no further need for precaution as to signals, and at 4 o'clock on the morning of Sunday, June 18th, the reveille sounded. All were immediately under arms except the Snake Indians, who had deferred the burial of their comrade until sunrise. All the relatives appeared in black paint, which gave them a diabolical aspect. I had been led to believe that Indians never yielded to the weakness of tears, but I can assure my readers that the experience of that morning convinced me of my error. The men of middle age alone restrained their grief, but the tears of the young men and of the squaws rolled down their cheeks as copiously as if the mourners had been of the Caucasian race. I afterward learned that the sorrow would not have been so intense if the boy had not been scalped. There is some superstition connected with that process. I think it had reference to the difficulty of the admission of the lad's spirit, under such circumstances, to the happy hunting grounds. [45]

[45]Unknown to the Author, apparently, weeping was a ceremonial and social custom among the Sioux and some other tribes of Indians, who cultivated the ability to turn the flow of tears on and off at will. One may reasonably question whether the weepers on the present occasion were animated by grief for the departed warrior or were merely exhibiting the behavior which the social code of the tribe demanded on such occasions. Father Louis Hennepin in 1680 named present-day Lake Pepin the "Lake of Tears" because here some of his Sioux captors "cryed all the night" over him. On still another occasion, several of the old men "laid their hands on my head and began to weep bitterly, accompanying their tears with such mournful accents as can hardly be expressed." Upon arriving at the village of his captors, an old man presented him with a pipe to smoke, rubbing his arms and head and "weeping over me all the while with abundance of tears." *New Discovery of a Vast Country in America.*

Captain Bourke records an instance of ceremonial weeping (this time by a Crow) on the march to the Rosebud. "While riding along side one of our scouts," he relates,

A grave was finally dug for the body in the bed of the stream and at a point where the horses had crossed and re-crossed. After the remains were properly covered, a group of warriors on horseback rode over the site several times, thus making it impossible for the Sioux to find the body.

This ceremony ended, our retreat began in earnest. Our battalion was, as nearly as I can remember, pretty well toward the head of the column. Between us and the Second Cavalry came the wounded on their travois and behind them came the mounted infantry. Looking backward occasionally, we could see small parties of Sioux watching us from the bluffs, but they made no offensive movement. As I rode along with Sutorius and Von Leuttwitz I observed a crowd of Crow Indians dismounted and standing around some object which lay in the long grass some distance to our right. The Lieutenant and I rode over there and saw the body of a stalwart Sioux war-

"I noticed tears flowing down his cheeks, and very soon he started a wail or chant of the most lugubrious tone. I respected his grief until he had wept to his heart's content, and then ventured to ask the cause of such deep distress. He answered that his uncle had been killed a number of years before by the Sioux and he was crying for him now and wishing that he might come back to life to get some of the ponies of the Sioux and Cheyennes. Two minutes after having discharged the sad duty of wailing for his dead relative, the young Crow was as lively as any one else in the Column." *On the Border with Crook,* 310.

CARRYING A DISABLED SOLDIER ON AN INDIAN TRAVOIS

Reproduced from General Charles King's *Campaigning with Crook.*

rior, stiff in death, with the mark of a bullet wound in his broad bosom. The Crows set to work at once to dismember him. One scalped the remains. Another cut off the ears of the corpse and put them in his wallet. Von Leuttwitz and I remonstrated, but the savages only laughed at us. After cutting off toes, fingers, and nose they proceeded to indecent mutilation, and this we could not stand. We protested vigorously, and the Captain, seeing that something singular was in progress, rode up with a squad of men and put an end to the butchery.

One big yellow brute of a Crow, as we rode off, took a portion of the dead warrior's person out of his pouch, waved it in the air, and shouted something in broken English which had reference to the grief the Sioux squaws must feel when the news of the unfortunate brave's fate would reach them. And then the whole group of savages burst into a mocking chorus of laughter that might have done honor to the devil and his angels. I lost all respect for the Crow Indians after that episode. I concluded, and I think with justice, that they are mostly braggarts in peace and laggards in war.

As we continued our march, having rejoined the head of the column, we heard a great rattling of small arms in the rear and concluded we had been attacked. The whole command halted and then we saw what the trouble was. A solitary and much frightened antelope had broken from cover far toward the rear and ran directly along our flank for more than a mile. Although at least five hundred men fired at the nimble creature, it ran the gauntlet in safety and at last found refuge in the thick timber of a small stream which we were obliged to cross. Owing to the condition of the wounded we were ordered to halt in an excellent camping place several miles from our wagon train. We were all pretty tired, and the whole command, except the pickets, lay down to rest early in the evening. During the night we were disturbed by some shots fired by our sentinels at what they supposed to be prying Sioux, but nothing serious resulted.

Next day we were en route very soon after sunrise and reached our wagon train on Goose Creek in good season. The officers and men left behind were glad to see us, and Major Furey, guessing that we must feel pretty thirsty as well as hungry, did all that a hospitable warrior could be expected to do for his famished comrades. That night, after having refreshed ourselves by a bath in the limpid waters of Goose Creek, we again slept under canvas and felt comparatively happy. We learned during the night that the General had determined to send the wagon train, escorted by most of the infantry, to Fort Fetterman for supplies, and that the wounded would be sent to that post at the same time. He had sent a request for more infantry, as well as cavalry, and did not intend to do more than occasionally reconnoiter the Sioux until the reinforcements arrived. This meant tedious waiting, and Mr. McMillan, whose health had daily grown worse, was advised by the surgeons to take advantage of the movement of the train and proceed to Fetterman also. "Mac," thinking there would be no more fighting, finally acquiesced, and, greatly to the regret of the whole outfit, left with the train on the morning of Wednesday, June 21st. We all turned out and gave Colonel Henry and the other wounded three hearty cheers as they moved out of camp. It was the last we were to see of them during that campaign.

CHAPTER XI

In the Shadow of the Mountains

IT is impossible to make any reader who is un-familiar with active military life feel what our command, from General to bugler, felt after the departure of the wagon train, when everybody knew that a period of inaction was to follow our recent exciting experiences. To add to the gen-eral monotony our Indian allies suddenly made up their minds that it would be good medicine for them to go home. The Crows, as usual, set the example and left us about the same time as the wagon train, leaving their wounded and a few squaws with us. The Snakes decamped a few days later, but with assurances of the strongest kind that they would rejoin us before the new cam-paign opened.

They also left their wounded behind. In fact, most of the latter were too badly injured to be removed. In order to break the sameness of the new condition of things the General moved us every day or so nearer to the base of the Big Horn Mountains. We had, therefore, grass, water, wood and brook trout in ever increasing abundance. The days from 11 o'clock until four became in-tensely hot, but the nights were deliciously cool. Fishing and hunting were about our only recreations, and even the most daring of hunters did not venture much beyond the limits of our picket posts as Indian signs were abundant on all sides of us.

Captain Vroom and Lieutenant Paul were the two literary men of the outfit, and their small, paper-covered circulating library found the rounds of the encampment, greatly to the detriment of the volumes. Schwatka's mind, then, as since, ran on science. He had no love for light literature, and he lay awake of nights thinking of the North Pole and Sir John Franklin's bones. Lieutenant L——, newly married, was still desperately in love, and saw his adored one in every flower that sprang by fountain shaw or green. He was a most delightful companion at that period of his life.

Bourke, always entertaining, occasionally condescended to tell us about his Arizona experiences, while brave old Lieutenant Lawson, eccentric but beloved, would nod drowsily over the camp fire, and, having listened to the narratives of the other warriors without attempting to conceal his indifference, would yawn out dismally, in the midst of some heroic recitation of adventure—"Did you now?" Then the young officers would start him on his exploits in the Kentucky Brigade during the Civil War, and, stealing off one by one, unperceived by the old man, would enjoy his discomfiture when he finally realized the situation.[46] There was not in the camp a bottle of beer, a glass of whisky or even a cigar, but there was plenty of government tobacco and this was about all the luxury the command could boast of at that time.

Perhaps my feelings about this period may be best described by the following passages from a letter written to the paper I represented from Cloud Peak Camp:

"The days run into one another unmarked, except for their length. In your civilized world Sunday chapters off the time, gives you a weekly beginning and end, freshens you up, as it were, every seventh day; but here that day is like every other—sultry, lazy, lonely and cheerless. No Charley O'Malley or other Irish dragoon could ever flourish in an atmosphere so irksome. Indian solemnity appears to oppress everybody, and the fierce, solemn-browed old hills appear to frown reproach on all that is light, or gay, or happy. Sad, desolate old hills, that have no history, old as the Pillars of Hercules, massive as the Apennines, snow-robed like the Alps, and yet without

[46]Joseph Lawson was a native of Ireland, who served during the Civil War successively as second lieutenant and captain in the Eleventh Kentucky Cavalry. In July, 1866 he was appointed first lieutenant in the Third U.S. Cavalry Regiment, and was promoted to captain in September, 1876. He died January 30, 1881.

a memory save that of the nomadic Indian with his hideous painted visage, his wolfish howl and his vermin-garrisoned wigwam. Around their gigantic figures are no gleams of the heroic past; no Hannibal with his mighty oath and mightier achievement; no Scipio with his Roman genius and terrible revenge; no Caesar with his devouring ambition and swarming legions—nor Horace, nor Virgil, nor Tasso, nor Dante with their deathless symphonies and souls of poetic fire; nor Rienzi with his eloquence; nor Angelo with his creative glory; nor Bonaparte with his eagle pinions, catching on their golden plumage the fame of the ancient world. These mountains that we look upon to-day are mere heaps of rock, sand, and clay, destitute of all that can appeal to the imagination from the magic lights and shades of antique story. But despite the historic barrenness, our mountains are not without their natural attractions, pine-tree forests, foaming cataracts, gloomy cañons, and towering pinnacles showing almost at every step

> A red deer's wild and rocky road;
> An eagle's kingly flight.

"Besides, they have that mysterious gold-concealing reputation which charms the adventurers, and which has led many a would-be Monte Cristo to sail 'neath alien skies and tread the desert path in pursuit of the world's *ignis fatuus*, only to find a tomb in the bowels of the wolf and the raven, or leave his miserable bones, those ghastly landmarks of mortality, to grin solemn warning at those who may follow his fatal trail. But thousands will follow that trail, even though they tread on skeletons at every step. The love of gold is stronger in men than the fear of death.

"Yesterday we received the first mail that has reached us since May 29th. It was rather small, no newspapers whatever having come except a few for headquarters, and even these were old. Dearth of reading matter is the greatest deprivation we endure. Nobody expected that Crook was going to make an all-summer affair of this campaign, but it looks very like it now. Our wagons are to bring supplies for four months, which looks somewhat tedious. Meanwhile a kind of informal post will be established here, or in this vicinity, under the name of Camp Cloud Peak (Goose Creek is not sufficiently heroic it would appear), so that our scouting parties can draw for supplies whenever they get run ashore, which will be pretty often. Everybody sighs for a renewal of active work, as the time then will not appear so long. Loafing hangs heavily upon us, for, unlike nearly all other campaigners, we are utterly cut off from the feminine world, which means civilization, and will be until we return to Fort Fetterman. Mars, when coming on this campaign, left Venus at home to look after the house."

On the morning of the 23d of June a party of four or five men, mounted and having a couple of pack mules, heavily laden, with them, were challenged by the pickets on the south side of the camp. They proved to be Lieutenant Schuyler, a brother of the Hon. Eugene Schuyler of diplomatic fame,[47] of the Fifth Cavalry, a couple of orderlies, a packer and an old miner, named Captain Graves, who had come all the way from Fort Fetterman to join us, traveling generally at night. They had met our wagon train and the wounded en route, and therefore had little trouble in finding us. The Lieutenant was then serving on Crook's staff, and brought some interesting information.[48] He told us, among other things, that

[47]Eugene Schuyler (1840–1890) was a native of Ithaca, New York and a graduate of Yale University, where he obtained the degree of Ph.D. in 1861. He subsequently studied law and practiced it for a short period in New York City, but in 1867 he entered upon a diplomatic career, in which he won much distinction. A scholarly man, he published several books and numerous magazine articles. *Dictionary of American Biography.*

[48]Lieutenant Walter S. Schuyler, a West Point graduate in the class of 1870, had served under Crook in Arizona during the earlier seventies. At the commencement of the Sioux campaign of 1876 he was stationed at Fort Hays, Kansas, where in early June he was summoned to rejoin his old commander in the capacity of Aid-de-Camp. He was brevetted for gallantry in action in Arizona

General Merritt with the Fifth Cavalry had been ordered to observe the Cheyennes at the agencies and prevent them from joining their friends already in the field. Nothing, he said, had been heard from General Terry's brigade since Custer left Fort Lincoln at the head of the Seventh Cavalry. Alas! Custer was even then, as Schuyler told us the news over a tin-full of coffee, marching up the Rosebud from the landing on the Yellowstone to his death! He had started from that point at noon on the 22d, and the first act in the immortal tragedy of the Little Big Horn had begun. But we knew nothing of all this at the time, and were, accordingly, happy.

On Saturday, June 24th, the General moved the command still nearer to the mountains, so that a musket shot could easily reach the camp from the foothills. It was a delightfully romantic spot, nothing more beautiful, at least at that season, this side of Paradise. We reveled in the crystal water, and slept beneath the grateful shade of the trees that fringed the emerald banks of those beautiful tributaries of Tongue River, that winding Daughter of the Snows.

in 1872 and 1874, and in the action against Indians in the Big Horns, November 25, 1876. He served as a colonel of New York Volunteers during the Spanish-American War of 1898, and in February, 1903 became lieutenant-colonel of the Second U.S. Cavalry Regiment.

Colonel Anson Mills, ever restless and enterprising, made an informal reconnaissance from camp on the afternoon of Sunday, June 25th. He went up some distance in the foothills with a small party, and, returning to camp, reported a dense smoke toward the northwest, at a great distance. He called the attention of several to it and all agreed that it must be a prairie fire or something of that kind. It was a prairie fire, sure enough, but it was kindled, as we knew afterward, by the deadly, far-sweeping musketry of the vengeful savages who annihilated Custer and his devoted band on the banks of the Little Big Horn! Even while we gazed, perhaps, the tragedy was consummated, and the American Murat had fought his last battle.

But the monotony of camp, despite the beauty of the surroundings, became more intolerable than ever. Officers who in times of excitement would take no notice of trifles became irritable and exercised their authority over their subordinates in a decidedly martinetish manner. This, as a matter of course, produced friction and occasional sulking. One field officer became particularly morose, and another, criticising him, used to say: "Major———— is the most even tempered man in this whole brigade, he's always in bad humor!"

On the 28th of June, in a letter to my paper, I relieved my mind on this branch of the subject as follows:

"To banish dull care, we are advised to go fishing. Oh, Isaac Walton, gentle, complacent old fraud!, even your patience would become exhausted sitting on the pebbly banks of Goose Creek, rain dripping from your garments, your teeth chattering, waiting for a bite. Even Nimrod's pastime grows monotonous in this vastness of mammoth desolation and preternatural silence. So oppressive, when away from camp, is the latter sensation that I fancy a shot fired by the man in the moon would be heard among these mountains. We virtually pine for something to read and would not cast away even a dime novel, a poem by Walt Whitman, a lecture by Deacon Bross, or a tract by Brother Moody.[49] Rather than this should last, welcome anything—tornado, earthquake, flood or storm.

"To a man used to the bustle of a great city, camp-life, inactive, is the most infernal of bores.

[49]William Bross was a prominent figure in the political and business life of mid-nineteenth-century Chicago. Active in the Second Presbyterian Church, he was a leading promoter of Lake Forest University. "Brother Moody" was Dwight L. Moody (1837–99), perhaps America's most noted evangelist in the thirty-year period which ended with his death.

"I have been astonished at the few amusement resources displayed by the officers of this outfit. Only for the occasional rubbing up given them by commanding officers, subalterns would sink into a Van Winklish lethargy and be eternally lost to glory and the service. Nowhere does the little brief authority of man display itself in such capers before high heaven as in the regular army of this Republic. In sooth, a man to be either an officer or a private in Uncle Sam's legions must say: 'Be calm, be calm, indignant heart' almost every day of his life; must muzzle his tongue, quell his spirit, and hug to his breast that granite idol, discipline. In military parlance, the corporal 'sits down' upon the private; the sergeant upon the corporal; the lieutenant upon the sergeant; the captain upon the lieutenant; the major upon the captain; the lieutenant-colonel upon the major; the colonel upon the lieutenant-colonel; and the General upon the whole pile. Thus, the nethermost man gets pretty well flattened out if the others are in bad humor, and at no time are commanding officers so cross and contrary as when lying around camp, tormented by blue devils, and nothing to do.

"A more unromantic looking set of military heroes the eye never rested upon than ours. Dust, rain, sun and sweat have made havoc of the never very graceful uniforms. The rear portions of the men's pantaloons are, for the most part, worn out. The boots are coffee-colored. Such a thing as a regulation cap is not to be seen in the whole camp, everybody from the General down wearing some kind of a sombrero, picturesque enough, but rather unmilitary. Every face is parched, nearly every beard unshorn, and the eye is wearied by the unending display of light-blue pants and dark-blue shirts, all in a more or less dilapidated condition. Our hours are regulated by the bugle, our only means of ascertaining the time. The mornings are chilly, the days hot and the nights wondrously cool for the latter part of June. But we generally have a lovely mountain breeze, highly invigorating and vastly agreeable except when it grows unruly and blows down our tents. I wish some enterprising company would lift these superb mountains en masse, move them to Chicago, and plant them for all time on the northwestern prairie, say five miles from Lawndale. How grand it would be to have the Big Horn giant scanning his tremendous countenance in the resplendent mirror of Lake Michigan."

But more stirring days were rapidly, and all unknown to us, approaching. Some half-breeds came into camp on June 30th and reported that Indian runners had told them of a fight between the hostiles and "pony soldiers" (cavalry), in which the latter had been wiped out. We imagined

that the story had reference to our own fight on
the Rosebud, and our officers, long familiar with
the Indian habit of exaggeration, paid little or no
attention to the second-hand intelligence. Yet, as
it turned out, the Indian story was absolutely
correct. The "pony soldiers," under the ill-fated
Custer, had been, indeed, wiped out.

The General, ever inclined to be active, determined to organize a party to enter the Big Horn
Mountains for the double purpose of hunting and
exploring. Thus was my desire to penetrate those
picturesque ranges to be gratified.

CHAPTER XII
Across the Snowy Range

ON Saturday morning, July 1st, General Crook, with Colonel Mills, Major Burt, Lieutenants Bourke, Schuyler, Carpenter, Lemley, half a dozen packers and some newspaper correspondents left the camp on a hunting and exploring expedition into the mountain ranges. The entire party were mounted on mules, and went provisioned for four days. The weather was very fine and we were not annoyed by the heavy rain-storms which prevail there at that season. Two hours' ride brought us to the plateau of the eastern slope, and we found a rich table land, carpeted thick with grass, begemmed with countless flowers and watered by innumerable ice-cold streams. Thick pine forests covered most of the ground, but there were numerous natural parks laid out by the hand of nature with a grace and beauty seldom seen in the artificial works of landscape gardeners. From the plateau we could see three or four snowy ranges, the breezes from which rendered the July atmosphere cool and bracing as the early May zephyrs in less elevated latitudes.

Not a man of the party had ever been two miles into the mountains previously, and we fol-

lowed the trail left by the Snake Indians after
they left us for Wind River Valley on June 19th.
This led us into the very roughest parts of the
Big Horn Range, for the Snakes took the most
inaccessible route in order to avoid the hunting
parties of the Sioux, who periodically go into the
mountains to cut lodge-poles and kill game. Our
mules, nevertheless, were equal to all emergen-
cies, and by 3 o'clock in the afternoon of our
first day out we reached a lovely dell on the main
branch of Goose Creek, where we went into camp
until the dawn of Sunday. Starting forward again,
we reached the beginning of the Snowy Range
about 10 o'clock and were considerably impeded
in our course by the melting snows, which converted the mountain valleys into so many quag-
mires in which our animals floundered about at
every step. As we ascended higher we noticed
several immense layers of quartz, some of which
gave indications of gold, but not in quantities
sufficient to justify a rush of people in that direction with the expectation of growing rich in a
day or a week. In fact, the gold indications were
no greater than those to be observed in almost
every great chain of mountains on the continent.

A gentleman of our party who had traveled
much in Europe, particularly in Switzerland, said
that the cañon through which we moved reminded him in almost every feature of the St. Goth-

ard Pass. Below us were the dark, green woods and golden streams, above us and around us were the eternal snows and the tremendous rocks, from which and through which burst and thundered a thousand cascades, forming the headwaters of the splendid rivers that fertilize the slopes of that mountain region throughout its entire extent. Picturesque lakes, none of them completely frozen over, and all of immense depth, so far as we could judge, met the eye at almost every half mile, so that there was no difficulty in recognizing the inexhaustible reservoirs that fed the countless torrents which swell the volume of the Big Horn and Tongue rivers.

At 3 o'clock in the afternoon we reached the highest pinnacle of the Snowy Range, almost on a level with Cloud Peak, and saw several other immense ranges toward the west and north, which, however, looked more like cloud banks than the mountains of Idaho, Utah and Montana. Resting on this crest for half an hour, we began to descend the western slope and struck into one of the loveliest cañons that can be imagined, indented by a glorious stream and garnished by groves of cedar through all its extent. In the middle of this wild paradise we halted and went into camp. General Crook and Lieutenant Schuyler shot a couple of mountain sheep, genuine big horns, so that our commissariat was well supplied. We had along three or four pack mules, which carried the heavier portion of our bedding and subsistence. The mosquitoes bothered us terribly while the sun continued visible, but at night the intense cold compelled them to cease their labors and allow us repose.

The General felt anxious to get back to camp by the Fourth, so he announced that he would allow us until noon the next day to prospect for gold and do such hunting as we felt disposed for, after which our homeward march would begin.

At 5 o'clock on Monday morning Colonel Mills, Lieutenant Lemley, Messrs. Wasson, Davenport and the present writer left the camp and rode down the cañon to the west until we reached a point six miles distant from where Crook had established his headquarters. There the party got separated in an unaccountable manner, and Colonel Mills and myself found ourselves alone. We supposed that the others had ridden forward to a prominent mountain peak about six miles farther on, and we determined to proceed in that direction. As we advanced, the valley progressed in beauty. We passed lake after lake and stream after stream. The trees increased in size and in variety, and the vegetation assumed a tropical richness. We saw hundreds of bear, elk and buffalo tracks, indicating that the country was full of large game, but the beasts kept successfully out of sight. Dozens of American eagles rose majestically from the rocks and soared proudly above us, screaming with all their might, for, doubtless, they had never seen white men before.

We kept on until we reached the base of the mountain, which was our objective point, but still we saw nothing of our late companions, which very much surprised us. Having gone so far, we determined to ascend the peak, the lower part of which was covered with large juniper trees, the crest being a bare rock which rose several hundred feet above the forest. We tied our mules to the trees about two-thirds of the way up the hill and then scaled the remainder of the almost perpendicular ascent. Thoroughly exhausted with the heat and climbing, we finally reached the summit, and each of us uttered an involuntary exclamation of astonishment. We had actually crossed the Range, and stood upon the western-most outpost of the Big Horn Mountains.

Below us, to the west, lay the tremendous valley of the Wind River and Big Horn, bounded by a wall of mountains half covered with snow, while two other ranges of similar character rose beyond it. We observed the great river winding around to the northwest, where it meets the Yellowstone, while the Grey Bull and countless other streams, running from east and west, were distinctly discernible. Along the Big Horn River for fifteen miles on either side appeared a strip of rough, sterile lands, similar to what I had already seen in Wyoming, but the western slope of the mountains and the mouths of the cañon were natural gardens, studded with evergreen groves and beautified by parks in which the grass appeared to be several feet high, looking rich as green velvet. The water courses ran from every rock, and the noise of the rushing waters could be heard in the sublime solitude, the only sounds that broke the awful stillness of that beauteous desert.

The lakes studding the valleys looked like pieces of the blue sky which had fallen from the heavens, as if to contrast their ethereal beauty with the lovely earth beneath. My enthusiasm was aroused, and looking down the slope and along the cañon I said to Colonel Mills: "Bring along your Italy." The Colonel laughed, but acknowledged that even in his extensive experience he had never looked upon anything so picturesque. He pointed out to me several ledges of quartz, and remarked that gold almost invariably accompanied that peculiar geological formation. He also took a sketch of the locality for the benefit of the service. Then we took a last lingering look at the scene and prepared to descend to where the mules were tied to the juniper trees, a thousand feet below where we stood.

Having found the animals, we faced toward the camp, Colonel Mills acting as guide. We had not proceeded down the slope very far when, on reaching an opening in the forest, we saw two huge bull buffaloes grazing at some distance, and the killing instinct common to masculine humanity immediately suggested the beasts as victims. The mules were tied up again. We approached the edge of the wood, leveled our rifles, and in a minute both bisons were wounded. Mills killed his at the first shot, but, being a young hunter, it took three cartridges to settle my buffalo. Then we cut out their tongues, as we had no means of carrying any other portion, and proceeded on our journey. We reached our camp in the cañon at 3 o'clock and found that Crook had been gone some hours, but had left one of his scouts behind to show us his trail, as he struck out a new route over the mountains which we found much more practicable than the one we first came over.

We overtook the rest of the party at 6 o'clock and went into camp for the night. Then we learned that Lieutenant Lemley and Mr. Davenport had missed us in the woods and turned back, supposing that we had done the same, while Mr. Wasson's mule was so tired that he could urge it no farther and he was obliged to return. Thus, by accident, Colonel Mills and I had the honor of being about the first pale faces that ever crossed the Big Horn Range completely from the eastern to the western slope. Had we known that the rest had turned back, to confess the honest truth, we should have done the same. The gold prospectors examined some of the streams and lakes, but found no great encouragement, although there were plenty of indications. We saw some Indian trails, but none of very recent appearance.

Next morning, after experiencing a July snowstorm during the night, we resumed our march, and without further adventure reached camp about noon on the centennial Fourth. We had nothing but coffee wherewith to drink to the memory of George Washington, but we had a banquet on elk, deer, and mountain sheep, killed by Crook and his officers during the time that Mills and I were wandering through the cedar cañon. Taken altogether, the trip was a delightful experience.

Captain Graves of Montana with a company of some thirty miners followed our trail into the mountains, determined to decide the gold question once for all. The Captain told me that his party had explored every stream on the eastern slope of the range from Crazy Woman's Creek to Tongue River and had not found a single grain of gold. He thought that if the precious metal existed in that region at all, it must be in the Wind River Valley, where the streams from both mountain ranges converge. Reports since made by prospectors, government surveying parties and others have confirmed the statements of this experienced miner, who first broke ground with the '49ers in California. Several men experienced in mining have tried their hands at prospecting, but nothing except disappointment has come of it.

Apart, however, from this question of gold, there is no richer tract of country in America, and scarcely any more beautiful than the portion skirting those mountains and contained in their valleys. The summer season is short, it is true; the winters are long and rather cold, but an industrious population would soon conquer the difficulties produced by these circumstances. Hundreds of thousands of cattle could be raised there, grain could be grown in abundance with powerful streams in such profusion, manufactories would soon spring up, and prosperity would be unlimited. These were about the sum total of my observations at the time, and most of my humble predictions have since been fulfilled. No gold in paying quantities has been discovered. There are, as yet, no manufactures, but cattle now graze on those ranges by the myriad and agriculture has grown apace. The land is no longer a howling wilderness.

Chapter XIII

The Sibley Scout—A Close Call

THE day after the return of Crook's party from their hunt the General, who expected the wagon train and reinforcements from Fetterman to appear every moment, determined to send out a reconnoitering party along the base of the mountains northwestward to locate, if possible, the Indian village, and to take a general observation of the country. Lieutenant Frederick W. Sibley of Troop E, Second Cavalry, with twenty-five picked men drawn from the regiment was detailed to accompany the scouts, Frank Gruard and Baptiste Pourier, on the reconnaissance. John Becker, a mule packer who had had some experience as a guide, was also of the party. The scouts had ventured forward on our projected route about twenty miles two nights previously, but, having seen several parties of Sioux, returned to camp and made their report. An officer came around to my tent on the morning of Thursday, July 6th, and informed me of the plan. He said that the party would proceed toward the Little Big Horn River, and if no Indians were discovered there they would proceed still farther, feeling their way as cautiously as possible.

As I was sent out to see the country and write

173

it up, and not to dry rot around camp, something insupportable to most newspaper men, I made up my mind to accompany Lieutenant Sibley, who was at that time as fine a type of the young American officer as could be found in the service, and I know that he has not gone backward since. His father, Colonel Sibley, a retired army officer, had died in Chicago, and several members of the family still reside in that city. I had, of course, to obtain General Crook's permission to accompany the party. The General seemed somewhat surprised at my request and hesitated about letting me go. However, he finally consented, but warned me that I might get into more trouble than, perhaps, I anticipated. Lieutenant Bourke asked me what kind of an epitaph I would like him to write for me, and the other officers rallied me good-naturedly about my proposed trip. I felt elated at having obtained leave to go, and hastened to inform Sibley, who expressed himself much pleased at my resolution. Grim Captain Wells only said to his orderly, "Bring Mr. Finerty a hundred rounds of Troop E ammunition." This command was much more eloquent than an oration.

The party mustered at noon beyond the creek. Each man took a double supply of cartridges and as much food as would last for some days. I think it was a mistake to start in daylight, but the scouts seemed anxious to get forward, as the General was impatient for definite information of the Sioux. The scouts led us to camp on Big Goose Creek, distant about thirteen miles from Crook's headquarters, and there we remained until about sundown. After we had saddled up Pourier thought he observed a horseman watching us from a shallow ravine. Gruard started off in hot pursuit, but was unable to come up with the suspicious object, which ran off like the wind, and was soon lost sight of in the increasing gloom. The incident rendered the scouts rather uneasy, but they finally reached the conclusion that the object they saw was a stray elk.

We moved forward rather circumspectly through the long grass, and I can still remember how we startled scores of sage hens from cover as we advanced. All kept strict silence. We marched, for the most part, over the old Fort C. F. Smith Trail, Gruard keeping a sharp lookout from every vantage point ahead. The full moon rose behind us at about 8 o'clock, rendering every object as distinct as if it had been daylight. We looked like a phantom company marching through that great solitude, with the lofty sierra of the Big Horn looming up grandly on our left flank. We continued thus to ride in almost dead silence, save for the occasional crunching of our horses' hoofs over the pebbles in the

water courses we had to cross, until perhaps 2
o'clock in the morning. Then we halted at a
point supposed to be only a few miles from the
valley of the Little Big Horn, at least forty miles
from Crook's main body, and bivouacked among
some small, grass-covered bluffs. Our horses were
half lariated, and pickets were posted on the
heights to prevent surprise by the Indians, who,
we rightly calculated, could not be very far off.

Early on the morning of Friday, July 7th, we
were again in the saddle, pressing on cautiously
toward where the scouts believed the Indian village to be. When we had reached a point several
miles from our late bivouac and close to the Little
Big Horn River, Gruard, motioning us to halt,
ascended a rocky mound directly in our front,
leaving his horse slightly below the crest. We
observed the intrepid scout's movements with
some interest, because we knew we were in the
enemy's country and might encounter Indians
at any moment. Scarcely had the scout taken a
first cautious look from the crest of the ridge
when a peculiar motion of his hand summoned
Baptiste Pourier to his side. Baptiste dismounted
also, leaving his pony below the crest.

He joined Gruard and both scouts keenly observed the country from between the rocks on
the summit of the bluff through their glasses.
Their observations finished, they mounted their

ponies and came galloping back to us in hot haste. "Be quick, and follow me for your lives," cried Gruard. We mounted immediately and all followed his lead. He led us through bluffs of red sandstone which formed, as it were, the footstool of the mountain chain, and we were obliged, sometimes, to make our horses leap down on rocky ledges as much as six or seven feet, per- haps, in order to follow his course. We soon reached a bluff of sufficient size to conceal our horses on its westerly side, while those of us who were provided with field-glasses—namely, Sibley, Gruard, Pourier and myself—went up into the rocks and waited to see what was coming.

"What did you see, Frank?" asked Sibley of the scout, after we had settled down to make our observations.

"Only Sitting Bull's war party," Frank replied. "I knew they would be here around the Little Big Horn without coming at all."

We did not have long to wait for confirmation of his words. Almost as he spoke, groups of mounted savages appeared on the bluffs north and east of us. Every moment increased their numbers, and scattered out in the Indian fashion they seemed to cover the hilly country far and wide. Most of them were in full war costume, which added greatly to the picturesque character of the scene.

"They appear not to have seen us yet," observed Gruard. "Unless some of them hit upon our trail of this morning, we are comparatively safe." Gradually the right wing of the war party approached the ground over which we had so recently ridden. We watched their movements, as may be supposed, with breathless interest. Suddenly an Indian attired in a red blanket halted, looked for a moment at the ground, and then began to ride around in a circle. "Now we had better look out," said Gruard. "That fellow has found our trail, sure, and they will be after us in five minutes."

"What, then, are we to do?" asked the young officer in a calm, steady voice.

"Well, we have but one chance of escape," said Gruard. "Let us lead our horses into the mountains and try to cross them. But, in the meantime, let us prepare for the worst." Then we left the rocks and went down among the soldiers, who, poor fellows, seemed ready to face any fate with manly courage.

Lieutenant Sibley said to them: "Men, the Indians have discovered us. We will have to do some fighting. If we can make an honorable escape, all together, we will do it. If retreat should prove impossible let no man surrender. Die in your tracks, because the Indians show no mercy."

"All right, sir," was the simple and soldierly reply of the men, and without more ado the whole party followed the officer and the scouts up the rough mountain side, which at that point was steep and difficult to a discouraging extent. The Indians must have seen us by that time, because they were scarcely more than a mile distant, and numbers of them had halted and appeared to be in consultation.

We continued to retreat until we struck an old Sioux hunting trail on the first ridge of the mountains. "This path leads to the Snowy Range," said Gruard, who had hunted in that region when a captive among the Sioux. "If we can reach there without being overtaken or cut off," he continued, "our chances are pretty fair." Most of the trail was fairly good, and we proceeded in a direction west of north at a brisk trot. Having traveled five miles or so, and seeing no Indians following us up, Gruard came to the conclusion that the savages had given up the pursuit, or else did not care about attacking us among the mountains, as they are not much accustomed to the more elevated ranges. Our horses were pretty badly used up and some of the men were suffering from hunger and thirst. Therefore, it was deemed best for us to halt, make coffee and allow our horses to recuperate on the abundant herbage around. We selected a shady spot, and were glad to stretch our weary limbs under the umbrageous trees. But, a very little later on, we came near paying with our lives for the privilege of brief repose.

Our halt lasted an hour, possibly longer, because we had begun to believe that the Indians would not follow us into the recesses of the mountains, and grew, for the time being, rather careless. It was afternoon, I think, when we again saddled up and pushed forward, feeling much invigorated. We crossed what Gruard thought was the main branch of Tongue River, or else a tributary of the Little Big Horn, flowing clear, cold and deep through the mountain valleys, and were within full view of the superb Snowy Range. The same splendid type of scenery that I had observed when out with Crook's hunting party farther southward was visible on every side. The trail led through natural parks, open spaces bordered by rocks and pine trees on the mountain sides. At times the country grew comparatively open. We were riding in single file, the scouts leading, and kept tolerably open order. Suddenly John Becker, the packer, and a soldier who had lingered somewhat in the rear rode up to the Lieutenant, exclaiming: "The Indians! the Indians!"

Gruard and the rest of us looked over our right shoulders and saw a party of the red fiends in their war bonnets riding rapidly along that flank at no great distance. We had reached a sort of narrow plain in the mountain range, with woods upon our left, woods upon our front, and high rocks and timber on our right. "Keep well to the left, close to the woods," said Gruard to Lieutenant Sibley. Scarcely was the warning uttered when from the rocks and trees upon our right, distant perhaps 200 yards, came a ringing volley. The Indians had fired upon us, slightly wounding the horses of two or three of the soldiers and also the animal which I rode. "Fall back on the woods!" cried the scout, and every horse was wheeled toward the timber on the left. My horse stumbled from the shock of the bullet, but recovered its feet almost immediately and bore me in safety to the edge of the timber, under the rapid Indian fire, which, fortunately for us, did not at the moment possess the essential quality of accuracy.

There was no need to urge our horses to cover because they were badly stampeded by the firing, after the manner of most American horses, and we were soon dismounted in the edge of the woods. Lieutenant Sibley, before we tied the animals, made some of the soldiers fire upon the Indians, which had the effect of confining them to the rocks. The savages did not come up to their ordinary marksmanship during this affair, for not a man of ours was seriously wounded, although they succeeded in injuring several other horses by their subsequent volleys, some fatally. We soon had such of the horses as could keep their feet tied to the trees near the verge of the wood, where, also, Lieutenant Sibley formed us into a semi-circular skirmish line, and matters soon became exceedingly hot in our front. The trees and fallen timber, particularly the latter, served us admirably for breastworks and we blazed away for some time with right good will.

The Lieutenant warned us not to waste our lead, and we slackened fire somewhat. We could see, occasionally, the Indian leader, dressed in what appeared to be white buckskin and wearing a gorgeous war bonnet, directing the movements of his warriors. Gruard thought he recognized in him White Antelope, a Cheyenne chief famed for his enterprise and skill. He led one charge against us and every man on the front of the skirmish line fired upon him and his party. We did not know until long afterward that our volley put an end to his career, but so it was. White Antelope led no more charges after that day. His death was a fortunate thing for us because it damped the spirits of his men and rendered them more cautious than they would have otherwise been. But he did not fall until he had made it exceedingly interesting for our little party battling there in the edge of the woods.

The Indians lay low among the tall rocks and pine trees and kept up an almost incessant fire upon our position, filling the trees around us with their lead. I could hear their bullets rattling against the pine tree trunks like hail-stones on the roof of a barn, and it was not comfortable music either. Not a man of our party expected to leave that spot with life, because all well knew that the noise of the firing would bring to the attack every Sioux and Cheyenne within reach, while we were fully fifty miles from any hope of re-inforcement. The savages evidently aimed at our horses, thinking that by killing them all means of retreat would be cut off from us.

Meanwhile, their numbers continued to increase and they seemed to swarm on the open slopes of the hills within the range of our vision. We could distinctly hear their savage, encouraging yells to each other, and Gruard said that Sioux and Cheyennes were allied in the attacking force, all of whom appeared to be in great glee at the prospect of a scalping entertainment at our expense. They had evidently recognized Gruard, whom they heartily hated, because they called him by his Sioux name, Standing Bear, and one savage shouted to him: "Do you think there are no men but yours in this country?"

The Indians were prodigal of their ammunition, but we reserved our fire until a savage showed himself. Then we would let him have it without stint. Thus we fought and kept them at bay, for Indians rarely ever seriously attempt to take by storm a position such as we occupied, for several hours, but we could tell by the extension of their fire from our front to the right and left flanks that they were being reinforced from the villages in the neighborhood of the Little Big Horn, and we felt that unless a special providence interfered we could never carry our lives away from that spot. We were truly looking death in the face, and so close that we could feel his cold breath upon our foreheads and his icy grip upon our hearts.

Nevertheless, I remember that in one of the intervals of the firing, doubtless the one that followed the fall of the Cheyenne chief, I picked a few specimens of the mountain crocus and forget-me-not growing within my reach and placed them between the leaves of my note-book, where they are preserved almost perfectly to this day. And yet I felt anything but indifferent to the fate that seemed to await me and would have given the world, did I have the power of its bestowal, to be back safe and sound in Crook's camp again. Life seemed particularly sweet throughout that eventful day. Close acquaintance with death is not a pleasing sensation.

As the volume of the Indian fire seemed to increase, "no surrender" was the word passed from man to man around the thin skirmish line. Each one of us would, if we found it necessary, have blown out his own brains rather than fall alive into Indian hands. Doubtless, if we had remained long enough the Indians would have relieved us of all responsibility on that score. A disabling wound would have been worse than death. I had often wondered how a man felt when he thought he saw inevitable, sudden doom upon him. I know now, for I had little or no idea that we could effect our escape and, mentally at least, I could scarcely have felt my position more keenly if an Indian knife or bullet had wounded me in some vital spot. So, I think, it was with all the command, but nobody seemed, therefore, to weaken. It is one thing, however, to face death in the midst of the excitement of a general battle. It is quite another thing to face him in almost cold blood, with the certain prospect of your dishonored body being first mutilated in a revolting manner and then left to feed the wolf or the vulture among the savage mountains. After a man once sees the skull and cross bones as clearly as our party saw them on the afternoon of Friday, July 7, 1876, no subsequent glimpse of grim mortality can possibly impress him in the same manner.

Well, the eternal shadows seemed to be fast closing around us. The Indian bullets were hitting nearer every moment and the Indian yell was growing stronger and fiercer when a hand was laid on my shoulder and Rufus, a soldier who was my neighbor on the skirmish line, said: "The rest are retiring. Lieutenant Sibley tells us to do the same." I quietly withdrew from the foot of the friendly pine tree which, with a fallen trunk that lay almost across it, kept at least a dozen Indian bullets from making havoc of my body, and prepared to obey. As I passed by Sibley, who wanted to see every man under his command in the line of retreat before he stirred himself, the young officer said: "Go to your saddle bags, with caution, and take all your ammunition. We are going to abandon our remaining horses. The Indians are getting all around us, so we must take to the rocks and thick timber on foot. It seems to be our only chance of escape." I did as directed, but felt a pang at leaving my noble animal, which was bleeding from a wound in the right side. We dared not shoot our surviving horses for that would have discovered our movement to the enemy.

Gruard advised this strategy, saying that as the Indians occupied the passes east, west and north of us—all of them being difficult at the best —we could not possibly effect a retreat on horseback, even if all our animals had escaped unwounded. If the grass had happened to be a little bit dryer, and it would not take long to dry as there had been only a light thunder shower during the afternoon, the Indians, in Gruard's opinion, would have tried to burn us out of the timber. He bluntly told the Lieutenant that the position was untenable at such a distance from Crook's camp, and even if a man could succeed in getting through to the General we could not expect timely relief, and all would be over with us long before an attempt at rescue could be made. Therefore, Gruard said, if Lieutenant Sibley did not choose to take his advice, upon the officer should rest the responsibility of whatever might happen.

There was no time to be lost if we meant to get away at all, and certainly there was nothing to gain, but everything to lose, by remaining where we were. Sibley, although very averse to retreating, finally yielded to the calm advice of the scout, whose great experience among the Sioux rendered him familiar with all the methods of Indian warfare. The arguments used by Gruard were warmly seconded by Baptiste Pourier, one of the most reliable scouts on the frontier, who was acquainted from childhood with the subtle tactics of the savages.

When the retreat was decided on we acted with an alacrity which only men who have at some time struggled for their lives can understand. A couple of scattering volleys and some random shots were fired to make the savages believe that we were still in position. As we had frequently reserved our fire during the fight, our silence would not be noticed immediately. We then retired in Indian file through the trees, rocks and fallen timber in rear of us. Our horses were, evidently, plainly visible to the Indians, a circumstance that facilitated our escape. We retreated for perhaps a mile through the forest, which was filled with rugged boulders and the trunks of fallen pine trees through which no horse could penetrate, waded one of the branches of Tongue River up to our waists, and gained the slippery rocks of the great mountain ridge, where no mounted Indians, who are as lazy on foot as they are active on horseback, could pursue us. Then, as we paused to catch our breath, we heard in the distance five or six ringing volleys in succession. It was most likely the final fire delivered by the Indians before they charged our late position with the hope of getting our scalps.

"That means we are safe for the present," said Gruard, "but let us lose no time in putting more rocks between us and the White Antelope." We followed his advice with a feeling of thankfulness that only those who have passed through such an ordeal can appreciate. How astonished and chagrined the reinforced savages must have been when they ran in upon the maimed horses and did not get a single scalp! Even under such circumstances as we were placed in, we could not help indulging in a laugh at their expense.

But we had escaped one danger only to encounter another. Fully fifty miles of mountain, rock, forest, river and cañon lay between us and Crook's camp. We were unable to carry any food upon our persons. The weather was close, owing to the thunder-shower, and we threw away everything superfluous in the way of clothing. With ravening Indians behind us and uncounted precipices before us we found our rifles and what remained of our 100 rounds of ammunition each a sufficient load to carry. The brave and skillful Gruard, the ablest of scouts, seconded by the fearless Pourier, conducted our retreat through the mountain wilderness and we marched, climbed and scrambled over impediments that at any other time might have been impossible to us until about midnight, when absolute fatigue compelled us to make a halt. Then we bivouaced under the projections of an immense pile of rocks on the very summit of some unknown mountain peak, and there witnessed one of the most terrible wind and hail storms that can be imagined. The trees seemed to fall by the hundred, and their noise as they broke off and fell, or were uptorn by the roots, resembled rapid discharges of field artillery.

To add to our discomfort, the thermometer suddenly fell several degrees and being attired in summer campaign costume only we suffered greatly from the cold.

Almost before dawn we were again stumbling through the rocks and fallen trees, and about sunrise reached the tremendous cañon cut through the mountain by what is called the southern branch of Tongue river. Most of the men were too much exhausted to make the descent of the cañon, so Gruard, finding a fairly practicable path, led us to an open valley down by the river, on the left bank, as hard as we could walk, for if discovered there by any considerable body of Indians we could only halt and, worn out as most of the little band were, die together. Fortune favored us and we made the right bank of the stream unobserved, being then, according to the calculations of the scouts, about five and twenty miles from Crook's encampment. In our front toward the east we could see the plain through which Tongue River flowed, where, no doubt, as it was then a fine game country, hostile Indians abounded, while our only safe avenue of escape was to cross the stream and climb the enormous precipice that formed the right side of the cañon.

But the dauntless Gruard was equal to the emergency. He scaled the gigantic wall diagonally, and led us along what looked like a mere squirrel path not more than a foot wide, with an abyss of perhaps 500 feet below and a sheer wall of rock 200 feet high above us. After about an hour's herculean toil, we gained the crest and saw the point of mountain, some twenty miles distant, where lay our camp and comrades. This, as may well be imagined, was a blissful vision, but we were half dead from fatigue and some of us were almost famine stricken. Yet the indefatigable Gruard would not stop until we reached the eastern foot-hills, where we made, so to speak, a dive into the deep valley to obtain water, our only refreshment on that hard, rugged road. The leaves from the pine trees made the hillsides as slippery as glass, and where there was neither grass nor tree the broken stones and shale made walking absolutely painful.

Scarcely had we slaked our thirst when Gruard led us up to the hills again, and we had barely entered the timber belt when the scout uttered a warning "hush" and threw himself upon the ground, motioning us to do the same. He pointed toward the north and there, wheeling around the base of the point of the mountain we had doubled so shortly before, appeared another strong party of the Sioux in open order. The savages were riding along quite leisurely, and although fairly numerous were evidently only the advance or rear guard of some larger party. This sight made us desperate. Every man examined his carbine and looked to his ammunition. We all felt that life would be too dearly purchased by further flight, and following the example of the brave young Sibley and the gallant scouts we took up a position among the rocks on the knoll we had reached, determined, if called upon, to sell our lives as dearly as possible.

"We are in pretty hard luck, it would seem," said Sibley, addressing me, "but d—— them, we'll show the red scoundrels how white men can fight and die, if necessary. Men," he said, addressing the soldiers, "we have a good position; let every shot dispose of an Indian!"

At that moment not a man among us felt any inclination to get away. Desperation and a thirst for vengeance on the savages had usurped the place of the animal instinct to save our lives. In such moments mind rises superior to matter and soul to the nerves. But fortune spared us the ordeal of another fight in our weakened condition. Our position, as the Lieutenant had said, was a good one. On the left or north of us there was a difficult precipice, which hung above the stream, of whose waters we had just drunk to satiety. The woods grew quite thinly on our front toward the east, and south of us was an almost open slope. Our rear was well secured by an irregular line of huge boulders, and rocks of good size afforded us fair shelter in nearly all directions. There was also some fallen timber, but not enough to make a serious blaze if the enemy should try their favorite maneuver of burning us out. The Sioux, fortunately for them and, no doubt, for us, too, failed to observe our party and did not advance high enough on the hills to find our trail. They kept eastward, following a branch of Tongue River.

The excitement over, we all again felt thoroughly worn out and fell asleep, all except the tireless and ever vigilant scouts, and awoke at dark feeling somewhat refreshed, but painfully hungry. Not a man of us, whatever the risk, Sioux or no Sioux, could endure the mountain route longer, so we took our wearied, jaded lives into our hands and struck out for Crook's camp across the Plains, fording Big Goose Creek up to our armpits at 3 o'clock in the morning, the water being as cold as the melting mountain snows could make it. Two of the men, Sergeant Cornwell and Private Collins, absolutely refused to ford the creek, as neither could swim and the current was exceedingly rapid. Sibley threatened and coaxed them alternately in vain, but those men, who could face bullets and tomahawks without flinching, would not be induced to cross that stream. They begged to be allowed to hide in the bushes on the north side of the creek until horses could be sent after them. Sibley, after providentially escaping so many dangers, could not sacrifice the rest of his command for two obstinately foolish men, and the scouts urged him to push on. This he did reluctantly, but there was no alternative.

We judged that our main camp must still be some dozen miles away on Little Goose Creek, but every step, chiefly because of the toil attending the previous mountain journey, became laborious. My readers can judge for themselves how badly we were used up when it took us four hours to accomplish six miles. The rocks had broken our boots and skinned our feet, while starvation had weakened our frames. Only a comparatively few were vigorous enough to maintain a decently rapid pace. About 5 o'clock we saw some more Indians toward the east, but at some distance. We took no pains, whatever, to conceal ourselves, which, indeed, would have been a vain task on the nearly naked Plain, and the savages, if they saw us, which is highly probable, must have mistaken us for an outlying picket, and being only, comparatively speaking, a handful, kept away.

At about 6:30 o'clock we saw two horses grazing on a little knoll, and the carbines glittering in their boots on the saddles proclaimed the riders to be cavalry-men. Presently the men rose out of the long grass and made for their guns, but we hailed them and they recognized us. They were men of the Second Cavalry who had obtained permission to go hunting and who were bound for Tongue River, where they would have certainly fallen in with the Sioux. Lieutenant Sibley sent them into camp for horses and some rations, and also told them to ask for an escort to proceed as far as Big Goose Creek for the two men who had stopped there. Most of Sibley's men threw themselves on the ground, unable to move farther, and awaited the arrival of the horses. Within an hour and a half Captains Dewees and Rawolle of the Second Cavalry came out to us with led horses and some cooked provisions. They greeted us most warmly, and having aided us most kindly, proceeded to pick up Sergeant Cornwell and Private Collins, who were found all safe, concealed in the thick undergrowth of Big Goose Creek, and who reached camp a few hours after ourselves. It was 10 o'clock Sunday morning, July 9, 1876, when we rode in among the tents, amid congratulations from officers and men alike.

Thus, after passing through scenes of great peril and privation our little band found itself safe in Camp Cloud Peak, surrounded by devoted and hospitable comrades. After we had somewhat recovered from our great fatigue and refreshed ourselves by a most welcome bath in the creek

we were obliged to relate our experiences again
and again for the benefit of the entire outfit. All
agreed that Frank Gruard, for his good judgment
and the skill with which he managed our retreat,
deserved to take rank among the foremost of
scouts and plainsmen. Nor did quiet, intrepid
Baptiste Pourier lack admirers around the camp-
fires of Crook's brigade. The oldest among Indian
fighters, including such officers as Colonel Royall
and Lieutenant Lawson, concurred in saying that
escape from danger so imminent and so appalling,
in a manner so ingenious and successful, was almost without a parallel in the history of Indian
warfare. It was fortunate, they said, for our party
that an officer possessing the coolness and good
sense of Lieutenant Sibley had command of it. A
rash, bull-headed commander would have disregarded the advice of Gruard and Pourier, and
would thus have brought ruin and death upon
all of us. Colonel Royall, in the absence of General Crook, who was in the mountains on a hunt,
was kind enough to say that while a spare horse
remained in his regiment it would be at my disposal, in lieu of the one I had lost in the Sibley
Scout, as the reconnaissance has ever since been
called by the American army.

Chapter XIV

The Custer Massacre

WHEN we returned to camp General Crook was, as I have said, up in the mountains over our camp on another hunt. Colonel Royall, who had heard further reports of a massacre of our cavalry by Indians, and rendered doubly careful by the late unpleasant experience of Sibley's party, sent a few companies of the Third after the General. They met him and his followers returning to camp, fairly laden to the earth with elk, deer, and mountain sheep, which proved a great blessing to our people.

Crook received all the news with his customary placidity and then set about cleaning himself up after his long turn in the mountains. He felt morally certain, however, that some dire disaster had befallen a portion of Terry's command and he feared the impetuous Custer was the victim. His fears were sadly realized on Monday morning, July 10th, when Louis Richard and other half-breeds came in from Fetterman with the official account of the catastrophe. With it came a characteristic dispatch from General Sheridan to Crook, in which the former said, referring to the Rosebud fight: "Hit them again, and hit them harder!" Crook smiled grimly when he read the telegram, and remarked: "I wish Sheridan would come out here himself and show us how to do it. It is rather difficult to surround three Indians with one soldier!" And this was all he said upon the subject then.

The official story of the Custer disaster was put into a few words, but no account that I have heard or read, either on or off the Plains, equals in clearness and succinctness the story of the Crow Indian scout, Curley, who alone of the immediate command of General Custer survived the memorable disaster of June 25, 1876. The following is the gist of Curley's statement:[50]

Custer, with his five companies, after separating from Reno and his seven companies, moved to the right around the base of a high hill overlooking the valley of the Little Horn, through a ravine just wide enough to admit his column of

[50]Strictly speaking the destruction of General Custer's command was not a massacre, since it involved only soldiers fighting in open battle. Yet after the lapse of almost eighty years it continues to intrigue the popular mind and to challenge the resources of historians, so that almost no year passes which does not witness the publication of one or several articles and books devoted to the subject. The Author's discussion presents one viewpoint which was more or less prevalent sixty years ago. A convenient more recent and more authoritative account is Colonel W. A. Graham's *The Story of the Little Big Horn*, first published in 1926 and several times reprinted since then, most recently in 1952. The story told by Curley, the Crow scout, is no longer seriously credited.

fours. There were no signs of the presence of Indians in the hills on that side (the right) of the Little Horn, and the column moved steadily on until it rounded the hill and came in sight of the village lying in the valley below them. Custer appeared very much elated, and ordered the bugles to sound a charge, and moved on at the head of his column, waving his hat to encourage his men. When they neared the river the Indians, concealed in the undergrowth on the opposite side of the stream, opened fire on the troops, which checked the advance. Here a portion of the command were dismounted and thrown forward to the river, and returned the fire of the Indians. During this time the warriors were seen riding out of the village by hundreds and deploying across Custer's front and to his left, as if with the intention of crossing the stream on his right, while the women and children were seen hastening out of the village in large numbers in the opposite direction.

During the fight at this point Curley saw two of Custer's men killed, who fell into the stream. After fighting a few moments here, Custer seemed to be convinced that it was impracticable to cross, as it only could be done in column of fours exposed during the movement to a heavy fire from the front and both flanks. He therefore ordered the head of the column to the left, and bore diagonally into the hills, down stream, his men on foot, leading their horses. In the meantime the Indians had crossed the river (below) in immense numbers, and began to appear on his right flank and in his rear; and he had proceeded but a few hundred yards in the new direction the column had taken when it became necessary to renew the fight with the Indians who had crossed the stream. At first the command remained together, but after some minutes' fighting it was divided, a portion deploying circularly to the left and the remainder similarly to the right, so that when the line was formed it bore a rude resemblance to a circle, advantage being taken, as far as possible, of the protection afforded by the ground. The horses were in the rear, the men on the line being dismounted, fighting on foot. Of the incidents of the fight in other parts of the field than his own, Curley was not well informed, as he was himself concealed in a deep ravine from which but a small part of the field was visible.

The fight appeared to have begun, from Curley's description of the situation of the sun, about 2:30 or 3 o'clock P.M., and continued without intermission until nearly sunset. The Indians had completely surrounded the command, leaving their horses in ravines well to the rear, themselves pressing forward to the attack on foot. Confident in the great superiority of their numbers, they made several charges on all points of Custer's line, but the troops held their position firmly and delivered a heavy fire which every time drove them back. Curley said the firing was more rapid than anything he had ever conceived of, being a continuous roll, or, as he expressed it, "like the snapping of the threads in the tearing of a blanket." The troops expended all the ammunition in their belts and then sought their horses for the reserve ammunition carried in their saddle pockets.

As long as their ammunition held out, the troops, though losing considerably in the fight, maintained their position in spite of all the efforts of the Sioux. From the weakening of their fire toward the close of the afternoon the Indians appeared to believe that their ammunition was about exhausted, and they made a grand final charge, in the course of which the last of the command was destroyed, the men being shot where they lay in their positions in the line, at such close quarters that many were killed with arrows. Curley said that Custer remained alive throughout the greater part of the engagement, animating his men to determined resistance, but about an hour before the close of the fight he received a mortal wound.

The Crow said, further, that the field was thickly strewn with the dead bodies of the Sioux who fell in the attack—in number considerably more than the force of soldiers engaged. He was satisfied that their loss exceeded 200 killed, besides an immense number wounded. Curley accomplished his escape by drawing his blanket around him in the manner of the Sioux and passing through an interval which had been made in their lines as they scattered over the field in their final charge. He thought they must have seen him, for he was in plain view, but was probably mistaken by the Sioux for one of their own number, or one of their allied Arapahoes or Cheyennes.

In most particulars the account given by Curley of the fight is confirmed by the position of the trail made by Custer in his movements and the general evidences of the battle field. Only one discrepancy is noted, which relates to the time when the fight came to an end. Officers of Reno's battalion, who, late in the afternoon, from high points surveyed the country in anxious expectation of Custer's appearance, and who commanded a view of the field where he had fought, say that no fighting was going on at that time—between 5 and 6 o'clock. It is evident, therefore, that the last of Custer's command was destroyed at an earlier hour in the day than Curley relates.

Much doubt was expressed at the time as to the truth of Curley's tale, but the famous Sioux chief,

Gall, who had an important command among the hostiles during the battle, on being taken over the field in 1888 by the officers at Fort Custer confirmed the statement of the Crow scout. Custer, according to Gall, did not succeed in crossing the river. He saw at a glance that he was overpowered, and did the only thing proper under the circumstances in leading his command to higher ground where it could defend itself to some advantage. Even in that dread extremity his soldier spirit and noble bearing held the men under control, and the dead bodies of the troopers of Calhoun's and Keogh's companies, found by General Gibbon's command lying in ranks as they fell, attested the cool generalship exhibited by the heroic leader in the midst of deadly peril.

It had always been General Custer's habit to divide his command when attacking Indian villages. His victory over Black Kettle on the Washita was obtained in that manner, but the experiment proved fatal to Major Elliot and a considerable squad of soldiers.[51] It was the general opinion in Crook's command at the time that had an officer of more resolution been in Major Reno's place he would have attempted to join Custer at any cost. Reno was, no doubt, imposed upon by Indian strategy, and his re-

[51]For the battle of the Washita, November 27, 1868, see Custer's *My Life on the Plains,* Chapter 10.

treat to the bluffs was, to say the least of it, premature. But in the light of after events it does not seem probable that he could have reached the fatal heights upon which Custer and his men perished. Had Custer taken his entire regiment into the fight he might still have sustained a repulse, but would have escaped annihilation. It is always a tactical error to divide a small command in face of the enemy. This was Custer's error. Applying the same principle on a larger scale, Napoleon erred when he detached Grouchy after Ligny. That fault cost him his crown and liberty. Reno, at the Little Big Horn, was Custer's Grouchy.

Some prominent army officers, and others, have held that Custer did not obey the order of General Terry. This point has given rise to controversy and I think it only fair to reproduce the commanding officer's instructions to General Custer, issued on the day that he marched from Rosebud Landing. The order was as follows:

"The Brigadier-General commanding directs that as soon as your regiment can be made ready for the march, you proceed up the Rosebud in pursuit of the Indians whose trail was discovered by Major Reno a few days since. It is, of course, impossible to give any definite instructions in regard to this movement, and, were it not impossible to do so, the Department Commander places too

much confidence in your zeal, energy and ability
to wish to impose upon you precise orders which
might hamper your action when nearly in contact
with the enemy. He will, however, indicate to you
his own views of what your action should be, and
he desires that you should conform to them unless
you shall see sufficient reason for departing from
them. He thinks you should proceed up the Rosebud until you ascertain definitely the direction in
which the trail above spoken of leads. Should it
be found, as it appears to be almost certain that
it will be, to turn toward the Little Big Horn, he
thinks that you should still proceed southward,
perhaps as far as the head waters of the Tongue
River, and then turn toward the Little Big Horn,
feeling constantly, however, toward your left, so
as to preclude the possibility of the escape of the
Indians to the south, or southeast, by passing
around your left flank. The column of Colonel
Gibbon is now in motion for the mouth of the Big
Horn. As soon as it reaches that point it will cross
the Yellowstone and move up at least as far as the
forks of the Big and Little Big Horn. Of course its
future movements must be controlled by circumstances as they arise; but it is hoped that the Indians, if upon the Little Big Horn, may be so
nearly inclosed by the two columns that their
escape will be impossible. The Department Commander desires that on your way up the Rosebud

you should thoroughly examine the upper part of Tulloch's Creek, and that you should endeavor to send a scout through to Colonel Gibbon's column with information of the result of your examination. The lower part of that creek will be examined by a detachment of Colonel Gibbon's command. The supply steamer will be pushed up the Big Horn as far as the forks of the river are found to be navigable for that space, and the Department Commander, who will accompany the column of Colonel Gibbon, desires you to report to him there, not later than the expiration of the time for which your troops are rationed, unless, in the meantime, you receive further orders."

Custer marched only twelve miles up the Rosebud on June 22d. On the succeeding day he made thirty-three miles. Then Indian signs began to show themselves and the trail became hot. On June 24th Custer marched twenty-eight miles, halted and waited for reports from his scouts. At 9:25 o'clock that night, according to Reno's report, Custer called his officers together and told them that beyond a doubt the village of the hostiles had been located by the scouts in the valley of the Little Big Horn. It would, therefore, he said, be necessary to cross the divide between the Rosebud and the Little Big Horn, and in order to effect this without being discovered by the Indians a night march would be necessary. The command resumed its march, and began crossing the divide at 11 o'clock P.M. Three hours later the scouts informed Custer that the divide could not be crossed before daylight, so the command halted and made coffee. The march was resumed at 5 A.M., the divide was crossed at 8 o'clock, and the command was in the valley of one of the branches of the Little Big Horn. Some Indians had been seen, and as all chance of surprising the village was, therefore, at an end, Custer resolved to march at once to the attack.

Commands were assigned on the march, and Reno had Troops M, A and G placed under his orders; Colonel Benteen received command of Troops H, D and K; Captain McDougall with Troop B escorted the pack train, and Custer took with himself the fated Troops C, E, F, I, and L.

Reno claimed that he received no definite orders from Custer, but moved with the companies assigned to him along with the rest of the column and well to its left. He saw Benteen moving with his battalion still farther to the left, and the latter officer told Reno that he had orders to sweep everything before him. He did not see Benteen again until 2:30 o'clock, when the survivors of both battalions, together with Captain McDougall's troop, rallied on the bluffs above the Little Big Horn River.

Custer carried his battalion to the right, and in this order all moved down the tributary creek to the Little Big Horn Valley. When Custer saw all the signs of the presence of a large village, previous to the division of his command, he became greatly elated, and waving his hat above his head he, according to the statements of some of the soldiers who were detached with Reno and Benteen, shouted: "Hurrah! Custer's luck!" But luck turned its back on the hero of sixty successful charges that bloody day. His long, yellow locks had been cut shorter than was his wont for the sake of convenience, and after the tragedy some of the officers who survived likened the dead hero to Samson. Both were invincible while their locks remained unshorn.

Horned Horse, an old Sioux chief, whose son was killed early in the fight, stated to the late Capt. Philo Clark, after the surrender of the hostiles, that he went up on a hill overlooking the field to mourn for the dead, as he was too weak to fight, after the Indian fashion. He had a full view of all that took place almost from the beginning. The Little Big Horn is a stream filled with dangerous quicksand, and cuts off the edges of the northern bluffs sharply near the point where Custer perished. The Indians first saw the troops on the bluffs early in the morning, but, owing to the abruptness and height of the river banks,

Custer could not get down to the edge of the stream. The valley of the Little Big Horn is from half a mile to a mile and a half wide, and along it for a distance of fully five miles the mighty Indian village stretched.

Most of the immense pony herd was out grazing when the savages took the alarm at the appearance of the troops on the heights. The warriors ran at once for their arms, but by the time they had taken up their guns and ammunition belts the soldiers had disappeared. The Indians thought they had been frightened off by the evident strength of the village, but again, after what seemed quite a long interval, the head of Custer's column showed itself coming down a dry water course, which formed a narrow ravine, toward the river's edge. He made a dash to get across, but was met by such a tremendous fire from the repeating rifles of the savages that the head of his command reeled back toward the bluffs after losing several men who tumbled into the water, which was there but eighteen inches deep, and were swallowed up in the quicksand. This is considered an explanation of the disappearance of Lieutenant Harrington and several men whose bodies were not found on the field of battle. They were not made prisoners by the Indians, nor did any of them succeed in breaking through the thick array of the infuriated savages.

Horned Horse did not recognize Custer, but supposed he was the officer who led the column that attempted to cross the stream. Custer then sought to lead his men up to the bluffs by a diagonal movement, all of them having dismounted, and firing, whenever they could, over the backs of their horses at the Indians, who had by that time crossed the river in thousands, mostly on foot, and had taken the General in flank and rear, while others annoyed him by a galling fire from across the river. Hemmed in on all sides, the troops fought steadily, but the fire of the enemy was so close and rapid that they melted like snow before it and fell dead among their horses in heaps. He could not tell how long the fight lasted, but it took considerable time to kill all the soldiers. The firing was continuous until the last man of Custer's command was dead. Several other bodies besides that of Custer remained unscalped, because the warriors had grown weary of the slaughter. The water-course, in which most of the soldiers died, ran with blood. He had seen many massacres, but nothing to equal that.

If the troops had not been encumbered by their horses, which plunged, reared and kicked under the appalling fire of the Sioux, they might have done better. As it was, a great number of Indians fell, the soldiers using their revolvers at close range with deadly effect. More Indians died by the pistol than by the carbine. The latter weapon was always faulty. It "leaded" easily and the cartridge shells stuck in the breech the moment it became heated, owing to some defect in the ejector. It is not improbable that many of Custer's cavalrymen were practically disarmed because of the deficiency of that disgracefully faulty weapon. If they had been furnished with good Winchesters, or some other style of repeating arm, the result of the battle of the Little Big Horn might have been different.

What happened to Custer after he disappeared down the north bank of the river has already been told in the words of Curley and Horned Horse. Not an officer or enlisted man of the five troops under Custer survived to tell the tale. The male members of the Custer family, George A., Colonel Tom and Boston, were annihilated. Autie Reed, a young relative of the General, who, like Boston Custer, accompanied the command as a sightseer, was also killed.[52] Mark Kellogg, of the St. Paul

[52]Autie (Armstrong) Reed was the son of Custer's half-sister, who married David Reed of Monroe, Michigan. In 1938 the present Editor interviewed Mrs. C. W. Hockett of Detroit, who had grown up at Monroe and who still retained lively recollections of her girlhood associations there. Concerning young Reed she related: "General Custer's nephew George Armstrong Reed, was among those killed. We used to call him Autie. Autie was the life of the party. He went to all the dances and we thought a great deal of him. It had been his ambition to join his

and Bismarck press, the only correspondent who accompanied the Custer column, nearly succeeded in making his escape. The mule he rode was too slow, however, and he was finally overtaken and shot down. Had he succeeded in getting away, his fame would have rivaled that of the explorer, Stanley.

Among the many distinguished people who fell in that dreadful conflict was Brevet-colonel Keogh, who had previously fought for the Pope under Lamoriciere, in Italy, and who attained the rank of colonel in the volunteer service because of gallant and meritorious conduct throughout the Civil War. He was a noble-hearted gentleman, the *beau ideal* of a cavalry commander, and the very soul of valor.[53] There also died Captain Calhoun,

Uncle and at last the time had come when he was seventeen and he was permitted to go. I remember him so well. I used to like to go over to his house. They had a room literally filled with Indian costumes and things that his Uncle had sent them. I used to love to dress up in these war bonnets. . . . Almost the last time I saw Autie was when a girl friend and I went to a fire (it was the custom in those days to run to fires) and he was there." *Burton Hist. Collection Leaflet,* Vol. 9, May 1939 issue, p. 11.

[53]Captain Myles W. Keogh, numerously brevetted for services in the Civil War and subsequently. Frederic F. Van de Water, author of *Glory Hunter: A Life of General Custer,* characterizes him as "once a papal Zouave, a divil-may-care Irishman with mustache and imperial and an unholy thirst which he could curb only by placing all his cash in the hands of Fennigan his striker and actual guardian."

Custer's brother-in-law; Captain Yates, Col. W. W. Cooke, the regimental adjutant; Lieutenants Crittenden, Smith, Riley, Harrington, McIntosh and several others.

Reno crossed the Little Big Horn, accompanied by some of the scouts, and charged down the valley a considerable distance. He finally halted in the timber and was, as he subsequently claimed, attacked by superior numbers. He remained in position but a short time, when he thought it advisable to retreat across the river and take up a position on the bluffs. This movement was awkwardly executed, and in scaling the bluffs several officers and enlisted men were killed and wounded. The Indians, as is always the case when white troops retreat before them, became very bold and succeeded in dragging more than one soldier from the saddle. Captain De Rudio, an Italian officer exiled from his country for political reasons, and a scout, unable to keep up with Reno's main body, concealed themselves in the brush and the Indians passed and repassed so close to them that they could have touched the savages by merely putting out their hands. They were fortunate in remaining undiscovered, and joined Reno on the 27th, after the arrival of Terry and Gibbon.

Col. F. W. Benteen, now retired and residing at Atlanta, Ga., has, at the request of the author, given the following statement relative to the movements of his battalion after parting from the main command:

"There was to have been no connection between Reno, McDougall and myself in Custer's order. I was sent off to the left several miles from where Custer was killed to actually hunt up some more Indians. I set out with my battalion of three troops, bent on such purpose, leaving the remainder of the regiment, nine troops, at a halt and dismounted. I soon saw, after carrying out the order that had been given me by Custer and two other orders which were sent to me by him through the sergeant-major of the regiment and the chief trumpeter, at different times, that the Indians had too much horse sense to travel over the kind of country I had been sent to explore, unless forced to; and concluded that my battalion would have plenty of work ahead with the others. Thus, having learned all that Custer could expect, I obliqued to the right to strike the trail of the main column and got into it just ahead of McDougall and his pack train.

"I watered the horses of my battalion at a morass near the side of the road, and the advance of McDougall's packs got into it just as I was pulling out from it. I left McDougall to get his train out in the best manner he could and went briskly on, having a presentiment that I'd find hot work very soon. Well, en route, I met two orderlies with messages, one for the commanding officer of the packs and one for myself. The messages read: 'Come on. Be quick' and 'Bring packs;' written and signed by Lieutenant Cooke, adjutant of the regiment. Now, knowing that there were no Indians between the packs and the main column, I did not think it necessary to go back for them—some seven or eight miles—nor did I think it worth while waiting for them where the orders found me, so I pushed to the front at a trot and got there in time to save Reno's outfit. The rest you know."

Reno, Benteen and McDougall, having effected a junction, fortified themselves on the bluffs and stood off the whole Indian outfit, which laid close siege to them until the 27th. Several desperate charges of the savages on the position were handsomely repulsed. The troops, especially the wounded, suffered terribly from thirst, and during the night a few daring soldiers succeeded in getting some water out of the river in their camp kettles, at the peril of their lives. One of those brave men was Mr. Theodore Golden, then of the Seventh Cavalry and now a resident of Janesville, Wisconsin.

The situation of the closely beleaguered troops was growing desperate when the infantry and light artillery column of General Gibbon, which was accompanied by General Terry, came in sight on the morning of the 27th. The soldiers of Reno, at this inspiring vision, swarmed out over the rough-and-ready breastworks, cheering the heroes of Fort Fisher and Petersburg vociferously. Many wept for joy and the chivalrous Terry and the gallant Gibbon did everything in their power to cheer up the wearied soldiers in their hour of misfortune. The Indians did not attempt any further attack after the rescuing party arrived. They, too, were tired out, and had expended a vast quantity of ammunition. They drew off toward the mountains, first burning such irremovable impedimenta as remained in their village. A part of their tepees had been burned in the fight with Custer.

General Gibbon, after a brief rest, set out to see what had become of that officer. Reno's men felt certain that something dreadful had happened to their comrades, because during the afternoon of the 25th and the morning of the 26th they had recognized the guidons of the Seventh Cavalry, which the savages were waving in an ecstasy of triumph.[54] General Gibbon had to march several miles before he came upon the

[54]Two of these guidons are still preserved: the one belonging to Captain Keogh's Company was recaptured by General Mills at the Slim Buttes battle, September 9, 1876 and preserved in his family until recently, when it was given to the Little Big Horn Battlefield Museum. See Col. W. A. Graham, *The Colors of the Seventh at the Little Big*

field of blood. The sight that met his eyes was a shocking one. The bluffs were covered with the dead bodies of Custer's men, all stripped naked, and mostly mutilated in the usual revolting manner. The General's corpse was found near the summit of the bluff, surrounded by the bodies of his brothers and most of the officers of his command. The Indians, who had recognized his person, and who respected his superb courage, forebore from insulting his honored clay by the process of mutilation.[55] The Seventh Infantry, Gen-

Horn. The other, found by Sergeant Ferdinand Culbertson of Company A, Seventh Cavalry beneath the body of a slain soldier, June 28, 1876, was presented to the Detroit Institute of Arts in 1895. In 1952 it was deposited with the Little Big Horn Battlefield Museum on indefinite loan. Still other Custer guidons were recaptured at Mackenzie's destruction of Dull Knife's village, November 25, 1876. Bourke, *On the Border with Crook,* 393. Information concerning their subsequent disposition has not been found.

[55]Despite numerous statements to the contrary, the Indians, aside from scalping, inflicted relatively few indignities upon the slain soldiers of Custer's command. Lieutenant James H. Bradley, General Terry's chief scout, who was the first responsible officer on the scene following the battle, distinctly states that apart from scalping "in possibly a majority of cases there was little mutilation." Even in such cases as there was mutilation of the bodies, Bradley thought it the result of blows with knife or other weapon to finish a wounded man, rather than a deliberate mutilation. Although nearly all of the bodies were stripped, half a dozen or so were not. Custer's body was undefiled, as the Author states. For Bradley's report see Colonel W. A. Graham, *The Story of the Little Big Horn,* 162–67.

eral Gibbon's regiment, buried the gallant dead where they fell, marking the graves of all that could be identified. Custer's remains and those of his relatives, together with those of most of the officers, have since been removed. The brave General is buried at West Point, from which he graduated, and on which his glorious career and heroic death have reflected immortal luster.

Three hundred and fifteen enlisted men and seventeen commissioned officers, together with several civilians, scouts and others, perished in this unfortunate battle. Charley Reynolds, the scout, whose name is still a household word upon the Plains, fell dead by the side of his beloved chief.

After performing the sad duty of burying the dead the wounded were placed on mule litters and Generals Terry and Gibbon slowly and sadly retraced their way to Rosebud Landing on the Yellowstone, where, like Crook, they awaited reinforcements, and made no forward movement until August.

Chapter XV

The Fight on the War Bonnet

ON July 12th the Snake Indians, 213 men, commanded by their grand old chief, Washakie—an Indian who greatly resembled the Rev. Robert Collyer, except for the darkness of his complexion—and his two sons rejoined us according to promise.[56] They were welcome, as we had been seriously annoyed every night owing to the enfilading of our camp by small parties of Sioux from the woods in the foot-hills. They did little damage, but they rendered the herding of our horses and mules more difficult. One night a Sioux warrior, more daring than his comrades, stole in between our pickets and attempted to run off some horses. He was discovered in time. Several shots were fired. The whole camp was alarmed, and there was a rattle of fire-arms in the dead hour of night from one end of our lines to the other. But the nimble Sioux escaped in the darkness, leaving his hunting-knife behind him. He got none of our animals.

[56]Robert Collyer famous as a reformer and preacher, was pastor of Unity Church, Chicago, from 1859 to 1879. In the latter year he became pastor of the Church of the Messiah in New York, serving as pastor or pastor emeritus until his death in 1912. *Dictionary of American Biography.*

On July 13th our wagon train arrived from Fetterman, escorted by seven companies of infantry from the Fourth, Ninth and Fourteenth regiments. These, with the companies that had remained with Crook, made a respectable battalion of well-seasoned foot soldiers. Among the officers who joined us with this detachment was Captain Burke of the Fourteenth, a very popular man.

But with the wagon train there also came the devil in the shape of a peddler who sold whisky. Two abandoned females disguised as mule drivers also came into camp. Such of the soldiers as had money got drunk with amazing promptitude, but they were not many. General Crook got angry when he learned what was going on, ordered the whisky barrels seized and the harlots put under arrest, to be sent back with the first train. A captain got intoxicated on duty, neglected to place his pickets properly, was tried in the field, deprived of his command, and ordered, under arrest, to Fort Fetterman. This gallant but unfortunate soldier, for whom I entertained a sincere regard, was subsequently dismissed from the service, that being the finding of the field court martial. I suppose there was no way out of it, but I have always considered the sentence too severe. The pickets are always commanded, in the immediate sense, by good sergeants, and our non-commissioned officers are the best in the world. Therefore the danger from the captain's neglect was not great; but, of course, discipline had to be maintained. I wish the court martial had had the power to order the whisky peddler flogged. He was the greater culprit of the two.

The severity in the case mentioned had the effect of restoring order and thenceforth no officer touched whisky, chiefly because there was none to touch except what the surgeons had in their medicine chests. At this time I changed my mess to Troop A, Third Cavalry, then commanded by First Lieutenant Joseph Lawson, an Irish Kentuckian and as gallant an old gentleman as ever drew a sword. He was an original in every way, and joined the Union army on principle at a time when nearly all his neighbors of fighting age were donning the rebel gray. Lawson was absolutely without fear, but his many peculiarities induced his brother officers to quiz him when they had nothing else to do. He bore it all with supreme good nature, and on the day of battle showed the whole brigade that an officer need not always hail from West Point in order to gain that place in the affections of his soldiers which dauntless courage alone can win.

It was, I think, on July 14th that General Crook was surprised by the appearance in his camp of a sergeant named Bell and two private soldiers, named Evans and Stewart, of the Seventh Infantry, who came with dispatches from General Terry. They also brought details of the Custer fight, with which we were already familiar. Those brave men traveled at night and lay by in the day time so as to avoid any parties of the Sioux who might be prowling around the country. They had come from Rosebud Landing on the Yellowstone, where Terry's force then lay, and had crossed no large Indian trail of recent formation while en route. This convinced the General that the main body of the hostiles was still in the locality where Custer had fallen, and where the Sibley scout had located them. Crook was very reticent at this period of the campaign, but, judging by subsequent events, I think he delayed moving against the Sioux until the Fifth Cavalry could arrive to reinforce him, or perhaps he had arranged some combination with Terry, as the latter's three soldiers were sent back with dispatches, two days after their arrival in our camp. I was glad to learn, subsequently, that they reached their destination without misadventure.[57]

[57]The three soldiers were Private James Bell, William Evans, and Benjamin F. Stewart of Company E, Seventh U.S. Infantry. All were awarded medals on December 2, 1876. General Mills places the date of their arrival at Crook's camp as "about June 30," and definitely states that they brought to Crook the first report of Custer's defeat. *My Story*, 410.

The General employed his scouts and Indians in reconnoitering the enemy, whose hunting parties they could see down Tongue River nearly every day. Crook was very impatient to attack, but our cavalry horses were, for the most part, in poor condition, and he wished to have the assistance of General Merritt's fresh and splendid regiment before making a forward movement, which he wished to be decisive. I know that General Crook afterward regretted this delay because the brilliant General Merritt, with his Fifth Cavalry, was detained by an unexpected movement of the Cheyennes at Red Cloud Agency and had to do battle with them on War Bonnet Creek. Maj. T. H. Stanton of the pay department brought information to Merritt on Saturday, July 15th, that eight hundred warriors of the band mentioned, fully armed and equipped, would leave the Agency early on Sunday morning for the purpose of joining the hostiles in the Big Horn region.

Captain Charles King, U.S.A., then with the Fifth Cavalry, thus clearly defines the situation in his excellent description of the operation: "To continue on his [Merritt's] march to Fort Laramie and let them go would have been gross, if not criminal, neglect. To follow by the direct road to the reservation, sixty-five miles away, would have been simply to drive them out and hasten their movement. Manifestly there was but one thing to be done, to throw himself across their path and capture or drive them back, and to do this he must, relatively speaking, march over three sides of a square while they were traversing the fourth, and must do it undiscovered."

Well, General Merritt did it undiscovered. He is a man of quick decision, and soon had seven troops of his gallant regiment in rapid motion to intercept the enterprising Cheyennes at their favorite crossing on War Bonnet Creek. Buffalo Bill accompanied him as chief of scouts. After a difficult night march Merritt had his command in position at dawn and succeeded in keeping it perfectly concealed. Lieutenant Hall, his quartermaster, marched all night to overtake him and his wagons were plainly visible, some miles away at sunrise. A large body of Indians, watching the wagons, was visible also. The train drew nearer, the Indians following it up behind the bluffs, so as to be out of view, but this action on their part inadvertently exposed them to Merritt, of whose presence they were utterly unconscious.

The General waited for the proper moment to strike and it came when two mounted couriers, evidently detached from the train, came riding along the trail not far from where he was lying in wait. The Indians, impatient for blood, swooped down upon the two soldiers, but Merritt was too quick for them. He sent forward a small party to check the charge of the Cheyennes. Buffalo Bill was in the van and reaped the brightest laurels of his adventurous life that morning by slaying Yellow Hand, the Indian leader, in single combat. The other Cheyennes came on rapidly to the assistance of their friends, and then Merritt, unmasking his whole force under Carr and Mason, hurled it upon them like a thunderbolt. The savages were taken totally by surprise and were driven back upon the Agency in wild disorder. They thought Merritt must have dropped from the clouds. He followed them to the Agency and placed them under an effective guard, after which he renewed his march to reinforce General Crook.

Merritt's action on the War Bonnet was worthy of his well-won fame as a general, but it prevented him from joining Crook's command until the beginning of August and by that time the Sioux, having exhausted nearly all the game at the base of the mountains, made a general break for the north, scattering themselves over many trails so as to confuse pursuit.

About July 20th General Crook sent a man named Kelly, a hanger-on of the pack train, with dispatches to General Terry, informing the latter, as I was told, of his probable future course of action and leaving it optional with him to make a junction of the two commands or not. The General offered Kelly a small escort, but he declined with thanks and told me afterward that nothing less than a regiment would be of any use, whereas by going alone and on foot he could travel all night, sleep in the undergrowth on the streams he would follow in the daytime, and thus reach his destination in safety. "You see," said Kelly, "I am fairly familiar with the country and can guide myself, when it ain't cloudy, by the stars. When I can't see the stars I can follow the cañons, and I cannot run into an Indian village because their dogs always bark at night and so give warning of their whereabouts. Indians never keep watch on dark nights, leastways the Sioux don't, and I know what I'm talking about. Another thing, I won't be bothered with a horse or a mule either. More men have lost their lives on this frontier through their horses whinnying to the Indian ponies out of cover or through the mules braying than through any other cause. Then an Indian will go to hades after a horse, but when it's a man afoot and he carries a good gun Mr. Indian is not so eager to follow him up, because the man afoot has the advantage of cover. Of course if I ran into a whole heap of Indians that would be a different matter. I'd get through all right anyhow, never you fear."

Kelly was an eccentric fellow, young, tall and well built. He was to receive good pay for his mission, but it took him a day or two to fully make up his mind. He started out one evening wearing only moccasins on his feet, but the cacti pierced the deer hide and he returned for his shoes. He started again, Gruard accompanying him some distance. At last Kelly saw, or thought he saw, an Indian on a bluff ahead of him. "What am I going to do with that fellow?" he inquired of Frank. "Better go up there and ask him," replied the Scout. Kelly turned back again, but he made a third attempt and nobody expected him to succeed in it, yet he did. He followed out his own program, marched down the Rosebud Cañon in the night time, and slept during the day. Finally, after dodging some Indian villages he reached the Yellowstone, and aided by a log floated down to where General Terry's camp was situated and delivered his dispatches. This I learned after we met General Terry in August. I inquired for Kelly, whom I found with the wagon train cleaning a rifle, and he succinctly related, as given above, the story of his remarkable adventure. He had determined, if he fell by accident into the hands of the Sioux, to play off as a madman, because the savages rarely ever injure a maniac, whom they regard as being under the special protection of the Great Spirit. Kelly, in my opinion, was near enough to the crazy line to play the role to the entire satisfaction of the Indians.

We learned with no little dismay, about the end of July, that General Crook, when he would resume the campaign, intended to abandon his tents and bivouac his command during the remainder of the season. He would also rely upon his pack train only, allowing no man to carry more than a single blanket and limiting clothing of every kind to the most meager dimensions. Toward the end of the month four Crow Indians came in from Terry's camp and reported the Sioux still in strong parties around the Little Big Horn and the northern tributaries of Tongue River. General Crook, at this news, became very impatient to attack, and immediately made a movement some ten miles to the northwestward along the foot-hills of the great range. The scouts saw several outlying parties of Indians, but not the main body.

The General became convinced that the savages were playing some trick, and, seemingly, deter-mined to attack them with his inferior forces. He became very restless, and quite evidently was much annoyed by the slow advance of Merritt, for which he could not then account. Merritt, as has already been shown, was not in fault, but on the contrary had, by his bold diversion on War Bonnet Creek, prevented a most potent reinforcement of the hos-tiles by the discontented Cheyennes of the Agen-cies. No advices concerning General Merritt's action had reached our camp, so that we were all profoundly ignorant at that period of the great service which he had rendered.

General Crook, under the circumstances, appeared to be greatly exasperated. He seemed to swing like a pendulum between a desire to fight at any cost and an innate feeling that to risk a battle with an outnumbering band of savages so recently and signally victorious would be very rash, and might, as in the case of the gallant Custer, result in disaster. Orders were actually given to march directly on the Little Big Horn and engage the Sioux, when, on the afternoon of August 2d, a courier from Merritt arrived announcing that he was approaching rapidly at the head of ten troops of the excellent Fifth Cavalry. This courier was Charley White, the familiar friend of Buffalo Bill, a tall, stout, fair-complexioned, long-haired, pock-marked man of about thirty-five, whose chief desire was to imitate the celebrated Bill in every particular. Buffalo Bill was a great favorite with General Sheridan and generally accompanied that immortal hero whenever he went to hunt or scout upon the Plains. On one occasion Sheridan was annoyed to find that Bill had gone East to arrange for the exhibition which has since become world famous as the Wild West Show. Charley White appeared instead. "Who the ——— are you?" asked Sheridan, in his abrupt, impetuous way.

"When Cody is not here," replied Charley, "*I* am Buffalo Bill."

"The d——— you are!" cried Sheridan. "Buffalo Chip, you mean!"

Charley felt crushed, and the unfortunate nickname clung to him until the day of his gallant death at Slim Buttes.[58]

After delivering his message to our General, Charley White rode around our camp and was hailed by soldiers, packers and train men by the title bestowed upon him by Fighting Phil.

"You fellows look as if you didn't have any chuck [the frontier word for rations] in a month," said he to Tom Moore.

"Get off your horse," said Tom, "and we'll relieve your famine in a pair of minutes."

White accordingly dismounted and we all surrounded him. He related the whole of Buffalo Bill's exploit with great glee, and made us think that the days of Achilles and Hector had been renewed in Merritt's fight on War Bonnet Creek. Poor fellow! Buffalo Bill seemed to him a bigger man than all the generals of the United States Army.

The courier from Merritt had met Crook's brigade on the northernmost branch of Tongue

[58]General King, in response to the request of Buffalo Bill Cody, recorded an appreciative account of White's career and of his death in the Slim Buttes battle. King,

River, about one good march from the field where
Custer died. It was understood in the camp, but
on what authority I now forget, that Crook had
arranged a rendezvous with Terry on that stream
for the very day on which Merritt's advance was
reported. But the hero of Fort Fisher failed to
keep the tryst.[59]

The Sioux scouting parties had hovered around
us at a safe distance for days. They avoided
fighting, but fired the mountains and the Plains
for miles upon miles, making it next to impossible
to observe any object, however prominent, through
the thick and pungent cloud of smoke. The scouts
of our command found it difficult to determine
whether the hostiles had retired into the Big Horn
fastnesses or retreated toward the British possessions. Finally, those experts of the wilderness
came to the conclusion that Sitting Bull had
adopted the latter alternative. They had located

however, gives his name as James White. *Campaigning
with Crook*, 113–17.

[59]In December, 1863–January 15, 1864 General Terry
distinguished himself by the capture of Fort Fisher, North
Carolina. For this success, "the supreme accomplishment
of his military career," he received the thanks of Congress
and promotion to the rank of brigadier general in the
regular army. At the time of the 1876 campaign he was
serving as commander of the Department of Dakota. On
March 3, 1886 he was promoted to the rank of major
general and on April 9 was made commander of the Department of the Missouri, with headquarters at Chicago.
Dictionary of American Biography.

one broad and well-defined trail which led toward the north, but they also suspected that the hostiles had left a strong war party near the mountains to observe our movements and gather up what game they could find in that fecund region.

General Crook, impatient to form a junction with Merritt and feeling sure that the Indians were trying to outwit him, moved out with all his force from Tongue River camp on the morning of August 3d, and fell in with Merritt's column on Goose Creek, after a march of twenty-five miles, that evening. This movement raised our force to nearly 2,000 fighting men, most of them in excellent condition. Our wagons, including those of General Merritt, amounted to 160, and it was determined to park them all and place them under command of Major Furey, with orders to retire on Forts Fetterman and Laramie by easy marches. The General decided not to detail any troops to guard the wagons as the discharged soldiers, drivers and hangers-on, all well armed, numbered fully 200 men—sufficient to defend the train against any ordinary party of hostile Indians.

Orders were issued that no man should take with him a change of clothing, but each person was allowed to carry 100 rounds of ammunition and four days' rations on his horse or person. A single blanket and a saddle blanket with a poncho, if he were lucky enough to possess one, must serve for covering. The saddle always constitutes the pillow of the cavalryman and the knapsack of the foot soldier on the Plains. Lieutenant Bubb, chief of the commissariat, with Tom Moore, chief packer, as assistant, was placed in command of the pack train. It carried fifteen days' rations for each soldier and all the reserve ammunition.

It blew great guns on the night of August 3, 1876 and more than half the tents were leveled to the ground, greatly to the discomfort of the weary troops. It was to be our last night under canvas for some time, and rude old Boreas made us feel his power. A terrible red glow lit up the clouded midnight sky, and looking westward in amazement we saw the whole front of the Big Horn Mountains on fire! Although the conflagration was many miles distant from our camp the strong west wind bore the pungent timber smoke upon us in blinding volumes and countless wild animals, driven frantic by fear, careered through the fiery darkness like beings of another world, some of them uttering weird sounds of unreasoning terror. It was a superb, if awe-compelling, scene. The prairies, ignited by the burning brands from the sierra, were also in a flame, and preparations were made to fight fire with fire in Indian fashion, if it became necessary. Our Indian allies burned over a large belt of prairie west of our camp early in the evening, so that we felt comparatively secure. But the smoke and cinders were stifling and few could sleep in comfort under such conditions.

Generals Crook and Merritt, together with the various battalion commanders, held a long consultation during the evening. I had had time to observe the new arrivals in the course of the day and they impressed me favorably. General Merritt was quite tall, rather spare and nearly beardless. He had a florid complexion, keen eyes of grayish hue, and small but comely and resolute features. General Carr, then lieutenant-colonel of the Fifth Cavalry, was short, fairly stout, full-bearded, and lavish, while in conversation, of graceful and energetic gestures. The other officers, I learned subsequently, took very little part in the deliberations.

Before the council broke up Buffalo Bill, the Hon. W. F. Cody, was summoned by the General in command. He was then in the prime of a matchless manhood. In form, as in face, he had hardly his peer on the American continent. He was dressed in full frontier costume, buckskin breeches, long riding boots, blue shirt, colored neckerchief and broad, white sombrero, with the usual snake band. His long, silky brown hair, with a suspicion of dark auburn glinting through it, fell over his shoulders in graceful profusion, and his dark, exceedingly expressive and handsome eyes seemed to blaze with martial ardor. As the meeting of the officers was a council of war I could not get within privileged ear shot, and I knew military etiquette too well to make myself intrusive; but I met Cody immediately after adjournment and had quite a long talk with him. He would not, of course, say anything about what had passed in the General's tent, but I remember that he felt doubtful of striking any Indians with the force we then had.

"If they want to find Indians," said he, "let them send a battalion, which I am willing to guide, and I'll engage we'll have our fill of fighting before reaching the Little Missouri. The hostiles will never face this outfit unless they get it in some kind of a hole, and there are plenty of them in this country. Crook ain't going to run into them, though. He served in Arizona too long for that."

"Have you scouted here before?" I asked of the formidable frontiersman.

"Not exactly here," said he, "but a man who is educated to prairie life is at home anywhere. Lieutenant Lawson, there, can tell you how I once guided him correctly through a country I had never set eyes on before."

Mr. Lawson nodded a cordial assent and Bill retired to find such repose as he could under the circumstances.

Chapter XVI
Marching in Darkness

DAYLIGHT came at last, accompanied by the usual shrill bugle-call and the hoarse harangue of the Snake head-soldier as he roused the sleeping savages from their lairs to look after their neighing ponies. Clouds partially obscured the sun as we tightened our horse girths or swallowed our scanty allowance of ration coffee, bacon, and hard-tack. All our superfluous baggage was rolled into bundles and turned over to Major Furey, while we, like the highwaymen of old, had nothing except what we had on our frames and what we could impose on our sorry-looking steeds. The poor horses looked supremely miserable. Even those of the newly arrived fifth were completely played out by the scout in pursuit of the Cheyennes, the very thing that allowed the main body of the enemy to escape from the Big Horn without a battle. As for the animals of the Second and Third Cavalry, they had had no grain or corn since the beginning of June, and at least a third of them looked well fitted for the boneyard.

The infantry under Colonel Chambers appeared stout and soldierly and moved off at a swinging step three hours ahead of us. General

Merritt became chief of cavalry. Royall retained his old command of the second and third, and Carr led the fifth. The twenty-five companies were formed into five battalions, the Third and Fifth being strongest having two each, and the Second one. At 7 o'clock we were all in the saddle and moved in three columns via Prairie Dog Creek to Tongue River, following the track of the guides and the infantry.

Frank Gruard and Buffalo Bill were in advance with a select body of scouts. Colonel Stanton, paymaster, had chief command of the irregulars, while Major Randall, with the Chief Washakie, directed the Snake Indians. We made about twenty miles that day, passing over the old campground of June 9th, where the Sioux gave us that first salute. Everything around the place looked desolate, and it seemed to me as if years had elapsed since I saw it last. Since Merritt joined we had adopted the plan of forming a circular camp with our horses picketed in the center during the night so that in case of an attack no stampede of our stock could be effected.

To detail all the incidents of a march would be very tiresome both to me and to my readers, so I will glance only at the chief features of our second northward pilgrimage. We marched twenty-five miles farther down Tongue River on August 6th, crossing that sinuous stream—perhaps the crook-

edest in the world—no less than seventeen times,
which made the march tell severely on our ad-
mirable infantry, who, nevertheless, got into camp
just as soon as we did. Our course lay through
Tongue River Cañon, one of the most rugged
and dangerous passes in that land of difficult and
interminable defiles. The sun was hotter than on
any march during the campaign, and the thermometer must have ranged at 105° in the shade
from 8 A.M. to sundown. The men converted
Tongue River into a bathing reservoir, for our
soldiers lost no opportunity in the way of keeping
their bodies clean, especially when they marched
without even a change of underclothing.

Failing to cut across the Sioux trail at that
distance down the Tongue, Crook determined to
move westward through a dry cañon to Rosebud
Creek, and move down that rivulet some distance, as the southern part of the valley was a
favorite Indian resort. This gave us another
twenty-five mile march over a very broken country
full of rocky bluffs and clumps of pine trees and
having hardly sufficient water to refresh our
already used-up horseflesh. Finally, after halting
innumerable times because of the intolerable heat
and dust, which nearly asphyxiated man and
beast, we reached again the famous Rosebud
some six miles north of our fighting ground of
June 17th and about a mile and a half from the

point in the cañon to which Mills' battalion of the
Third Cavalry penetrated on the day of the conflict.

Subsequent investigation showed what a dreadful fate we escaped by obeying Crook's order to
file out of the trap by our left flank. Immense
piles of felled trees in our path and on the sides
of that savage ravine showed where the Sioux had
lain in ambush for our approach. Half a mile
farther on and not a man of our battalion would
have come out alive. The five companies of the
Second, following to support us, would have been
massacred without fail, for there was no room to
deploy or to rally. The Indians held the timber
barricades in front and flank. They would have
closed upon our unguarded rear and another
horror would have been added to the long and
ghastly catalogue of Indian-American warfare.
However, a miss is as good as a mile and we felt
duly thankful that we escaped being the awful
example of that unfortunate campaign.

We camped in a most beautiful valley, hemmed
in by thickly timbered hills which were blazing
like so many volcanoes, the Indians having fired
the woods, either by accident or design. That portion of the Rosebud vale is called the Indian
Paradise, and truly, for many miles, it deserves
that heavenly name. Two miles north of where we
bivouacked we found the site of the mammoth

Indian village, to protect which Sitting Bull fought on the 17th of June. It was situated in an expanse of the valley two miles square and protected by steep, rock-guarded eminences on every side. Crook's force could never have captured and held such a position, defended as it must have been, judging by the number of lodges, by at least 3,500 fierce, desperate, and well-armed warriors.

The scouts went down the Rosebud fifteen miles, and returned in the evening with intelligence of a fresh Indian trail leading diagonally from the Little Big Horn River toward the Yellowstone. This cheered us up somewhat and we lay down to sleep with the hope of a speedy encounter and a quick return, victorious, of course, to civilized existence. But, as usual, man proposes and God disposes. When the reveille sounded on the morning of the 8th no man could see his neighbor, owing to an abominable alliance between the fog and smoke. We felt our way down through the old Indian village for a few hours and then Crook ordered a halt, hoping for a gale to clear away the atmospheric obscurity.

We lay by until 6 o'clock that evening, when an obliging breeze sprang up and everything came out of the gloom smiling and picturesque. We knew that we had a night march before us to make up for lost time; so when the orderlies came galloping along the lines with orders to saddle up, we were not taken by surprise. Still following the Rosebud, we marched at dark, the cavalry on the flanks and the infantry and pack train in the center, but not far in advance, so that all might be within supporting distance. The moon did not rise for some hours and the evening was dark as Erebus. Intense silence pervaded the line of march, and not a sound was heard but the solemn tramp of the cavalry columns advancing through the gloom, except when a solitary jackass attached to the pack train gave vent to his perturbed feelings in a bray which amid the mountain echoes sounded like the laughter of a legion of mocking devils. The lonesome donkey repeated his performance so often and so loudly that he had to be muzzled, as he appeared determined to apprise the Sioux, if any were within hearing, of our approach. The mules were heard from occasionally, but on the whole their conduct was decorous and patriotic.

Does any reader remember his experience during a night march in total darkness? Of course thousands of my readers marched with Sherman and with Thomas, and know all about it. But a night march in the Indian wilderness of the North is one of the most impressive incidents of war. It is weird, *outre*, awe-inspiring. The vastness of untamed nature is around you and its influence is insensibly felt. You are on the track of a mysterious enemy. The country over which you are marching is to you an unread chapter. You see something like a black shadow moving in advance. You are conscious that men and animals are moving within a few paces, and yet you cannot define any particular object, not even your horse's head. But you hear the steady, perpetual tramp, tramp, tramp of the iron-hoofed cavalry, broken by an occasional stumble and the half-smothered imprecation of an irate trooper; the jingle of carbines and sling-belts, and the snorting of the horses as they grope their way through the eternal dust, which the rider can feel in his throat like the thick, stinking vapor of a champion London fog. Once in a while a match, struck by a soldier to light his pipe, would flash in the gloom like a huge fire-fly, and darkness would again assert itself.

In this manner we proceeded for quite a time when all of a sudden a tremendous illumination sprang up from behind us and lit almost the whole line of the valley. Reflected in it we could see the arms glistening as our battalion moved steadily along, and the bluffs, left and right, seemed like giants keeping watch and ward upon the pass. We turned in our saddles to observe the phenomenon and beheld a flood of flame, which, rushing like a charging battle-line storming some fated town, burst over the mountain crest behind us twenty miles away, flinging its lurid banner to the very arch of the firmament, almost as if the gates of hell had been flung open to allow the demons down under the sea to throw defiance at the power which hurled them from the heavens during the apocryphal battle which the genius of a Milton has portrayed in immortal words. I have seen some magnificent freaks of fire in my time, including the Chicago disaster[60] and the conflagrations in the Big Horn Range, but that sudden outburst of flame in the Plutonian gloom of Rosebud Valley surpassed in lurid splendor anything that I have ever imagined or beheld. It was something to be witnessed only once in a lifetime. Soon afterward the moon rose on our right and its chaste luster tamed down the infernal glow on the southward hills. We pressed forward until 2 o'clock, when we halted and lay down under our single blankets to catch the hasty sleep of Indian campaigners.

[60]The famed Chicago Fire of October 8–9, 1871.

CHAPTER XVII
Crook and Terry Meet

NEXT day we made twenty miles through one of the roughest countries I ever traveled over, still following the Rosebud. It looked like the bottom of an extinct lake. We were pursuing the Indian trail, but the Sioux had burned almost every blade of grass behind them so that our horses were nearly starved. That entire section of the valley is a huge coal-bed, one of the most extensive in America, and this accounts for the peculiar sterility of the surface soil. We saw huge lumps of coal sticking out of the sides of the cañon, while the ground in many places was black as ink from genuine coal dust. Some day, I thought, when the Sioux are all in the happy hunting grounds this valley will rival the Lehigh of Pennsylvania. But my observations of coal did not blind me to the fact that the weather had taken a change for the worse. A cold, disagreeable rain, accompanied by a chilling north wind, set in, and after a tramp of twenty-two miles we halted in a cross cañon, where, fortunately, some grass remained, lit fires amid the gigantic rocks cut into fantastic columns and corners by the action of waters which had subsided countless ages ago, and made ourselves as comfortable as it was possible to be in the most inhospitable looking country outside of Iceland or Siberia. Honestly, that part of the world looked utterly unfinished, just like a half-built house, raw, dirty, and cheerless. Darwin might have been able to find that 'missing link' somewhere along the Rosebud.

Soon after we halted, Captain Jack Crawford (Buffalo Bill's friend) and Captain Graves of Montana rode up to our dismal, smoky camp fire and handed me some private letters, for which I was duly grateful.[61] The gallant fellows left Fort Fetterman with dispatches for Crook on July 28th, reached our wagon train four days later,

[61]John Wallace (Captain Jack) Crawford, of Scottish descent, was born in Ireland in 1849. Brought to America by his parents in childhood, he worked in the Pennsylvania coal mines and grew up illiterate. He enlisted in the Union Army while still a mere boy and was badly wounded at Spottsylvania in May, 1864. During his consequent stay in a Philadelphia hospital he was taught to read and write by a Sister of Charity. Some years after the Civil War he went West, where he acquired the friendship of Buffalo Bill Cody and the skill of a scout. He was one of the first migrants into the Black Hills region following the Custer expedition of 1874, and in 1876 served as a scout for General Crook and Colonel Merritt. Later he served as a scout in the Apache warfare of the Southwest, at whose conclusion he established a ranch on the Rio Grande, which until his death in 1917 remained his permanent home. Military and other activities aside, he became widely known and popular as a writer of verse, stories, and plays, and for many years lectured and recited his poems. *Dictionary of American Biography.*

and despite every warning had followed our tortuous trail by Prairie Dog, Tongue River, the dry cañon and Rosebud until they came up with us in that home of storms.

The night came on cold as midwinter and we, provided with only summer outfits, shivered like palsy patients. It seemed to me as if the combined winds from "a' the airts" had concentrated on that wretched spot to give us sinners a foretaste of the inferno. Heat and dust are bad, but cold and mud take the vim out of a fellow and make him think of houses and stoves. We had seen neither since May 29th. Nevertheless, the morning of August 10th dawned on a comparatively happy set of mortals, for we were nearing the famed Yellowstone River, and that would at least be a change of scene. We had marched only twelve miles, however, when some of the scouts rode back to inform the General that the Sioux trail had suddenly diverged toward Tongue River. We were then marching over a portion of the route followed by Custer on his last fatal scout. His trail was cut deep into the soil and still looked fresh.

We halted on some high, grassy ground above the creek at the point where it turns due north, where we allowed the horses to have a lunch. Then we moved northward, and had not proceeded more than a mile when we observed a mighty column of dust, indicating a large body of men and animals in motion in our front, about three miles down the Rosebud. "They are Sioux!" exclaimed some of our officers. "If so, you will immediately hear music," others replied. Just then a solitary horseman separated himself from our vanguard and rode like the devil in a gale of wind down the river. It was Buffalo Bill, the most reckless of all frontiersmen. "He's going to reconnoiter," remarked Colonel Royall. "That's Bill's style, you know." At this point a handsome young Shoshone Indian, the only one of the reds for whom I entertained a shadow of liking, rode up and ejaculated: "How?" He looked down the road, and his piercing eyes glittered like jet in the sunbeams. "What's that?" I asked, pointing to the pillar of dust. "Heap pony-soldier [cavalry]. No Sioux—Sioux far off—run when pony soldier and good Indian come strong—heap strong now. Sioux no good—run away. Ugh!" and the young savage, with a ferocious grin distorting his comely features, lashed up his pony and disappeared over the ridge.

Within a few minutes Buffalo Bill, his long hair streaming on the wind, came galloping madly back to our lines. "What is it, Bill?" asked Colonel Royall. "Terry and his outfit," replied the scout. "He's got wagons enough to do an army corps. Were we going to catch Indians

with such lumber as that?" and he dashed off
to see Crook. It was true. Terry had been three
days marching from the Yellowstone, thirty
miles from where we halted. Crook immediately
ordered us into camp and Terry who, mistaking
us for Sioux because of the panic of his Crow
scouts who saw some Snake Indians in our van,
had formed line of battle, continued to advance.
The General and his staff rode up first and joined
Crook and his officers. It appeared to be a cordial
meeting, although I am rather of opinion that
Crook intended to operate alone and met Terry
just by chance. General Terry was then a fine-
looking man about fifty years of age. He had a
genial face, but looked like a fighter.

The principal thing that attracted my attention and that of all our force was the remnant
of the Seventh Cavalry. It came in, formed into
seven small companies led by Major Reno, a
short, stout man about fifty years old with a
determined visage, his face showing intimate
acquaintance with the sun and wind. The horses
were all in splendid condition, having been grain-
fed all along, but many of the officers and men
looked tired, dirty and disgusted, just as most
of Crook's column had appeared for many weeks.
The Second Cavalry, four companies called the
Montana Battalion under Major J. S. Brisbin and
a crowd of rather green infantry, most of them

recently from Detroit, followed, and after them came a light field battery of four guns and a huge wagon train.

The men of the respective commands saluted each other cordially, but there was no cheering or undue excitement of any kind. Every one felt that there was naught to cheer about. When you have seen one regiment of our soldiers in the field, you have seen all. There is hardly any difference in the caliber of the men, and as for uniform the absence thereof is a leading characteristic of the service. Perhaps this is all the better, for a more disfiguring costume than the fatigue dress of the United States Army the imagination of the most diabolically inclined of existing tailors could not conceive. Our Indian allies on the other hand, with their beautiful, glossy, abundant black hair, their ornamented leggings, and flowing, richly-colored blankets, together with their sleek, fat forms, presented a most picturesque aspect.

To be sure, they were more or less troubled with parasites, but so we became in a few weeks, without a change of under-clothes. It is a comfort to reflect that, probably, Julius Caesar, Pompey and Mark Antony picked gray-backs off their togas in olden times; that the Little Corporal certainly amused himself in driving the crawling enemy from his shirt about the morning of Lodi's murderous bridge, and that General Grant, with characteristic phlegm, routed them from his body by aid of blue ointment when he started the Rebs out of Vicksburg. As a correspondent I was doubly consoled to know that only one insect got into Washington from Manassas before Bull Run Russell, and that was the bug which occupied his hat when it was blown off his head while crossing the celebrated Long Bridge.[62]

Excuse this chapter on vermin, but Scotia's favorite bard devoted one of his neatest sonnets to the same subject. When a young lady full of romance is inclined to fall in love with a dashing soldier, let her conjure up this picture: A summer morning in the wilderness. A hero with a single shirt, 300 miles from a laundress. A willow tree and the warrior depopulating said garment in the shade thereof.

The Crows, Snakes and Rees, when they met, had a grand howl in concert, their enthusiasm

[62]"Bull Run" Russell was the famous correspondent of the London Times, characterized by one contemporary as "the most interesting correspondent of the largest, ablest, and most influential paper in the world." Editorial introduction to *The Civil War in America* (Boston, n. d.) Russell's candid reports upon the war-time scenes he currently viewed, along with his conviction, frequently expressed, that the Union would never be restored, found little favor in northern eyes. The Author's satirical comment suggests that this dislike rankled after the passage of more than a decade.

being in striking contrast with our indifference.
In fact, the shadow of a coming fizzle was already
upon us. Terry and Crook had a "big talk" that
evening. The former did not wish to deprive
Crook of command. The latter insisted that the
senior should take his proper place. Finally he
of Fort Fisher agreed to accept the glory thrust
upon him, but said that General Crook should
always share in his councils. The commander of
our column looked the picture of disgust. "This
command is now too large," he observed to a
friend. "We shall find no Indians while such a
force sticks together."

Among the newspaper men who either came
up with or followed Terry's command, were
James J. O'Kelly, now member of the British
Parliament, of the New York *Herald,* "Phocion"
Howard, of the Chicago *Tribune,* and Charles S.
Diehl, of the Chicago *Times.* They accompanied
Terry's column after it parted with ours on
Powder River.

General Terry, impressed with Crook's idea
of campaigning in light marching order, retain-
ing his pack train, sent all his wagons back to
Rosebud Landing under the escort of General
Nelson A. Miles and the Fifth Infantry. The combined columns, about 4,000 effective men, horse
and foot, were ordered to march eastward to
Tongue River on the Indian trail at daybreak.

We marched, accordingly, about fifteen miles, reached Tongue River, and went into camp in one of the beautiful valleys that abound in that region. We found the skeleton of a murdered miner, a bullet-hole through his skull and shoulder bone, and buried it. The man had been killed about the beginning of June and coyotes had eaten the body, the clothing being quite fresh and the hair on the head showing the mark made by the Sioux scalping knife. The hapless man's dead pony, which had been shot also, lay near him in a state of most offensive putrefaction. Such was the fate of him who sought for fortune in that demon-peopled land.

That night a terrific storm of wind and rain came up. We had no tents, and had to sleep in the puddles. You can imagine how we passed the night. Water saturated us at every point and the rain kept pouring down until the afternoon of the succeeding day, retarding our march and making every man of the command feel as if possessed of a devil. This, however, is glory, and no one must complain. Officers and men slept in rain and dirt, drank coarse coffee, and ate hardtack and raw bacon. All this is the concomitant of war and fame. The rays of the star of glory are made up of filth, hardship and disappointments. Fighting is the least of the evils attendant on a military career. And yet, the worst feature of a

summer campaign is paradise itself compared
with the untold miseries suffered by our troops
when engaged in a winter hunt after Indians.
But, after all, the best time to strike the savages
is when snows are deep and pony locomotion
almost impossible. To give some idea of the
severity of the fall and winter in that region let
me recall the fact that General Connor, when
operating against the Sioux in that same territory in 1865 had 300 horses frozen to death on
the picket lines the night of September 7th.[63]

On August 12th and 13th we continued our
northward march on the Tongue, losing horses
every mile of the way. When we reached Pumpkin Creek, about forty miles from the Yellowstone, we switched eastward toward Powder
River. The rain and mud made the marching
terrible, and some of Terry's young infantry lay
down exhausted in the dirt. Many of them had to
be placed on pack-mules or carried on travois.

---

[63]In the summer of 1865 General Patrick E. Connor led
an army from central Colorado into the Sioux country of
central Wyoming to open the Bozeman Road and to impress the Indians. On August 19 he established Fort
Connor (subsequently named Fort Reno) at the Bozeman
Road crossing of Powder River. Connor's conduct aroused
sharp criticism, leading to the recall of the troops and the
embitterment of the Indians. The following year General
Carrington reoccupied the region with an army whose experiences are related in Mrs. Carrington's *Absaraka,
Home of the Crows.*

Every company, almost, of the Second, Third and Fifth Cavalry had to abandon or shoot used-up horses. We made fully thirty miles over a most infernal country before halting. Chambers' "astonishing infantry," as Napier would have called them, made the full march, and not a man fell out of the ranks. In fact, they reached camp and were in bivouac before ourselves. The Roman legions or the army of Austerlitz never made better time than the splendid detachments of the Fourth, Fourteenth and Ninth Infantry. They and their gallant officers deserve unstinted praise for their magnificent foot work. This so-called creek was a miserable stream, full of alkali and about the color of the mud on city street crossings after a rainy spell. There was very little wood, and we had to sleep at night in pools of water and were thankful to get a chance to lie down even in that way.

We marched all day Tuesday, August 15th, along Pumpkin Creek through a terrible section.[64] The soil looked like the surface of a non-

[64]There is obviously some confusion in the Author's account of the march from the Tongue to the Powder. General King's narrative at this point suffices to resolve it. Instead of marching all day of the 15th along the Pumpkin, the army marched eastward at dawn along an Indian trail which soon left that stream, and at noon crossed the Divide between the Tongue and the Powder. Crossing the latter above its confluence with the Mizpah (a stream

atmospheric planet, hard, repulsive, sterile. It made one's heart sick to look at the place. But there were strong marks of mineral wealth, especially iron and coal, along the route. I am convinced that all that part of Montana is a tremendous coal region, which one day will yield untold wealth to some enterprising corporations. This kind of land continued until we struck the Powder River Valley, which, like all the valleys of the larger streams, is extremely fertile. But our animals were so exhausted that we hardly made more than a couple of miles an hour on the average. The horses staggered in the columns by scores, and most of the men had to lead their animals during three-fourths of the march. Very frequently a played-out horse would fall as if shot, and the rider was compelled either to abandon the equipments or pack them on a mule. All the led horses were in use owing to frequent deaths of the line animals, and dozens of dismounted cavalrymen toiled painfully along over steep, rugged hills in the rear of the column.

Our whole line of march from the Rosebud

coming from the southwest) the column marched down the Powder to the Yellowstone during the two days of August 16 and 17. *Campaigning with Crook,* 87–90. The hardships described as undergone in descending the Pumpkin were evidently encountered, instead, in the course of the westward march from the Pumpkin to the Powder.

to the Powder and Yellowstone rivers was dotted with dead or abandoned horses. Some of the newly-enlisted infantry grew desperate—their feet bleeding and their legs swollen from the continuous tramp—and refused to move a step. They had to be mounted on the ponies of the friendly Indians and carried along. One man, an officer's cook, without saying a word to anyone lay back under a tree to die. He was not missed for twelve hours, when General Terry, who is very kind-hearted, sent back the Crow Indians and some cavalry to see what had become of the poor fellow. They found him a raving maniac and bore him into camp strapped to an extra pony. Many of the young foot-soldiers seemed injured for life. Some of Terry's men could not keep up at all. Gibbon's veterans marched like Romans. Chambers' men rivaled O'Leary and Weston.[65]

[65]Edward Payson Weston, born in 1839, was one of the most notable athletes and perhaps the most renowned walker in the history of American sports. His numerous walking exploits, continued even into old age, still excite the reader's admiration and wonderment. In 1909 for example, at the age of seventy, he walked from New York to San Francisco, 3895 miles, in 104 days and 7 hours. Struck by a taxi cab and partially crippled in 1927, he died in 1929, aged ninety years. *Dictionary of American Biography*. O'Leary was another notable walker of the period, concerning whom detailed information has not been found.

Taken all in all, Crook's column had the tougher material, except as regards horses. What chance had we of catching Indians with such beasts? The animal I rode was a fair specimen. His shoulder was a mass of scabs and blood. He stumbled at every step, and I had to lead him more than half the time. When I got on his back I made a bargain with him: he was to carry me and I was to keep him from falling and breaking both our necks. Yet this poor devil of a horse was a superb, prancing, fiery, and most untamed steed compared with the ghastly skeletons that disfigured most of our cavalry companies. Such is war in the wilderness. Our Government ought to have had a supply of fresh horses on the Yellowstone so that we might follow hot on Sitting Bull's trail, which led direct to the Little Missouri River.

All Wednesday and Thursday we kept moving at snail's pace northward, along the glorious valley of Powder River, thickly timbered and covered with grass knee high. It has a uniform width of about four miles, the country on either side being sterile, except as regards mineral products. Finally, at 3 o'clock on the afternoon of August 17th we sighted the famed Yellowstone, a majestic stream, wide and deep, and camped on the angle made by the junction of Powder River, (the left bank) with that fine inland water-thoroughfare. From that grand river the part of Montana and Wyoming good for anything will undoubtedly be settled. At 5 o'clock the steamboat *Far West* came up from Tongue River, and the soldiers ran like a flock of overgrown children to see it. The poor fellows had not seen steam since May 18th, and this glimpse of civilization reminded them of home.

Some fresh, well-dressed infantry were on board, together with a couple of cannon. Also there was a colored cabin-girl, another reminder of the States. Dinah modestly covered her eyes when she saw all of the soldiers who were not on picket or on the river bank, about half the command, nude in the water. Lieutenant Von Leuttwitz of the Third Cavalry had just got on his shirt and was standing with his back toward the boat when the waves caused by the motion of the vessel flew over him, swept away half his clothing, and wet him thoroughly. He received a thundering cheer from the boys, and ran up the bank a la Adam before the fig leaves, swearing strange German oaths and damning the Yellowstone from the bottom of his heart. Every man who marched from Rosebud and Goose Creek washed his shirt, etc., allowed the garments to dry in the sun, and put them on without ironing. There was one great drawback to the common laundry, a dearth of soap. Despite this, I felt comfort in knowing that I was a little less like a ground-hog. Why do not our gallant militia, when in their summer camps, practice the noble art of washing without soap for a few days?

In concluding a letter to the paper I represented, about August 18th, I said:

"I think I mentioned the fact that Crook insisted on Terry assuming command while the two expeditions hung together. Terry is, therefore, responsible. Crook feels awfully disgusted. Sitting Bull has played all of us a shabby trick. Like a greedy gambler, he has won a large stake and then, when the chances are about equalized, he draws out and leaves us in the lurch. Probably I am disappointed in Mr. Bull, but he knows his own business best. I went to see Crook and his staff last night. Having no tents, it is rather difficult to discover the whereabouts of any one. After a long chase I finally came upon a group of seedy-looking fellows having all the appearance of brigands sitting on the wet grass under a cottonwood tree. They were Crook and his staff. I interviewed them, but could not obtain much information. The general idea was to follow the trail to the Little Missouri, and then nobody knew where. This makes the affair extremely unpleasant for all concerned. I think the game is up, and that there will be little, if any, fighting. I close this letter with a feeling of disgust and disappointment.

"Incertitude is the order of the day at present. Many camp followers, including some of the correspondents, are leaving the expedition. I have not yet made up my mind what is best for me to do. I hate to leave at this stage of the futile campaign, and yet by remaining I shall see very little else than mud, misery and rough country. One good battle and a decent wind-up to this wretched business would just suit me now. But I fear very much that the last shot of this section of the campaign has been fired. This comes of the official imbecility which at the outset sent an insufficient force to fight a powerful enemy, and in the end sent green troops to impede our movements and left us cavalry horses fit only for the purposes of a glue factory."

CHAPTER XVIII
Under a Deluge

WE were drying our saturated clothes on the bank of the Powder River, the filthiest stream in America or elsewhere, on the morning of August 24th. Thunder and everlasting wet had pursued us all the way from Tongue River camp, but the night of August 23, 1876, was the most utterly miserable so far experienced. Unfortunately, our camp had to be moved in order to give the horses fresh grass and our temporary shelters had to be abandoned in the midst of a torrent of rain. There was no very dire necessity for the move as General Terry had supplied our horses with grain for a few days, but the soldiers were obliged to follow the orders of the battalion commander all the same. The movement was attempted, to be countermanded when too late to do any good, and we went into camp about 200 yards from our first bivouac, in some lowlands under a range of sand hills, flooded with water and fully a mile from wood. Clothing and blankets were thoroughly soaked, and having neither tents nor camp fires most of the troops were in a most unenviable situation.

To keep dry was impossible and to keep warm was equally so; for a cold north wind set in at nightfall as if to drive the water more mercilessly into our bones. The officer with whom I messed and myself made a desperate effort to sleep, but met with almost utter failure. Our one army blanket and leaky poncho were no protection against the solid sheet of rain falling from the opaque clouds, and the eternal, infernal rat-tat-tat growing faster and heavier each second on the gum coverings made us think that the devil was beating his famous tattoo for our especial benefit. Cold may be warded off. Heat can be modified in some way, but without canvas it is impossible to combat the terrible rainstorms of that region. The oldest of the soldiers, men who had served all through our great war and some of the wars of Europe, declared that they had experienced nothing more distressing either under Havelock in India, Von Moltke in France and Germany, or Sherman in Georgia and the Carolinas.

Vivid flashes of lightning followed by tremendous peals of thunder added satanic grandeur to the misery. All the artillery in the world could hardly have produced such an indescribable uproar. The horses drew their picket-pins from the sodden soil and stampeded, plunging helplessly around in the swamps. Something that felt like an elephant walked over my bunk. I punched the creature with my carbine, and by the vigorous kick which it gave my saddle in return I became aware of the presence of a scared pack-mule. The lightning revealed the wretched troops gathered on the sheltered side of the low hills, huddled in groups and vainly trying to keep up some animal heat. A few of their remarks came fitfully to my ears and served to amuse me in some measure. One fellow had had enough of glory, and would either desert or secure his discharge before coming on another Indian campaign. Another damned whisky for leading him into the army.

"Now, George," said an Irish soldier, "wouldn't you just wish you had a little drop to mix with all this water?"

"No fear of you mixing it, Tim," George answered, "you always take it straight in Ireland."

"Bad luck to the ship that brought me over thin," Tim replied. "If I had taken my poor owld mother's advice and remained in Cashel it isn't like a drowned rat I'd be this night."

"Och, be J——, this is the most G—— damnablest outfit I ever struck in my twenty-five years of sarvice," said a Milesian veteran in disgusted tones. "Divil shoot the ginerals and the shoulder-sthraps all around. Shure they have no more compassion on a poor crayture of a soldier than a wolf has on a lamb!"

"A tough old lamb, you are, Jerry, sure enough," said another warrior. "A wolf would have to howld his head a long way from the wall afore he could eat you."

"We can't have even coffee, and must eat our bacon raw to-night," lamented a native American. "The confounded sage-brush won't burn, and the d—d rain won't let it."

In the midst of these flying remarks I suddenly fell asleep, and awoke perhaps an hour later to find water running over, under and all around me. To get up was useless, so I lay and soaked in my clothes until morning came, gray, cold and cheerless. Then I looked at Lieutenant Lawson, bundled up in his blanket beside me. He was just as badly off as I was, so we rose with great unanimity and made a break for Captain Meinhold's campfire, where we struggled with the rain-fiend for more than an hour. Everybody looked tired and haggard, but the situation was not without its ludicrous features. At about 7 o'clock the weather cleared a little and then, seated on a stone, a captain could be seen wringing out his shirt tail, a lieutenant wrestling with his one pair of stockings, and the non-commissioned officers and privates helping each other to dry their overcoats and saddle-blankets. As for underclothing and shoes being wet, they were too well used to that to mind it much. I had slept in the rain several times on the trip, but the experience of that night was the nearest approach to hell upon earth that I have known.

At 10 o'clock, our fifteen days' rations being all packed, the order to march came and Crook's column turned its back upon the Yellowstone. We marched up the west bank of Powder River, through unending coal-fields, about ten miles and went into camp on high ground. General Terry had resolved to cut loose from us and cross to the left bank of the Yellowstone. Crook had determined to follow the Indian trail to the Little Missouri River, and as much farther as it might lead. The Snake and Crow Indians, appalled by the hardships which they clearly saw in store for them, abandoned the column the moment we faced up the Powder River. They knew they were safe in going home, because the Sioux and their allies had evacuated the Big Horn country. Buffalo Bill, who had theatrical engagements in the East, and three newspaper correspondents, who did not relish so much water on the outside, forsook us also, and started down the Yellowstone on the steamer. Ute John, an Indian partially civilized, was the only redskin who remained with us, but all Crook's white and most of his half-breed scouts continued faithful.

The weather continued abominable as we resumed our march. We made another short march up Powder River on the 25th, and next day crossed to its right bank and marched twenty miles toward the Little Missouri, halting on a branch of O'Fallon Creek, which is distinguished by running through the most adhesive mud on the American Continent. We were following the Indian trail discovered on the Rosebud, which our junction with General Terry's column had prevented us from pursuing with greater alacrity. We reached O'Fallon Creek proper on the 27th and went into bivouac under a pelting shower. Several officers and soldiers began to show signs of approaching sickness, and a few cases of rheumatic and neuralgic fever were reported. The exposure told mostly on the older men and several of these, notably Captains Andrews and Meinhold, did not long survive the hardships of that campaign. I was hardy enough, and felt very little inconvenience except a sense of being abominably dirty. The rain and the heat of the bivouac fires had so shrunken my boots that I could not remove them. In fact, I was afraid to do so even if I could, because I would have been unable to get them on again. This was a common experience on that trip. Several men did not have their boots off for two weeks, at least.

Our march on the succeeding day brought us to Cabin Creek, why so called nobody can tell as nothing more substantial than an Indian tepee was ever erected thereon. That night we had thunder, lightning and a deluge. We gave up the idea of rest and were glad to keep even moderately warm.

The horses sank in the mud to their knee-joints, and soldiers' shoes were pulled off in trying to drag their feet through the sticky slime. "Can hell be much worse than this?" said an officer to me next morning. He was cleaning about twenty pounds of wet clay from his boots with a butcher-knife. His clothes were dripping, his teeth chattering, and his nose a cross between purple and indigo. If looking like the devil could make a man fit for the region he inquired about, that young lieutenant was a most eligible candidate.

The scouts reported the Indian trail growing fresher, so we moved ten miles farther east and encamped among a detached section of bluffs, chiefly cone-shaped, which were very picturesque. We found that the Indians were following the Sully Trail of 1864, which leads at that point directly to the Missouri. General Crook thought that the village might be on the headwaters of either the Glendive or Beaver creeks, and sent out the scouts, who remained absent over thirty hours, which compelled us to lie over for one day. On the morning of August 31st they reported no Indians at the point designated and we marched to Beaver Creek, about a dozen miles, so that the troops might have their bi-monthly muster for pay.

Beaver Creek is called the Indian branch of the Little Missouri, and runs through a lovely cham-

paign country. How General Hazen, in his famous
report, could call the section of territory from
Powder River to that stream a desert passes com-
prehension and excited general surprise.[66] A finer
locality for either grazing or tillage purposes could
hardly be imagined. With few exceptions the tract
indicated is an unbroken meadow-land. Timber is
scarce, but coal abounds in marvelous quantities.
Every cut made by the water and the sides of
every bluff, large or small, showed immense blocks
or veins of that mineral, thus settling the fuel
supply question beyond cavil. Our troops lit some
fires made of this material and found them admir-
able. We saw two burning coal ledges. The coal
is bituminous on the surface, but, doubtless, all
the other varieties can be found when mines are
opened there, which must be the case in the not
remote future.

[66]General William B. Hazen, a graduate of the U.S.
Military Academy in the class of 1855, was an upright and
capable soldier whose career was marked by numerous
controversies. That these were occasioned in large part by
the frankness with which he denounced dishonesty and
incompetence on the part of others seems clear. One such
controversy involved him with General Custer over the
respective conduct of the two officers during Custer's
Washita campaign of 1868. For it see *My Life on the Plains,*
the Lakeside Classics volume for 1952. In 1866 Hazen, in
response to orders, undertook a tour of inspection of the
region extending from the Missouri River to the Rocky
Mountains. His subsequent Report (published as House
Exec. Doc. 45, 39th Cong., 2nd sess.) provided an un-

If inexhaustible supplies of coal, water and grass cannot make a country rich the Americans have lost their renowned enterprise, and the pioneer spirit which, more even than the rifles of the continentals, made a gigantic nation spring from the waters of the Atlantic and converted a fettered colony into a proud republic, prosperous, limitless and invincible, is no more. We expected to find a Sahara, and we entered a land of promise. Our animals appreciated this fact as much as we did, for the starved creatures filled themselves to satiety with the succulent grasses of the Montana plains.

flattering picture of the region surveyed, and this and subsequent publications roused the animosity of railroad and other promoters seeking to profit from the development of the Plains country, concerning which the Report succinctly stated: "The country has little value, and can never be sold by Government at more than nominal rates. It will in time be settled by a scanty pastoral population. No amount of railroads, schemes of colonization, or government encouragement can ever make more of it."

Concerning the Plains Indians, General Hazen was no less outspoken: "The ideal Indian of the popular mind is found only in poetry and Cooper's novels. The Indian who now inhabits the Plains is a dirty beggar and thief, who murders the weak and unprotected, but never attacks an armed foe . . . he knows no sentiment but revenge and fear, and cares only to live in his vagrancy." Continuing, the Report recommended that the several tribes be assigned to reservations and rigorously pursued and punished when they strayed from them. The military methods recommended in this connection bear a startling resemblance to the procedure adopted by General Crook in 1876, and subsequently in Arizona.

CHAPTER XIX
Half-Rations and Horse Meat

WE made two marches north on Beaver Creek, about thirty-two miles, and, finding no Sioux, moved up Andrew's Creek, nearly due east, about twenty miles. Crook became satisfied that the Indians had crossed to the Little Missouri, and on September 4 we marched to that river on Custer's trail of 1874, perhaps eighteen miles east, and crossed it at 2 o'clock in the afternoon. The stream is sullen and muddy, like its large namesake, and has tremendous bluffs or buttes, which are filled with coal and iron veins on both sides. Wild cherries, plums, and buffalo berries grow in profusion on the banks, so our soldiers had quite a feast that evening. Many men were suffering from internal ailments and this timely fruit supply checked sickness of that nature to a great extent. It rained all day, as usual, and made night a thing of horror. We camped where Sully camped in 1862, and where Custer did ten years afterward, and on some of his later scouts.

It was an amphitheatrical valley, rock enchaliced, as it were, and would have been an excellent thing for some artist to sketch. By the way, our artistic brethren were not very enterprising on that campaign. A man capable of producing good sketches could have made a small fortune. But hard campaigning on very coarse food and sometimes insufficient would hardly enliven the genius of a city man gifted with the artist's magic skill. On the whole, I think the artists were sensible to remain in the land of the civilized. I never appreciated the force of the lines,

O solitude! where are the charms that sages have seen in thy face?

until I struck George Crook's Indian-hunting outfit. The wild freedom of the Plains sounds well in a comfortable parlor, but does not feel quite as nice when your hide is wet and clammy with rain, like the skin of a frog, and when you have as much mud on your person as would disgrace a stockyards' pig. I have seen an English regiment after returning from the Crimean war, hairy, patched up, and tanned, but so ragged, filthy, forlorn-looking a set of men as the soldiers of Crook's expedition I have never beheld. That they were not vermin-eaten is to me a bewildering mystery. Let civilization scratch itself all over when it hears that we had not three pounds of washing-soap in the entire command, and that no man, not even General Crook himself, had a second shirt to his back! I have seen that officer wash his own under-clothes in the Yellowstone and sit on the bank to let them dry.

General Gibbon cried out to our column when he passed us the day the junction was effected on the Rosebud: "Why, soldiers, you're even dirtier than my men!" I should think they were. Terry's men moved with 205 wagons, Sibley and A tents, together with a pack-train, while Crook's command had only rations on their mules and all the clothing they possessed on their frames. Terry's troops applied to Crook's a nickname unfit for ears polite, but which unmistakably referred to the dilapidated condition of the rear portion of their pantaloons. If any reader considers this picture overdrawn, I call upon any man in that column, from General Crook to the humblest private, to contradict me. I wish to let the American people know what their gallant army had to undergo in fighting those red scoundrels who have too long been treated as chiefs and equals.

Crook is severe, and I'd rather be with Terry as regards food, shelter, and clean flannel, but he goes for the Indians as one of themselves would do and has shown that an American army can stand, without much growling or the slightest approach to mutiny, more than any other troops upon this earth. At the same time I hope that the General, should he ever repeat that experiment, will allow a little more soap and an additional pair of stockings to each man. In referring to the army as American I do not wish it understood entirely in the native sense, for a large proportion of the rank and file was made up of the material that covered the British arms with glory in the Peninsula—the never war-absent Irish—and of Germans, whose slow bravery solidifies the Celtic ardor with Yankee coolness and makes the three elements a military body that, to use the words of a dashing American officer who had accompanied the column from the outset, "would go with the Balaklava six hundred into the mouth of hell and then brandish their carbines and call upon the Light Brigade to follow them and fight their way out at the other end."

A word about officers. Most of them are high-bred, manly, learned, good-humored, hospitable gentlemen, while a very few are narrow-minded, jealous, panctilious, swell-headed, irritable, excitable, and generally unfit for anything but retirement into private life. I am glad to say that the percentage of the latter grade is insignificant, and the sooner the army is rid of them the better. The high-toned, chivalric class of officers almost extinguish the others, but one disagreeable "shoulder-strap" is enough to disgust an entire regiment. As for bravery, the quality is so universal in the American army that no officer gets credit for fearlessness, which is regarded as a matter of course. Judgment, skill and dignified firmness are far more necessary. A hectoring, bullying officer never gains the respect and confidence of his men, were he as bold as Ajax, while the quiet, determined, yet courteous commander wins the hearts of his subordinates, and because of his moral influence is obeyed with all the more alacrity. Personally, I have nothing to complain of; but were I an officer serving under certain other officers, I think I'd feel like occasioning a special court-martial. Nothing appears so unmanly and uncalled for in any soldier as an insulting, snappish tone toward his inferiors, knowing, as he must know, how utterly helpless, according to the humiliating military code, they are. If an inferior officer resents the impertinence of his superior, he may obtain temporary satisfaction, but in the end he will be made to suffer.

In regard to the privates, they count for so many machines, and have no right to question orders, good or bad.

> Theirs not to reason why,
> Theirs but to do and die,

without resisting the higher power. Their only resource is the disgraceful one of desertion, and no wonder that some of them adopt even that vile mode of breaking their fetters. How a man of spirit, brought to enlist through intemperance or other folly, must burn and long to tear the windpipe out of some official bully who talks to him as though he were a dog. I admit some of the soldiers are roughs, just fit to be kicked around, but the greater number are good men enough, some of them men who have seen better days, and some who, in soldiering, have learned a lesson that will reform their lives.

We marched some thirty miles from the Little Missouri to Heart River on September 5th. We were within 160 miles of Fort Abraham Lincoln, and about 200 from the northern edge of the Black Hills. To accomplish either march, we had half rations for two and a half days only. I interviewed General Crook on the subject. This was what occurred:

"You are sending in a courier, General?"

"Yes, to Fort Abraham Lincoln. He will carry some mail and telegrams for the command," Crook answered.

"What do you propose to do now, General?"

He paused for a moment, and, pulling his peculiar beard, said very slowly: "We are five full marches from Fort Abraham Lincoln. We are seven, at least, from the Black Hills. By going to the Missouri we lose two weeks' time. By marching on the Hills we gain so much. I march on the Black Hills to-morrow. Between going to and coming back from Fort Abraham Lincoln we should lose more than half our horses."

"How much rations have you left?"

"Only two days' and a half half-rations, but we must make them last for seven, at least. It must be done. The Indians have gone to the Hills and to the Agencies. The miners must be protected and we must punish the Sioux on our way to the south or leave this campaign entirely unfinished."

I looked at him in some amazement, and could not help saying: "You will march 200 miles in the wilderness, with used-up horses and tired infantry on two and one-half days' half rations!"

"I know it looks hard," was the reply, "but we've got to do it, and it shall be done. I have sent a telegram for supplies to General Sheridan. The wagons will meet us at Crook City or Deadwood. If not, the settlements must supply our wants. Nobody knows much about this region, but it looks fair. We'll kill some game, too, perhaps, to make up for short rations. Half-rations will be issued after to-night. All will be glad of the movement after the march has been made. If necessary," he added, "we can eat our horses."

This suggestion fell upon me like a splash of ice water. I could hardly believe, even then, that such an alternative would present itself, but it did, as will be seen, very soon. We were encamped in a bleak and dreary spot. Everybody appeared to be gloomy, and even old Lieutenant Lawson admitted that he had never seen such hard times with his beloved Kentucky brigade.

"As for eating a horse," said he, after I had told him of General Crook's remarks, "I'd as soon think of eating my brother!" But hunger is a great sauce, and Lieutenant Lawson dined on horse steak, like the rest of us, before many days.

I wrote my dispatches that evening under a half blanket precariously supported by poles cut in the neighboring marsh, while the rain came down as if it had not rained before in several years. By great exertions the soldiers collected quite a lot of wood, and by the glare of the camp fires that night I could see the steam rising from the bivouac as thickly as it rises in a laundry on washing day. The soldiers were too tired to mind the deluge.

The weather did not improve on the three following days, and all the arroyos, or small ravines, were filled with water. The whole country was as wet as a sponge, but without elasticity. Our horses played out by the score and between two and three hundred dismounted cavalrymen were marching in the rear of the wonderful infantry battalion. Every little while the report of a pistol or carbine would announce that a soldier had shot his horse, rather than leave it behind with a chance of being picked up by straggling Indians. Some of the poor beasts fell dead from the effects of fatigue and want of proper forage, but a majority simply lay down and refused to budge an inch farther. My horse became a burden on my hands. Do what I would, I could not induce him to get out of his slow walk, and I tolerated him only because I could not get along without the writing material which was carried in the saddle-bags.

On the night of September 7th General Crook detached 150 picked men, fifteen from each troop of the Third Cavalry in the field, under Colonel Anson Mills and Lieutenants Emmet Crawford, A. H. Von Leuttwitz and Frederick Schwatka, accompanied by a train of fifty pack mules, with Commissary Bubb and Chief Packer Moore, to make a dash for the Black Hills settlements and bring back supplies to the famishing troops. It was my desire to have accompanied the party, but my horse was useless and I was compelled to remain with the main command. Not a stick of wood had we seen for eighty-six miles, and this, added to the cold, ever-falling rain, made life almost unendurable. There was hardly any coffee left, and this could not be cooked, while the poor remains of sugar and salt were absolutely washed out of the pack saddles by the falling flood. Hard tack had disappeared, and nothing remained on September 8th but to eat one another or our animals.

While trudging along through the mire on the morning of that day, leading our worn-out steeds, Lieutenant Lawson and I observed a small group of soldiers by the side of the trail busily engaged in skinning a dead horse and appropriating steaks from its hinder parts. This was the beginning of our horse rations. The men were too hungry to be longer controlled and the General wisely ordered that as many horses as would be necessary to feed the men be selected by the officers and slaughtered day by day. It was a tough experiment, but there was no help for it, and anything outside of actual cannibalism was preferable to starving slowly to death. Some of the men, before they began to destroy the horses for food, had taken to splitting the fat leaves of cacti, and when wood was procurable they roasted them at the camp fires. This induced a species of dysentery, from which a large portion of the command suffered during the remainder of the march.

Chapter XX
Fighting at Slim Buttes

AS we were about to break camp on the morning of September 9th a packer named George Herman rode up in hot haste to General Crook bearing a dispatch from Colonel Mills which announced that his detachment had attacked and captured, that morning, an Indian village of forty-one lodges, a large herd of ponies, and some supplies. The Sioux were still fighting to regain what they had lost, and the Colonel requested reinforcements. He was then seventeen miles south, at Slim Buttes, on a tributary of Grand River. General Crook at once selected one hundred men with the best horses from the Third Cavalry, fifty from Noyes' battalion of the Second and the Fifth Cavalry, and, accompanied by his staff and the commanding officers of the different regiments, rode forward to the assistance of his subordinate.

Mills, not anticipating an Indian fight, had allowed his men only fifty rounds of ammunition each and Crook was alarmed lest the Sioux should compel him to expend his last cartridge before assistance could reach him. I accompanied the advance, but my infernal beast broke down completely two or three miles from camp and I had to lead him the rest of the way. The road was so bad that the cavalry could not go at a very fast pace, so I was lucky enough to reach the captured village very soon after Crook got in. All was quiet then, for the Sioux had withdrawn to procure re-enforcements before Crook arrived, and, as subsequently appeared, did not know of his arrival at all. They fancied that Mills, like Custer, was all alone.

Approaching the scene of the fight, I saw a small ravine between gentle hills, in which the captured pony herd was corralled, while our cavalry horses were picketed along the slopes. Several large Indian tepees covered with canvas or buckskin were pitched on the east side of the northern slope, and showed the location of the village. A solitary tepee on the north side of the hill was used as a hospital, and there the wounded were placed. I met Mills as I led in my jaded hack and he showed me the position. He was surrounded by high, very steep bluffs on all sides but the east, and consequently the defeated Indians had a full chance to annoy him. It was noon when I met him and the fight had closed about 10 o'clock. The capture of the village was but the work of a few minutes. The Indian trail had been struck the previous afternoon, and was followed up to within four miles of the village when Mills went into camp. He reconnoitered with Gruard, and finding the location determined to attack next morning.

Of course it rained all night, and while yet dark the Colonel moved forward his detachment, together with the pack mules, two miles. Then he halted the packers, fearing their beasts' braying would alarm the Indians, dismounted all his cavalry except twenty-five men under Schwatka, and moved forward to fall on. Captain Jack Crawford of Omaha, a well-known scout, and some other guides went with Gruard and joined in the subsequent charge. Mills, arriving in the edge of the ravine where the redskins slept securely, as they thought, sent Lieutenant Schwatka with his twenty-five mounted men to drive off the pony herd. The ponies were stampeded at once, but rushed for the village and alarmed the Indians.

Von Leuttwitz and Crawford with fifty men each, on foot, surrounded the lodges and charged. There was a ripping of canvas and buffalo hide as the Sioux had no time to untie the strings of the lodges and therefore cut the tents with their knives. The soldiers fired a volley, which the Indians returned in a desultory way. Almost at the first shot Lieutenant A. H. Von Leuttwitz of Troop E, Third Cavalry fell with a bullet through his right knee joint. This gentleman had served in the Austrian and Prussian armies, had fought at Montebello, Magenta, Solferino, all through the Italian campaign of '59, had distinguished himself at Gettysburg and other great battles of our war, and had escaped comparatively unscathed. Yet his hour had come, and he fell wounded in a miserable Indian skirmish, the very first man. Colonel Mills and Lieutenant Crawford then led on the soldiers and made short work of the village, although the Indians kept up a scattering fire from the bluffs.

When daylight came the Sioux made matters much hotter, and the soldiers, who were much exposed on that bare bluff, were almost at their mercy. Mills sent back for his train, which came up with Moore, Bubb and R. A. Strahorn, all of whom behaved in a gallant manner during the skirmishing which followed. Lieutenant Crawford acted with fine judgment and was spoken highly of by the soldiers who participated in the affair. Schwatka did his work in a thorough manner and made a mark of which he may well be proud. But Mills is peculiar and occasionally the reverse of politic, which to some extent neutralizes his undeniable ability as an officer. Yet, for all that, Crook's column can never forget his brilliant dash on September 9, which saved it from much greater privation. He captured a large amount of dried provisions, 2,500 buffalo robes, and many other campaign luxuries which Indians appreciate as much as white men.

One of gallant Custer's guidons, Colonel Keogh's gauntlets, five horses of the Seventh Cavalry and several other relics of the fated regiment were among the prizes secured. A party of Sioux, unable to make their escape, took refuge in a sort of deep, brush-covered gully just above the site of the village on the eastern slope, dug intrenchments with their hands and knives, and could not be dislodged by Mills' detachment. In an attempt to drive them out nearly all the casualties occurred. Private John Wenzel of Troop A, Third Cavalry was killed and Sergeant Ed Glass of Troop E, one of the boldest non-commissioned officers in the army, was shot through the right forearm. Several other soldiers were wounded in attempting to carry this fatal den.

The firing of the Indians from the bluffs compelled the soldiers to throw up temporary breastworks, which saved them from particularly serious damage. The riding mule of Mr. Moore and a horse belonging to Troop I were shot from the lava bed arrangement. Mills, when he sent back for his train in the morning, had the good sense to send for re-enforcements at the same time. Crook arrived a little after 11 o'clock and immediately attacked the Indian burrow in the gully. In that affair he displayed to the fullest extent his eccentric contempt for danger. No private soldier could more expose himself than did the General and the officers of his staff. I expected to see them shot down every moment, for Charley White, the well-known scout, was shot through the heart just across the ravine, not ten paces from Crook. Kennedy of the Fifth Cavalry and Stevenson of the Second were wounded, the one mortally and the other dangerously, beside him, while many other soldiers had hair-breadth escapes.

The boys in blue, although unquestionably brave, did not quite relish the idea of being shot in the digestive organs by an unseen and ungetatable enemy, but their officers rallied them without difficulty, heading the assault, musket or carbine in hand. Besides General Crook and his staff, Major W. H. Powell and Major Munson of the infantry; Major Burke of the same branch of the service; Lieutenant Charles King of the Fifth Cavalry; and Lieutenant Rogers and the ever gallant Lieutenant W. Philo Clark of the Second Cavalry took desperate chances in true forlorn hope fashion. The guide, Baptiste Pourier, already so distinguished for bravery, fought his way into the cavern and succeeded in killing one of the male Indians, ingeniously using a captive squaw as a living barricade between himself and the fire of the other warriors. He took the scalp of the fallen brave in a manner that displayed perfect workmanship. Scalping is an artistic process and when neatly done may be termed a satanic accomplishment.

Crook, exasperated by the protracted defense

of the hidden Sioux and annoyed by the casualties inflicted among his men, formed, early in the afternoon, a perfect cordon of infantry and dismounted cavalry around the Indian den. The soldiers opened upon it an incessant fire, which made the surrounding hills echo back a terrible music. The circumvallated Indians distributed their shots liberally among the crowding soldiers, but the shower of close-range bullets from the latter terrified the unhappy squaws and they began singing the awful Indian death chant. The papooses wailed so loudly and so piteously that even the hot firing could not quell their voices, and General Crook ordered the men to suspend operations immediately. Then Frank Gruard and Baptiste Pourier, both versed in the Sioux tongue, by order of General Crook approached the abrupt western bank of the Indian rifle pit and offered the women and children quarter. This was accepted by the besieged and Crook in person went to the mouth of the cavern and handed out one tall, fine-looking woman, who had an infant strapped to her back. She trembled all over and refused to liberate the General's hand. Eleven other squaws and six papooses were then taken out, but the few surviving warriors refused to surrender and savagely re-commenced the fight.

Then our troops re-opened with a very rain of hell upon the infatuated braves, who, neverthe-

CHIEF AMERICAN HORSE

From a group photograph of Indian chiefs made in
Matthew Brady's studio in Washington.
Reproduced by courtesy of the Smithsonian Institution.

less, fought it out with Spartan courage against such desperate odds for nearly two hours. Such matchless bravery electrified even our enraged soldiers into a spirit of chivalry and General Crook, recognizing the fact that the unfortunate savages had fought like fiends in defense of wives and children, ordered another suspension of hostilities and called upon the dusky heroes to surrender.

After a few minutes' deliberation the chief, American Horse, a fine looking, broad-chested Sioux, with a handsome face and a neck like a bull, showed himself at the mouth of the cave, presenting the butt end of his rifle toward the General. He had just been shot in the abdomen and said, in his native language, that he would yield if the lives of the warriors who fought with him were spared. Some of the soldiers, who had lost comrades in the skirmish, shouted "No quarter!" but not a man was base enough to attempt shooting down the disabled chief. Crook hesitated for a minute and then said: "Two or three Sioux, more or less, can make no difference. I can yet use them to good advantage. Tell the Chief," he said, turning to Gruard, "that neither he nor his young men will be harmed further."

This message having been interpreted to American Horse, he beckoned to his surviving followers and two strapping Indians, with their long, but quick and graceful stride, followed him out of the gully. The Chieftain's intestines protruded from his wound, but a squaw—his wife, perhaps—tied her shawl around the injured part and then the poor, fearless savage, never uttering a complaint, walked slowly to a little camp fire occupied by his people, about 20 yards away, and sat down among the women and children. The surgeons examined the wound, pronounced it mortal, and during the night American Horse, one of the bravest and ablest of the Sioux chiefs, fell back suddenly and expired without uttering a groan.

Crook, after the surrender of the Chief, took all the survivors under his protection and ordered the dead and wounded to be taken from their late stronghold. Let the country blame or praise the General for his clemency. I simply record the affair as it occurred. Several soldiers jumped at once into the ravine and bore out the corpses. The warrior killed by Baptiste Pourier was a grim-looking old fellow, covered with scars and fairly laden down with Indian jewelry and other savage finery. The other dead were three squaws—one at first supposed to be a man—and, sad to relate, a tiny papoose. The captive squaws with their children came up to view the corpses. They appeared to be quite unmoved, although a crowd of half-savage camp followers, unkempt scouts, and infuriated soldiers surged around them—a living tide. The skull of one poor squaw was blown, literally, to atoms, revealing the ridge of the palate and presenting a most ghastly and revolting spectacle. Another of the dead females, a middle-aged woman, was so riddled by bullets that there appeared to be no unwounded part of her person left. The third victim was young, plump, and, comparatively speaking, light of color. She had a magnificent physique, and, for an Indian, a most attractive set of features. She had been shot through the left breast just over the heart and was not in the least disfigured.

Ute John, the solitary friendly Indian who did not desert the column, scalped all the dead, unknown to the General or any of the officers, and I regret to be compelled to state a few—a very few—brutalized soldiers followed his savage example. Each took only a portion of the scalp, but the exhibition of human depravity was nauseating. The unfortunates should have been respected, even in the coldness and nothingness of death. In that affair, surely, the army were the assailants and the savages acted purely in self defense. I must add in justice to all concerned that neither General Crook nor any of his officers or men suspected that any women or children were in the gully until their cries were heard above the volume of fire poured upon the fatal spot.

That was a peculiar picture of Indian warfare at Slim Buttes. There a dead cavalry horse lay on his side on the western bank of the bloody burrow, while Tom Moore's mule, his feet sticking up in the air, lay on his back about thirty yards nearer to the abandoned tepees. On the southern slope of the embankment, in the line of fire, face downward, the weight of his body resting on his forehead and knees, the stiff, dead hands still grasping the fully cocked carbine, two empty cartridge shells lying beside him, lay John Wenzel. He had been shot through the brain, the bullet entering the left jaw from below and passing out through the top of his head, by either American Horse or Charging Bear, after having fired twice into the gully. He, doubtless, never realized that he had been hit, poor fellow. Wenzel knew more about a horse than perhaps any man of Troop A, Third Cavalry, and used to attend to my animal before he was detailed, for the reason that he was well mounted, to accompany that, to him, fatal advance movement of Colonel Mills.

Diagonally opposite, on the northern slope, lay the stalwart remains of Charley White—Buffalo Chip, as he was called—the champion harmless liar and most genial scout upon the Plains. I saw him fall and heard his death cry. Anxious to distinguish himself, he crept cautiously up the slope to have a shot at the hostiles.

Some of the soldiers shouted, "Get away from there Charley, they've got a bead on you!" Just then a shot was fired which broke the thigh bone of a soldier of the Fifth Cavalry named Kennedy, and White raised himself on his hands and knees in order that he might locate the spot from whence the bullet came. As he did so one of the besieged Indians, quick as lightning, got his range and shot him squarely through the left nipple. Charley threw up his hands, crying out loud enough for all of us to hear him: "My God, my God, boys, I'm done for this time!" One mighty convulsion doubled up his body, then he relaxed all over and rolled like a log three or four feet down the slope. His dead face expressed tranquility rather than agony when I looked at him some hours later. The wind blew the long, fair locks over the cold features and the eyes were almost perfectly closed. The slain hunter looked as if he were taking a rest after a toilsome buffalo chase. Last, and also least, the slaughtered Indian papoose, only about two months old, lay in a small basket, where a humane soldier had placed the tiny body. Had the hair of the poor little creature been long enough, Ute John, I believe, would have scalped it also.

With all this group of mutilated mortality before them and with the groans of the wounded

soldiers from the hospital tepee ringing in their
ears, the hungry troopers and infantry tore the
dried Indian meat they had captured into eatable
pieces and marched away as unconcernedly as if
they were attending a holiday picnic. It was, indeed, a ghastly, charnel-house group, one which,
if properly put on canvas, would, more than anything I have read of or heard described, give the
civilized world a faithful picture of the inevitable
diabolism of Indian warfare. Most of our dead
were hastily buried by their comrades, but the
bodies of the Indians, both male and female, were
left where they fell so that their friends might
have the privilege of properly disposing of them
after we had left. The Sioux Indians so far
as known never place their dead in the earth, so
that leaving the bodies above ground was of no
particular consequence in their case. During the
afternoon American Horse and some of the
squaws informed Gen. Crook, through the scouts,
that Crazy Horse was not far off, and that we
would certainly be attacked before nightfall. The
General, under the circumstances, wished for
nothing better.[67]

[67]Crazy Horse, born probably about 1849, became before his early death one of the ablest leaders of the Sioux
tribes. When the Government in 1876 undertook to force
the hostile Sioux back upon the reservation the first blow
fell upon Crazy Horse's village near the mouth of Little
Powder River, which a detachment led by Colonel J. J.

Sergeant Van Moll of Troop A, Third Cavalry and some soldiers had carried the dead body of Private Wenzel, the carbine still clutched in the dead hands, to a place convenient to the small camp fire at which Lieutenant Lawson and I were trying to enjoy a tincup-full, each, of coffee made from some of the berries captured in the Indian village. They had picked the unexploded cartridge from the chamber and then wrested the weapon by main force from the stiff fingers of the corpse, whose face and fair sandy

Reynolds destroyed on March 17, capturing the Indians' pony herd. Crazy Horse followed the retiring army and recaptured the ponies. Three months later, June 17 his followers met and defeated General Crook's entire army in the battle of the Rosebud, compelling that veteran Indian fighter to retire and await the arrival of reinforcements before resuming his campaign. Crook's subsequent pursuit of Crazy Horse is described by our Author in the present volume. Defeated in the battle of Slim Buttes on September 9, 1876, Crazy Horse established winter quarters in the Wolf Mountains on the upper Rosebud, where on January 8, 1877 Colonel Nelson A. Miles attacked and broke up his village. With further resistance hopeless, Crazy Horse led his band of over 1,000 followers to the Red Cloud Agency near Camp Robinson, Nebraska, where on May 6 he tendered his submission to the Government. Suspicions of his intent to renew hostilities led to his arrest on September 5 and in the melee which ensued he was mortally wounded either by a knife or a bayonet thrust. Leader of a hopeless cause, he compelled the admiration of his white foemen. For fuller sketch see *Dictionary of American Biography* and references therein cited.

locks were covered and matted with blood. A grave was being dug and the Lieutenant was preparing to read the service for the dead when all at once we were fired upon from the bluffs, which surrounded us on all sides except the east. To occupy them thoroughly would have required an army corps, so that nobody was to blame for this second attempt on the part of the Indians to recapture their ponies and get back their tepees and other property.

The buttes called Slim are of an extraordinary shape, very lofty, and strongly resemble a series of mammoth Norman castles or a semicircular range of gigantic exposition buildings. They have tier upon tier of rocks, with the hardy northern pine growing in every crevice, contrasting the green with the gray and clothing the otherwise bare, stern, granite crags with a savage beauty. Along the ledges and among the pines the Sioux led their war ponies and began operations. No time was lost by Crook in meeting their attack. With the rapidity of an exploding shell the brigade, which had nearly all come up, broke into a tremendous circle of skirmishers, forming a cordon of fire around the horses, pack mules and captured ponies. General Merritt was Crook's second in command, and directed the movements of the troops in our section of the field. The Indian bullets whizzed in among us for a few minutes and the voices of our officers could be heard shouting: "Steady men! Take your proper intervals! Don't fire until you get the range! Forward! Double quick time! D—n it, Reilly, are you firing at the Black Hills? Never waste a shot, boys!", *etcetera,* as the infantry and dismounted dragoons trotted out to face the enemy.

Colonel Chambers with his officers and men made straight for the southern bluff, while General Carr with the Fifth Cavalry, also dismounted, made for the hills on the west and southwest. The Third Cavalry under Colonel Royall took charge of the northern and northwestern heights, while the Second Cavalry, under Maj. Henry E. Noyes protected the eastern flank, which was exposed on an open plain, and, being mounted, rode around by the northern end of the bluffs to checkmate any attempt Crazy Horse might make to cut off our rear guard under Sibley, which was driving the stragglers and used-up horses in before it. The bloodiest battles are not always the most picturesque. The evening fight at Slim Buttes was not particularly sanguinary, as regarded our side, but it was the prettiest battle scene, so acknowledged to have been by men who had witnessed a hundred fights, that ever an Indian war correspondent was called upon to describe.

When our men got within range their fire opened steadily. First it was the infantry "pop-pop-pop," slow but sure; then the livelier racket of the cavalry carbine, and finally the rapid, ringing discharges of the Winchester repeaters from the Indian lines, showing that Crazy Horse was neither dead nor deaf nor dumb. On the infantry front the rattle soon swelled into a well-sustained roar. The Fifth Cavalry caught the infection and the clangor soon spread nearly around the whole field. Our men, supplied with plenty of ammunition, resolved to silence the fire of the Indian enemy. Long wreaths of smoke, held low by the heavy atmosphere, enveloped the skirmish lines and showed more picturesquely as the evening advanced. Those wreaths gradually crept up from tier to tier on the bluffs as the soldiers continued to ascend. The combatants were finally shrouded in its sulphurous gloom. Through this martial vapor you could observe the vivid flashing of the fire arms, our boys creeping stealthily from ledge to ledge and the Indians, bold as ever, but utterly confounded, stunned and dispirited perhaps by the ceaseless fusillade, retiring before the stronger force, disputing every inch of ground as they retreated.

It was a matter of astonishment with every man on that trip how our men came off with such small loss, in the comparative sense. The best

explanation is that the Indians of the Plains generally fire from horseback, which may, in some
degree at least, account for the very common
inaccuracy of their aim in battle. Besides, in firing
down hill, unless the slope is gradual and free
from serious obstructions, the range cannot be
very accurate, while, *per contra,* the party moving
upward can see every prominent object clearly
defined against the artificial sky line. Every
time an Indian got killed or disabled his comrades
picked him up and carried him off. The infantry
must have done great execution, their long toms
—altered Springfields—reaching the enemy far
beyond the range of the carbine. The Fifth
Cavalry were very warmly engaged, and fired upon
the Sioux with great enthusiasm.

Driven by the forces named from their original
point of attack, the defeated Sioux came out
through the ravine in the northwestern angle of
the bluffs and charged the position of the Third
Cavalry. Like the Napoleonic cuirassiers at
Waterloo, they rode along the line looking for a
gap through which to penetrate. They kept up
perpetual motion, apparently encouraged by a
warrior, doubtless Crazy Horse himself, who,
mounted on a fleet white horse, galloped around
the array and seemed to possess the power of
ubiquity. Failing to break into that formidable
circle, the Indians, after firing several volleys,

their original order of battle being completely broken, and recognizing the folly of fighting such an outnumbering force any longer, glided away from our front with all possible speed. As the shadows came down into the valley the last shots were fired and the affair of Slim Buttes was over.

Our loss in the action was about thirty, all told. Those who died on the field were Private Wenzel of the Third Cavalry, Private Kennedy, of the Fifth Cavalry, and the ill-fated scout, Charley White. Most of the soldiers wounded, among them the celebrated sharpshooter, Edward Glass, a sergeant of the Third Cavalry, and Private Wilson of the same regiment, were disabled for life. The Indians must have lost quite heavily. Several of their ponies, bridled but riderless, were captured during the evening. Indians never abandon their war horses unless they should happen to be surprised or killed. Therefore many saddles, to use the Caucasian military phrase, must have been emptied. Pools of blood were found on the ledges of the bluffs, indicating the places where Crazy Horse's warriors paid the penalty of their valor with their lives.

I have heard the number of the Sioux variously estimated, but I cannot presume to verify any of the estimates made. There could not, in my opinion, have been more than from six to eight hundred of their fighting men opposed to us.

Had they been of equal number it is difficult to
say how, notwithstanding the unquestioned
courage of our troops, the affair might have
terminated. They had fresh horses, while ours
were entirely used up, and, therefore, the celerity
of their movements would have enabled them to
fling a superior force on any point of our widely-
extended circular skirmish line. I am convinced,
however, that no equal force of any color could
have beaten such men as composed Crook's
brigade on the day of Slim Buttes.

Night fell suddenly and Lieutenant Lawson
and I, each the proud and glad possessor of a
captured buffalo robe, lay down to sleep with our
half blankets over us, while Sergeant Van Moll
and a small party of Troop A proceeded to complete the burial of Private Wenzel, so rudely
interrupted in the afternoon by the attack of the
Sioux from the bluffs. The brave old Lieutenant,
a God-fearing Irish Presbyterian, would have
read the prayers over the remains, but he was
tired out, and my pious inclinations were utterly
subdued by a tendency to sleep which would
have required, at the time, all the horrors of
which Indian warfare is capable to overcome.
The Sergeant and the soldiers, one of them
holding some sort of an improvised lantern,
scooped out the grave with shovels borrowed
from the chief packer and Van Moll acted as

chaplain. They wrapped Wenzel's old overcoat around the body and laid him to rest as carefully as if he had been a major-general.

No useless coffin enclosed his breast,
  Not in sheet or in shroud they wound him;
But he lay like a warrior taking his rest,
  With his martial cloak around him.

American Horse, before he died, gave some information to General Crook about the war. Dr. McGillicuddy, who attended the dying chief, said that he was cheerful to the last and manifested the utmost affection for his squaws and children. The latter were allowed to remain on the ground after the dusky hero's death, and subsequently fell into the hands of their own people. Even Ute John respected the cold clay of the brave Sioux leader and his corpse was not subjected to the scalping process.

We broke camp early on the morning of September 10th, which was raw and drizzling. A gray mist enshrouded the bluffs and the muddy stream that ran through the battle field was swollen to an uncomfortable depth by the rains that had fallen in the mountains. The rear guard of the column consisted, that morning, of two troops of the Fifth Cavalry commanded by Captains Sumner and Montgomery, under Gen. E. A. Carr. They remained dismounted until all the rest of the command had filed by them, bound for the Hills. Scarcely had they mounted their

horses when they were attacked most determined-
ly by Indians secreted in the ravines that abound
in that region. But they were veterans, and coolly
held their ground. They lost many wounded, but
none killed outright. The Indians, on the other
hand, were unfortunate, and left five warriors
gasping upon the sod. Crazy Horse, convinced
that Slim Buttes was not the Little Big Horn,
drew off in despair and the remainder of the
march was made without molestation.

The rain continued throughout the day, turning the country into a quagmire. We were so
used to being wet to the skin that no man who
could keep his feet uttered a complaint, but our
eyes would often turn compassionately to the
long string of travois (mule litters) on which our
sick and wounded were being dragged toward
civilization. The chill, merciless rain poured
upon them constantly and neither poncho nor
blanket could keep it out. The General turned
over all the dried meat, coffee and other provisions
captured in the Indian village to those *hors de
combat,* so that we who were healthy, if otherwise
miserable, had to put up as best we could with
Indian pony steak which, at least, did not taste
of the blanket, like some of the old cavalry horses
we had been previously compelled to devour.

One of the most cheerful men I marched with
amid the pelting rain was Captain Charles King,
now celebrated as a military novelist, who was

then, if I mistake not, a lieutenant and regimental adjutant of the Fifth Cavalry. He was full of anecdote, but complained occasionally of the effect of serious wounds which he had received while fighting the Apaches in Arizona and which subsequently, compelled his retirement from active service.[68]

[68]Lieutenant Charles King possessed a distinguished lineage. His father, Rufus King, a West Point graduate in the class of 1833, won distinction as a journalist and soldier. In 1845 he removed from New York State to Milwaukee, then a small town in still-infant Wisconsin. Here he quickly attained leadership in journalism and politics, being one of the most influential and useful citizens of his developing city and State. At the outbreak of the Civil War he organized and for the first half of the war commanded the Iron Brigade, one of the most notable military organizations in the country's history. Imbued from his earliest childhood with pronounced military ideals, for practically two-thirds of a century (from the opening of the Civil War, when at the age of seventeen he served as an orderly on his father's staff, to the statewide celebration of his eighty-fourth birthday in 1928) Charles King lived for the United States Army. Incapacitated by an Apache arrow from active service, for many years he supported himself by literary work, in whose performance he achieved marked distinction. Meanwhile, for several decades he labored to perfect the Wisconsin National Guard, whose service in World War I was outstanding. It was the present Editor's privilege to enjoy several years of friendly association with General King during his later years, and to procure, among other things, the writing and publication of his lifetime memories ("Rufus King, Soldier, Editor and Statesman," and "Memories of a Busy Life,") in *Wisconsin Magazine of History,* Vols. 4–6).

CHAPTER XXI

Marching in the Mud

AT about noon on September 11th we entered a range of bluffs known as Clay Ridge. The rain fell in unending sheets as we wound through the serpentine defiles of that abominable sierra, our horses slipping in the mud when we remained on their backs and our boots absolutely sticking in the rotten soil when we dismounted. The ridge ought to be re-christened Church Spire Range, because the rocks are fashioned into fantastic pinnacles resembling the spires which pierce the clouds from the summits of sacred edifices. The number of steeples reminded me of Brooklyn, Beecher and the celebrated case which then agitated the public mind.[69] At last we reached the southern edge of Clay Buttes and saw through

---

[69]Henry Ward Beecher, perhaps the most notable American preacher of his generation and for forty years (1847–87) pastor of Plymouth Congregational Church in Brooklyn, was accused of adultery with Mrs. Tilton, one of his parishioners, about the year 1870. In 1874 the aggrieved husband sued Beecher for $100,000 damages and the ensuing trial of the case, which lasted six months, commanded nation-wide attention. Although a split jury failed to convict Beecher, his further influence was undoubtedly considerably affected by the scandal. He continued to serve Plymouth Church until his death March 8, 1887. *Dictionary of American Biography.*

the rising mist a dark blue wall a long distance in our front. Our guides made out Bear Butte on our left and the lofty peak of Inyan Kara on our right. We were within plain view of the Black Hills. They were not yet entirely visible—only their outposts, but the sight made us feel quite cheerful.

General Crook ordered Colonel Mills with a picked company of fifty men, all mounted on captured Indian ponies, to ride forward to the Black Hills camps and settlements for the purpose of ordering supplies to meet us after we had cleared the tedious defile of Clay Buttes. Mills was accompanied by Lieutenants Bubb and Chase. The intrepid scouts, Captain Jack Crawford and Frank Gruard, were sent in as government couriers.

Our march from Owl Creek to Willow Creek on September 12th was one of the worst of the campaign.[70] We were on the go from daylight until after dark, leading our miserable horses most of the way. Colonel Royall, as loyal an old soldier as ever placed foot in stirrup, hoofed it beside me mile after mile, never complaining but lightening up the dismal prospect of events with anecdotes of Mexico and the Civil War. We made over thirty-five miles on that march. Our only

[70]Present-day Moreau River was sometimes called Owl Creek.

guide to the position of camp was a fire kindled
by the headquarters staff of the General, who had
got in ahead. The darkness was so thick that, to
use the rude language of the tired soldiers, you
could cut it with a knife. We came up after the
Fifth Cavalry, but we could hear the commands
of the officers of that regiment as they sought to
place their men in position before ordering them
to dismount.

Finally our turn came. We were, to all appearance, on the brink of a deep ravine, fringed by
trees of some kind. I can hear old Royall's gruff
voice yet, calling out, "Colonel Mills, put your
battalion in camp beyond the creek." Our troop
led that night, and Lieutenant Lawson called out
"A Company, right into line!" The order was
obeyed. "Don't delay there," shouted Colonel
Royall. "Forward!"

"Forward!" repeated the old Lieutenant, and
not knowing but what we might be riding down a
precipice we moved ahead. The undergrowth
parted before us. My horse made a plunge in the
dark. Several other horses and riders did the
same and we all landed with a flop in about three
or four feet of water, thus adding to our misery.
We quickly spurred up the opposite bank, un-
saddled and unbridled our animals, and threw
ourselves down on the wet ground to rest. Hunger was forgotten, because indescribable fatigue

held us captive for the moment. When, two hours later, the tired orderly, Roberts, made a fire and fried some horse steak, Lieutenant Lawson and I felt in better appetite. But we had to wash down that strange repast with only the alkaline waters of Willow Creek.

On the road between Owl and Willow creeks, we had lost seventy horses and had buried in a big pit about the same number of saddles and other equipments. Before quitting the camp at Slim Buttes General Crook had caused all the immovable property of the Indians to be burned. It was a pity, but it could not have been helped. The order was thoroughly executed by Major W. H. Powell of the Fourth Infantry. Some of the soldiers managed to retain a few souvenirs but the weakness of their horse flesh compelled most of them to abandon their booty on the wayside. The poor dismounted cavalrymen had a terrible time of it and came straggling into camp until daylight, presenting a most pitiable appearance. What cheered the whole command up was the knowledge that the Belle Fourche was only five or six miles distant, and that, once there, we would be nearing civilization.

We were breakfasting on pony steak the morning of September 13th when we heard the lowing of oxen, which then seemed sweetest music to our ears. The effect on the troops was electrical.

The fatigues and privations of the march were forgotten by the light-hearted and easily-pleased soldiers. "Hurrah for old Crook!" "Hurrah for old Mills!" they shouted, like schoolboys who get an afternoon off. Neither of the officers named was very venerable, but when a soldier speaks of his superior as "the old man" you may be sure he is in good humor with him. The arrival of the beef herd, together with some wagon loads of crackers and vegetables from Crook City on the edge of the Hills, changed the aspect of affairs and made everybody feel happy. The beeves were speedily shot and butchered, and the soldiers were not long in satisfying their appetites upon the meat, which they roasted in Indian fashion on willow wands that served the purpose of toasting forks.

With the exception of what had been secured in the captured Indian village the command, from General Crook downward, had lived upon horse or pony meat for more than a week. Some of the soldiers, who had exhausted all their regular rations in an improvident manner, had begun earlier. As I sampled all kinds of equine meat on the trip I will give my opinion of that style of diet in brief: cavalry horse meat, played out, sore-backed subject, fried without salt, stringy, leathery, blankety and nauseating. Cavalry horse, younger than preceding and not too emaciated, produces meat which resembles very bad beef; Indian pony, adult, has the flavor and appearance of the flesh of elk; Indian pony, colt, tastes like antelope or young mountain sheep; mule meat, fat and rank, is a combination of all the foregoing, with pork thrown in.

Some of the soldiers were fortunate enough to shoot a few antelopes while on the march, but as there was neither bread nor salt hunger was general and the horses and ponies were killed, as I have said, by men regularly detailed for that purpose. Indeed, I saw a heap of the hind-quarters of Indian ponies in front of the Fifth Cavalry headquarters—a few wicky-ups—during the halt on Owl Creek, and the late Capt. W. Philo Clark of the Second Cavalry, acting as commissary, distributing the "beef" to the soldiers of the different commands. The kind-heartedness of some of the enlisted men was touching. All of his troopers loved Lieutenant Lawson, and one evening a private came to his bivouac with one of the hind-quarters of a fine, fat Indian pony colt, on which we dined sumptuously, although the old officer made wry faces and said again that he felt like a cannibal while eating horse flesh. But famine is, indeed, a stern master, and the campaign cured all who participated in it of any tendency toward epicureanism.

After passing Clay Ridge, Sergeant Van Moll and a corporal named Bessie obtained leave to go on a hunt for antelopes. Mr. Lawson enjoined them not to go too far from the column for fear of falling in with Indians. Night came, and they failed to return. The Lieutenant became uneasy, but nothing could be done until morning. After midnight we heard the sound of horses' hoofs and in the struggling, sickly moonlight Van Moll and Bessie rode up to our bivouac.

They had shot an antelope, but came near paying dearly for it. As they were traveling southward to join the column, after night had fallen, they heard the barking of Indian dogs, right in their path. They made a detour, but only succeeded in striking an Indian village, through which they had to ride at full gallop, their horses being in fairly good condition. The astonished Indians fired a few shots after them but did not attempt to make pursuit, probably because their ponies were turned loose to graze. The bold Sergeant, who was as truthful as he was courageous, declared that he had never had such a scare during all the years of his Indian experience. The Indian village was, doubtless, occupied by some of the savages who had fought us at Slim Buttes, and who were making for the Agency because winter and starvation were approaching.

The destruction of the game upon the Great Plains was about to settle a question that had puzzled the American Government for twenty years. The Sioux nation had never been thoroughly whipped in a pitched battle with our troops, but hunger tames the bravest and no general of the American army was better aware of that fact than George Crook. All other commanders had withdrawn from pursuit after following the hostile trail till their horseflesh played out, but Crook resolved to teach the savages a lesson. He meant to show them that neither distance, bad weather, the loss of horses nor the absence of rations could deter the American army from following up its wild enemies to the bitter end, and in bringing this home to the stubborn mind of Crazy Horse he achieved the crowning triumph of a campaign that might have, otherwise, seemed almost abortive.

This was the reason why he subjected his command and himself to hardships that under ordinary circumstances might have been easily avoided. He could not have worn out the obstinacy of the Indians in a more effective manner. But at the time he was rather unpopular with the soldiers, while many of the officers did not hesitate to criticise his campaign freely among themselves, in spite of the etiquette which generally restrains their utterances in regard to their com-

manders. The long absence of vegetables from
our scanty supplies told upon the health of many
of the troops toward the last and some cases of
scurvy, none of them very severe, were reported.
The eyes of the country were at that period fixed
upon Philadelphia, where the Centennial exhibition was in progress, or the toilsome cross march
of General Crook's brigade would have attracted
the national attention.

Our march from Willow Creek to the Belle
Fourche occupied only a couple of hours and was
devoid of any remarkable incident. The river was
pretty high, but we crossed to its southern bank
and went into camp. I should have said that before the passage of Clay Ridge General Crook,
whose campaign I had freely, but fairly, criticised
as a correspondent; seeing that I was dismounted,
very kindly lent me one of his own horses, the
same that had been wounded under him at the
Rosebud fight in June, and which had entirely recovered. Otherwise I should have been compelled
to tramp it all the rest of the way into the Hills,
something I was quite willing to do if necessary,
because there were not enough horses to go
round in the Third Cavalry. The regiment had
suffered very severely in regard to horse flesh,
and so also had the other cavalry organizations.
The brigade had abandoned or shot not less than
between five and six hundred horses since we

broke camp on Tongue River in the beginning of August. I have since heard that some of the apparently played-out beasts, when relieved from carrying their riders, rallied, lived on what they could find and were finally restored to the regiments to which they belonged, but I don't think they could have numbered very many.

Chapter XXII

Invading the Black Hills

THE order of the Lieutenant-General to General Crook, which reached the latter on the Belle Fourche, September 14th, commanded the brigade to march southward via the Black Hills and directed the Brigadier to meet Sheridan at Fort Laramie without loss of time. The command was turned over to General Merritt and on the night of the 15th, the expedition being then encamped on Whitewood Creek, Crook and his staff around a huge log fire drank farewell to their comrades in champagne procured from Deadwood and served in tin cups. Some Black Hillers of the prominent type assisted at the ceremony, General Dawson, United States Inspector of Internal Revenue, being the principal person.

Next morning Crook's party, consisting of himself and his personal staff, some infantry officers going home on leave, an escort of twenty men under Lieutenant Sibley, and the newspaper correspondents, whose mission ended with the cessation of war's alarms, and the "Hillers" turned their faces southward and, seeing that the fogs and damps had cleared away, like the idolators of the Orient worshiped the sun. Crook City, the northernmost picket of the Hills, was

distant sixteen miles and Deadwood lay about
the same distance beyond. We met a regular
caravan from the settlements proceeding to the
camp, bringing with them onions, cabbages, tur-
nips, potatoes and other vegetables, all of which
were grown in the neighborhood of the "cities"
already named. Oak groves and gentle uplands,
watered fairly, were the chief features of the
nearer landscape. Herds of cattle guarded by
grim-looking herders armed to the teeth, of
course, grazed with bovine tranquility among the
pretty dells of this northern Arcadia.

Behind rose the irregular and far from imposing wall of the Black Hills proper, pastoral in
their singular beauty, but entirely, at their first
view, destitute of that imperial grandeur which
marks the mighty range of the Big Horn, monarch of the northwestern mountains. Covered
thick with pine and fir trees, the Hills have a sable
appearance, which, for a wonder, makes their
title no misnomer. They are a ring-worm formation on the face of this earth, independent and
eccentric in construction, separated by hundreds
of miles of prairie or bad lands from all other
highlands, and neither the parents of lesser eminences nor the children of greater. Prof. Jenney
has expended the harsh vocabulary of science in
his report upon those highlands, and I, having a
horror of technical verbiage and a profound be-

lief that too much indulgence in the same leads
to thorough mystification and final softening of
the brain, refer the geologically curious to that
learned person's documents, if they desire more
thorough information.[71]

We were not long in reaching Crook City, a
rough-and-tumble place situated in the opening
of a wooded ravine, on the Whitewood. It contained about 250 houses, all frame or log, the
latter style of architecture predominating. An
explosion stirred the atmosphere and made the
hills shiver with sound as we approached. It was
a cannon which some enthusiastic parties fired in
honor of the General's visit. This performance
was repeated several times, and a fair-sized crowd
of hairy men and bilious women thronged around
the little cavalcade and indulged in stentorian or
shrill shouts of welcome. We were all forcibly
dismounted and led to an attack on Black Hills
whisky, which we found more formidable than
either Sitting Bull or Crazy Horse. Subsequently
dinner was served in the nearest approach to a

[71]On March 27, 1875 Professor Walter S. Jenney was
directed by the U.S. Commissioner of Indian Affairs to
conduct a geological and natural history survey of the
Black Hills region. Attended by a military escort of 400
men with 75 wagons, the party left Fort Laramie on May
24, 1875, concluding the survey the following October.
Chapters 5–7 of Jenney's final report, dated April 15,
1876, were printed as Senate Executive Doc. 51, 44th
Cong., 1st Sess.

hotel that the place could furnish, and if Crook City failed in many of the delicacies of the season it certainly did not fail in warmth of hospitality.

There was an appearance of depression about the settlement which showed a lack of prosperity, and some of the houses appeared untenanted. The mining gulches were either deserted or worked in a slow, unsatisfactory manner. The men, loafing around with their hands in their pockets, did not carry upon their faces the light of success. I made some inquiries and found that Crook City was on the wane. It started up, mushroom like, in May, but the main gulch having been washed out, it was found impossible to utilize the water in Whitewood Creek any further, and the energies of the populace were directed toward the work of turning the water power of Spearfish Creek, one of the finest streams in the Hills, into the first-named stream, so as to create the proper sluicing facilities for mining such gold as might exist in that district.

Crook City, according to my best information, has not improved its fortunes much beyond what they were in the fall of the Centennial year. More is the pity, too, because its kindly, open-hearted founders deserved all the success that courage and energy should win.

By the time the horses were fed General Crook was ready to proceed, and, followed by the usual

wild cheering, we rode on to Deadwood City over
a well defined and improved wagon road, through
a wooded tract just enough undulating to escape
being called a timbered prairie. On the right and
left, however, rose some lofty pinnacles of rock,
and ledges of quartz showed themselves at every
step. Heaps of the mineral, thrown around
promiscuously, as it were, appeared in the most
unexpected places, looking like deposits of petri-
fied snow. Quartz being the concomitant of gold,
its presence always indicates the strong proba-
bility of the presence of that precious metal, and
as regards quartz the Black Hills appear to be an
irregular mass of that mineral. We encountered a
number of horsemen and several wagons on our
way to Deadwood. Everybody was armed and the
men all wore huge spurs, which jingled like
sleigh bells after the first snow-fall. Some ranches
appeared at intervals, bearing the legend "sa-
loon" on their dingy fronts. As a rule it would be
better for the traveler to have some Indian lead in
his carcass than have a glass of ranch rot-gut in
his stomach.

About three miles from the city we met a group
of equestrians who were well mounted and dressed
in neat fashion. Their clean, civilized, respectable
aspect made us, by way of contrast, look like
white savages—veritable Goths and Vandals. I
am free to say that a seedier, more tattered and

generally disreputable looking group of cavaliers, from the General downward, than we were, never rode into any town, ancient or modern. The gentlemen who came to meet us were introduced by General Dawson as Mayor Farnum and the aldermen of Deadwood.[72] Half an hour's ride brought us to the suburbs of the mountain municipality. We passed by several groups of miners hard at work panning out gold dust, which, they told us, ranged from 10 to 85 cents per pan, the latter being very much in the minority. I had always looked with some degree of suspicion on the Black Hills business, and was considerably astonished to find a settlement of such proportions as that we were riding through. First we struck Montana City and then Lower Deadwood, and then Deadwood City, an artillery salute of thirteen guns being fired as Crook's countenance appeared in the latter place. The General acknowledged the universal enthusiasm, nearly all the population being in the main street, cheering, yelling and prancing around as if the day of jubilee had come, by lifting his weather-

[72]The town of Deadwood was laid out April 26, 1876, when a provisional government was organized and E. B. Farnum was chosen Mayor. The organization of the village of Deadwood was effected October 7, 1876, about the time of General Crook's visit. *South Dakota Hist. Collections,* XIV, 266. The Author's pages afford perhaps the best picture in existence of the infant mining center.

beaten hat and bowing right and left, after the manner of public men.

We drew up in front of the Grand Central Hotel, a wooden establishment kept by a burly Teuton, a la the knights of old returning from a crusade against the Turks and fleas in Palestine. Mayor Farnum did not say to General Crook what a certain mayor of Chicago said to King Kalakaua on the arrival of that dusky monarch in the city, "Now we'll take our leave until you put on a shirt and clean yourself up!" but he designated significantly the public bath house, for such a luxury existed even then in Deadwood, and pointed out the best ready-made clothing establishment in the town. The General took the hint, as did also the rest of us, and half an hour later the sluice leading from that bath house looked as if Powder River, of muddy memory, had been emptied into it. When we again appeared in public our appearance was not quite so forbidding as in the morning, but there was still considerable room for improvement.

Deadwood City in the fall of 1876 presented an appearance which combined in a singular manner the leading features of Cheyenne, Wyo., Braidwood, Ill., and McGregor, Iowa, at that period. Like Cheyenne, it possessed a multitude of variety theaters and a crowd of brazen and bedizened harlots, gambling hells, drinking dives and other moral abominations. Like Braidwood, it had a long, straight frame or log house street, just as it is popularly believed a snipe has one long, straight digestive apparatus, destitute of ramifications. Like McGregor, Deadwood was shut in by high wooded hills which seemed to choke off the air currents and to massively protest against any extension of the city's width. The tendency was to force the place along the ravine and convert it into a geometrical line— length without breadth. A couple of fires and a first-class cyclone which swept the long street described, have since partially cured Deadwood of its tendency to burrow in the valley.

Nuggets and gold dust, quartz and placer mining made up the conversation of those times in what might be called Deadwood society. I was shown specimens of gold in all forms until I felt like a jaundiced patient. Everything I looked at turned yellow, and I thought of Midas and the unpleasant fix that gentleman got himself into when he touched any object. The placer mines were already giving signs of exhaustion, and, as most of the experts predicted then, Deadwood had finally to rely upon the quartz mines and the men with capital enough to work them for such prosperity as she now enjoys.

The arrival of Crook's army in the neighborhood caused quite a flutter among such mer-

chants as had supplies for military needs, and
every kind of speculator from a photographer to
a three-card-monte man was soon on the road to
Whitewood Creek, where lay Crook's brigade,
commanded by the able and gallant Merritt.

After dark, all Deadwood and the surrounding
settlements, over 2,000 people, turned out and
gave Crook an ovation. It was very noisy. The
General had to address the crowd from the hotel
balcony. He made an off-hand speech which
showed intimate acquaintance with the habits
and sentiments of the mining fraternity. Neither
did he hesitate to crack a few bluff jokes about
the Indian troubles, which, as the phrase goes,
were well received. Afterward he was ushered to
the Deadwood theater, where he was formally
addressed and presented with the freedom of the
city. When that much was disposed of, Crook,
who abhors hand-shaking, was subjected to the
pump-handle nuisance at the front door of the
dramatic temple. He survived it all, not without
some wry faces, I imagine. The General appeared
to be very much liked by the miners, his long
residence on the Pacific Coast having familiarized
him with hundreds of the brotherhood.

In the evening I took a stroll around the city
and visited everything of interest. Wearing cavalry pants and looking altogether like one of
Uncle Samuel's boys out of repair, the hardy and

hearty miners took it for granted that I was earn-
ing thirteen dollars per month fighting "Injuns."
As I wished to post myself on the country I did
not undeceive them, but was compelled to swal-
low enough forty-rod to kill an ordinary alder-
man. The effects of that accursed beverage were
apparent for a week later, and I was not the only
awful example. But as I am now making my own
confession I'll say nothing about other people's
follies. As Mickey Free would poetically observe,
"Their failin's is nothin' to me."[73]

I visited half a dozen hells, where I noticed
some Chicago toughs, all engaged in the noble
art of faro or some other thimble-rigging devilment. In that lively time Deadwood sports killed
off a man or two every night. Between them and
the Sioux it was a hard matter to keep the population of the place up to the maximum standard.
Women, as in Cheyenne, acted as dealers at
many of the tables and more resembled incarnate
fiends than did their vulture-like male associates.

---

[73]Mickey Free was a well-known scout of somewhat du-
bious reputation who served under Crook in Arizona.
Captured in childhood by the Apaches, he had grown up
and married among them and according to Britton Davis
"had become to all intents and purposes an Apache."
During Davis' time of service in charge of the San Carlos
Reservation, Mickey Free assisted him in the capacity of
interpreter. Britton Davis, *The Truth about Geronimo,*
the Lakeside Classics volume for 1951, 55–59 and index
entries.

I observed that decided brunettes or decided blondes were more engaged in evil works than their negative fellow-women. Most of the miners would prefer playing faro or monte with men, for the women were generally old and unscrupulous hands whose female subtlety made them paramount in all the devices of cheating and theft. I observed one of them—a brunette, either French or Italian, something of the Latin order anyway —with some attention. She had a once-handsome face which crime had hardened into an expression of cruelty. Her eye glittered like that of a rattlesnake and she raked in the gold dust or chips with hands whose long white fingers, sharp at the ends, reminded one of a harpy's talons.

Every gambler appeared to play for gold dust. Nobody took greenbacks, and the gold-scales were in constant requisition. They allowed twenty dollars for every ounce of gold and placed greenbacks at the regular discount.[74] Not alone

[74]Prior to 1934 the general rule prevailed that paper money should be redeemable in coin upon demand. On numerous occasions, however, payments in specie (or metallic money) had been suspended for shorter or longer periods, or in various more or less limited areas. Most notable of these suspensions began in New York City, Dec. 30, 1861, as a consequence of conditions produced by the Civil War. By 1865 the "Greenback" or paper dollar had fallen in value to less than one-half its face value in gold. Resumption of specie payments was not achieved until January 1, 1879. Meanwhile the subject had become, and

in gaming, but also in commercial transactions was dust used. A miner swaggered up to the bar with five or six others and called for the drinks. They were supplied and he tossed his buckskin wallet to the bartender, who weighed out the requisite amount of dust and handed back the balance. I am inclined to believe that this display of crude bullion was made a good deal for effect, to make people believe that gold was as plentiful in Deadwood as were sands on the seashore.

for two decades remained, a hot political issue, culminating in the Free Silver campaign of 1896. It is noteworthy that our Author seems unaware of the subsequently celebrated "Crime of 1873," a myth which agitated the minds of millions of voters in subsequent political campaigns. In 1934 the redemption of paper currency in gold was indefinitely suspended, introducing economic and price revolutions with which the current reader is painfully familiar.

Chapter XXIII
Closing the Campaign

AS nearly every horse-shoer in Deadwood happened to be on a spree the night of Crook's reception, Lieutenant Clark, our acting quartermaster, had to go around with a posse of soldiers and sober up sufficient of the boys to get our horses shod. This operation consumed several hours and it was nearly daylight before we got to bed. We did not start very early next morning, and at breakfast I read a copy of *The Black Hills Pioneer*—a neat little sheet, which contained a very good account of our recent campaign and of Crook's oratorical effort on the preceding night.[75] It "blew" a little about the hills, and advertised the Cheyenne and Sidney

[75]The first issue of *The Black Hills Pioneer* was published at Deadwood, June 8, 1876. Its contents are reprinted in *South Dakota Hist. Colls.*, XI, 494–506.

Among other items, one which may perhaps be characterized as an editorial begins: "Some pap-sucking Quaker representative of an Indian doxology mill, writes in *Harper* for April about settling the Indian troubles by establishing more Sunday Schools and Missions among them," and concludes: "It is enough to make a western man sick to read such stuff. . . . You might as well try to raise a turkey from a snake egg as to raise a good citizen from a papoose. Indians can be made good in only one way, and that is to make angels of them."

routes in sensational style. I did not notice any politics in its pages.

At 8 o'clock we were in the saddle and en route for Custer City. We moved on through a forest road, meeting ranches every mile or two and encountering or overtaking wagon trains moving to and fro between Deadwood and the railroad settlements. We passed by several mining camps, most of which reported fair progress. We met a wagon train from Red Cloud, loaded with supplies for the expedition, on Box Elder Creek, escorted by three companies of the Fourth Artillery under Major Smith. It seemed strange to meet that branch of the service—nearly always on coast duty—so far inland. Like nearly all soldiers, they were hospitable, and we had a pleasant time for an hour or two. I had not come in contact with the Fourth Artillery since June 3, 1866, when I saw them at Buffalo patrolling the Niagara River in order to save Canada from a Fenian invasion.[76]

General Crook is a regular path-finder, and when we started on Monday, the 18th, after mak-

[76]The relatively short-lived Fenian agitation originated under the leadership of John O'Mahoney with the objective of supplying aid and equipment to the Irish Revolutionists against British rule. In 1865 an Irish Republic was organized in New York City and futile efforts to promote the Irish Revolutionary cause followed. In 1866 an invasion of Canada from Fort Erie resulted in the defeat of the

ing Castleton, about forty-two miles from Deadwood, we took a regular cut-off, marching in the
direction of Harney's Peak. At Castleton we
found great preparations being made both for
gulch and ledge mining, but matters were in too
undeveloped a condition to glean much important information. It was evident, however, that
something had been discovered there or people
would not be going to so much trouble. The
inhabitants of Castleton numbered about 200,
mostly practiced miners. They had some strips
of cultivated ground and several herds of cattle.
They were people of great expectations, like
nearly all of their class.

Our cut-off lay through a superbly parked
country resembling the Big Horn foot-hills, over
which towered in craggy sublimity the haughty
crest of Harney's Peak. We followed the course
of Castle Creek and its tributaries, streams that
are as transparent as the air on a sweet May
morning. The grass and the leaves were green
and nature was clothed in loveliness. Birds sang
amid the shady groves and trout leaped in the
rivulets. The squirrels frisked from tree to tree

Canadian troops and in the prompt arrest of the raiders
by the American Government upon their return to Buffalo. Several subsequent attempts to raid Canada were
made. O'Mahoney died in January, 1877 and the Fenian
movement came to its close. *Dictionary of American History.*

and there was an exhilaration in the atmosphere
that made us triumph over time and recall the
days of happy boyhood, when every leaf and
flower charmed us into many a wildwood ramble.
How gloriously the sympathetic genius of a Burns
or a Moore would have sung of that lovely scene!

At noon we had reached the broad plateau
above Hill City, from which we had a superb view
of Harney's Peak. The "city" was like Sweet
Auburn, a deserted village, tenanted by one solitary mortal, who kept a ghostly-looking ranch for
the benefit of travelers. We asked this stout-
hearted hermit why the place had been abandoned, and he answered sententiously, "Indian
scare and no gold dust." We continued our ride
to Custer City. I have seen more sublime, but
never more charming, scenery. The hand of
nature never shaped anything more beautiful
than the groves and parks that then ornamented
every foot of that enchanting road. The soil was
not rich, but the queen of beauty might have
fixed her throne securely there, at least while
summer lasted.

The sun was dipping into the western cloud
banks on the evening of September 18th when
we entered Custer City and received a warm
greeting from the inhabitants. Captain Teddy
Egan of the Second Cavalry, a renowned Indian
fighter, was there with his troop of gallant grays,

the same which led the charge on the village of Crazy Horse on St. Patrick's Day in the Morning, 1876.

The hotel experience at Custer could hardly be called pleasant. The partitions were thin and a sick infant made the veterans, who had slept with the war yells of the Indians ringing in their ears, lie awake most of the night. After having slept for several months in the open air it is very difficult to come back to the ways of civilization, especially such as was then furnished on the frontier. Couriers from General Sheridan to General Crook arrived during the night with dispatches which requested the latter officer to meet the former at Fort Laramie within forty-eight hours.

Captain Egan, at General Crook's request, furnished horses from his splendid troop to the Commanding Officer, Colonel Chambers, Colonel Stanton, Surgeon Hartsuff, Major Powell, Major Burt, Lieutenants Clark, Bourke, Schuyler, four correspondents, including myself, and an orderly. The General determined to leave his escort and pack train behind with orders to follow by easy marches under Major Randall and Lieutenant Sibley. The officers and others selected to accompany the General sprang upon the backs of Egan's superb grays early on the morning of September 19th and set out on a forced ride of

106 miles, the distance between Custer City and Camp Robinson. How soul stirring it is to ride at full speed on a swift, strong horse, after lumbering along for weeks on some jaded sorry hack! It is like changing from a stage coach to a lightning express. We made first-class time until the General got tired of the road and resolved to strike out a short-cut trail to the South Cheyenne River. This led us into a handsome, but rugged, country which retarded our progress to a great extent. Custer City civilization had told on a few of the party, and Surgeon Hartsuff's hands were full in attending to the wants of the disabled. But there was no time for extra halts, and those whose stomachs were not in good repair had to take their horseback punishment without growling.

About 2 o'clock in the afternoon we reached the banks of a charming, sparkling mountain stream. The General, with his usual luck as a hunter, ran across and shot a fine, fat deer and we all enjoyed a hunters' dinner. That being over, we again saddled up and followed our experienced leader through the ever winding defiles of the wooded hills. The sun was low in the west when we emerged from the southern rim of the Black Hills group, and we found great difficulty in getting our horses safely across the marshy bottom lands running along the handsome stream whose course we had followed to

the Great Plains. As we cleared the last of the
foot-hills we saw not more than a quarter of a
mile in our front the waters of the South Cheyenne River, and felt recompensed for the toil of
our journey.

After fording the famous stream we found ourselves on an unbroken prairie, and soon struck
the main wagon road leading from Buffalo Gap to
Red Cloud Agency. We increased our pace to a
round trot and then broke into a gallop, which
we kept up for a number of miles. In all my
equestrian experiences in the great West I never
enjoyed anything more heartily than that wild
ride in the evening shadows across the plains of
the South Cheyenne. I wished for a horse that
could gallop without ever tiring, and the others,
with perhaps the exception of the unimpassioned
Crook, felt all the mad ardor of the chase or the
charge. Egan's grays did credit to the old Second
Dragoons, and covered the ground with a swinging stride that showed good blood and good
grooming.

We continued our ride until 10 o'clock that
night, when we reached a branch of War Bonnet
Creek, where we halted to water the horses. It
was decided to keep on, as there was no time to
be lost, and we did not halt again until 2 o'clock
on the morning of the 20th. We picketed the
horses, lay down on the frosty ground, put the

half blankets we had along over us, and, tired out as we were, slept soundly until about 4 o'clock. The General called us at that hour and away we went again. At daylight General Crook pointed out to me a box-shaped formation on a ridge of bluffs some twenty miles away and said that beneath it lay Red Cloud Agency and Camp Robinson.[77]

The rest of the road lay through a rough and barren strip of country not far removed from the condition of bad lands, and we were so covered with dust that it was next to impossible to tell whether we were young or old, soldiers or citizens, miners or robbers. We were about as hard a looking set of customers as ever rode through that country.

As we rode into the Agency a large body of soldiers from the neighboring post were standing around the saw mill. One of them shouted to the General: "Hello, where the d— have you fellows been?" One of the staff answered sharply, and instantly, "In Hades of course!" and the soldier, recognizing under all that dust and dirt a shoulder strap, disappeared in double quick time. The poor fellow was not to blame if he mistook us for a squad of highwaymen.

[77]Camp, or Fort Robinson was built in 1874 at the Red Cloud Agency on White River in Nebraska. It was the scene of the killing of Crazy Horse, September 5, 1877.

Thousands of Indians flocked to see us, tall, powerful savages with lowering visages, all anxious to have a good look at the Gray Fox, as they called General Crook. The latter remained only a short time, and set out for Fort Laramie attended by a small escort. Our horses were used up, so we had to wait the arrival of Randall and Sibley before proceeding farther. They arrived during the afternoon of the 21st, and I, meanwhile, was the guest of Captain Hamilton and Lieutenant Andrus of Troop H, Fifth Cavalry. I also received much courtesy at the hands of as dashing and handsome a young officer as ever graced the service of the United States, Lieut. John A. McKinney of the Fourth Cavalry, who fell gloriously in battle with the tribe of the Cheyenne chief, Dull Knife, on Clear Fork of the Powder River the following 25th day of November.

The officers stationed at Fort Robinson gave us all a hospitable reception on the night of September 21st. They crowded the commodious sutler's store, and enjoyed themselves in true military fashion. All formality was dropped for the occasion and officers of all ranks mingled in the closest good-fellowship. It was a most delightful reunion, and no two men were more beloved in that brilliant assemblage than they who are now but ashes and a memory, John A. McKinney and Philo Clark.

Our party, under Major Randall, marched for Fort Laramie on the 22d. We enjoyed the hospitality of General Mackenzie, whose fate has been a sad one, at his camp between Red Cloud Cañon and Rawhide Creek on the night of the 23d. He had most of his regiment, the Fourth Cavalry, with him, and informed us that he thought there would be a winter campaign. Mackenzie, was then a noble specimen of the beau sabreur, tall, well built and with a frank, handsome face. Some of the fingers of his right hand had been lost in a Virginia battle, and on that account the Indians called him "Bad Hand."[78]

I reached the railroad, from Fort Laramie, on September 27th and reported at the headquarters

[78]Ranald S. Mackenzie was born in New York City, July 27, 1840. He graduated from the U.S. Military Academy at the head of his class in 1862 and within three years (not yet twenty-five years old) was commander of a cavalry division in the Army of the Potomac. Of him General Grant wrote in his *Personal Memoirs:* "I regarded him as the most promising young officer in the army. Graduating at West Point as he did during the second year of the war, he had won his way up to the command of a corps (division) before its close. This he did upon his own merit and without influence." Subsequent to the Civil War, Mackenzie, reduced to the rank of Colonel of the Fourth U.S. Cavalry, served on the western and southern frontiers until he was retired for disability incurred in the line of duty in 1884. Failing health terminated his life on January 19, 1889. The winter campaign of 1876, which he foretold to the Author, was conducted by Crook with General Mackenzie in command of the cavalry contingent

of the Chicago *Times* about a week later. Mr. Storey, who was by no means liberal of praise, gave me his best congratulations and I settled down again for a while to the routine of journalism and city life.

of the army. On November 25, 1876 on the headwater of Powder River he thoroughly defeated Dull Knife's band of hostiles, and this, along with other factors, led to the surrender of Crazy Horse and the termination of the war. *Dictionary of American Biography.*

Chapter XXIV

Dull Knife and Crazy Horse

THE prediction of the late Gen. Ranald S. Mackenzie, a soldier whose premature death is mourned by the nation as well as by the army, that there would be a winter campaign against the hostiles turned out to be prophetic. Early in November, 1876, General Crook made up a column consisting of six troops of the Fourth; two of the Fifth; two of the Third and one of the Second Cavalry; four companies of the Fourth Artillery, acting as infantry; six companies of the Ninth, two of the Fourteenth and three of the Twenty-third Infantry, together with some guides and Indian scouts, to operate chiefly against Dull Knife's band of fierce Cheyennes, who were believed to be somewhere on the Powder River or some of its very numerous branches.

The scouts discovered an Indian trail leading up the valley of Crazy Woman's Fork toward the mountains, and Crook immediately detached Mackenzie to follow it up. That intrepid soldier carried out his orders to the letter and struck the hostile village after a cold, dismal march through deep snow on the morning of November 25th. He attacked immediately and met with a brilliant success. Dull Knife's band was almost wiped out.

Their tepees and other property were burned, their pony herd captured, and the Chief himself escaped with great difficulty. He soon afterward surrendered at Red Cloud Agency, and appeared upon the war-path no more. The gallant death of Lieutenant McKinney, already mentioned, and of several soldiers attested the desperation with which the brave Cheyennes, although surprised, had fought. Most of the survivors of the tribe were subsequently sent to the Indian Territory, from which they made their escape by an unparalleled march. They were placed in the guard house at Camp Robinson, broke jail, escaped to the bluffs, killed a number of soldiers, and were finally slaughtered to a man by a few companies of the Third Cavalry. Very few of Dull Knife's people now remain to menace civilization, but the gallant band has left behind a name of terror, at which the white settlers of the conquered territory still grow pale.

The Sioux hostiles under Crazy Horse, who carried with him a majority, perhaps, of the warriors, became convinced, after Crook's march through rain and mud from Tongue River to the Yellowstone, from the latter stream to the Little Missouri, and from Heart River to Slim Buttes and the Black Hills, that their game was up, and concluded to surrender to the General. They did so during the winter of 1876 and the spring of

1877. The negotiations were mainly conducted by Col. George M. Randall, Col. T. H. Stanton, the late Capt. W. P. Clark and Capt. John G. Bourke. They were elaborate and very successful. Starvation had taught the hostiles a lesson that war of itself could not impart. They were keen enough to recognize that they could no longer depend on game for their subsistence. Peace was thus restored to the Big Horn and Black Hills regions, which were soon afterward thrown open to settlers by the Government.

Thus of all the Sioux who, in the pride of numbers, had held their own against Crook and destroyed Custer in the summer campaign of 1876, there remained hostile only those under Sitting Bull and his immediate lieutenants, Black Moon, Rain-in-the-Face, Spotted Eagle, White Eagle and Gall; and even they had retreated for protection beyond the British line. It remained for General Miles to settle with them a few years later, as will be seen.[79]

Crazy Horse did not remain long tranquil at Red Cloud Agency. He was a wily, desperate and ambitious savage, the terror of friends and foes alike. He found that he was a bigger man on the

---

[79]The original edition of the Author's book contains a second part, not included in the present reprint, devoted to General Miles' campaign of 1879 along the British border.

CHIEF DULL KNIFE

From a photograph by William H. Jackson.
Reproduced by courtesy of the Smithsonian Institution.

war-path than at the agencies, and this made him frantic. He formed a conspiracy to murder General Crook and his escort, but a friendly Indian warned the General just in time to prevent a tragedy. All the malcontents were to attend a council that was to have been held, wearing blankets under which the weapons of death would be concealed until Crazy Horse gave the signal for their use. He never got the opportunity. The friendly Indians conspired to kill the turbulent chief, and one of them, No Flesh—a noted Sioux of peculiar physical appearance— actually set out to assassinate Crazy Horse.[80] The latter had gone to the Rosebud Agency, where the Brule Sioux chief, Spotted Tail, the ablest of Indian leaders, had him arrested by his scouts

[80]General Mills, who assumed command of Camp Sheridan in April, 1875, records some interesting information about Spotted Tail and No Flesh. The former seems to have enjoyed the respect of both Indians and whites. He became a great favorite of Mrs. Mills, who frequently entertained him, while steadily withholding the like hospitality from No Flesh, who was a sub-chief under Spotted Tail, and who aspired to the like treatment accorded the latter. No Flesh painted some pictures for Mrs. Mills showing his exploits as a warrior. One of these graphically depicting the killing of a cavalry captain and a soldier is reproduced along with the foregoing data in General Mills' book, *My Story*. Spotted Tail returned Mrs. Mills' hospitality by staging a dog feast in her honor. She attended and danced with the squaws, but to her subsequent regret could not muster courage to partake of the feast.

and sent back to Red Cloud. When confronted with the guard house, Crazy Horse drew his knife and fought desperately. Little Big Man, as great a scoundrel as ever took a scalp, pinned the chief in his arms. Some soldiers also interfered, and in the melee a bayonet was thrust into the side of Crazy Horse, who died hurling curses at the pale faces and the Sioux renegades.

Trouble threatened for a time, but the death of the Indian hero, the bravest of all the brave hostiles, quelled the spirit of the tribes. They fell into apathy, and in that condition, for the most part, they have remained ever since. It is not likely that they will ever again give much trouble to the government, especially as the reservation question has been settled, in a measure, satisfactorily.

Although our regular army suffered cruelly during the war of 1876, it inflicted perhaps equal punishment on the enemy, and that, too, under circumstances the most adverse. Had the force sent against the hostiles under Crook, Terry, Gibbon and Custer in May of that year been of the strength attained by the army when the two department commanders united their forces on the Rosebud in August, or had either been as strong, individually, as he became in the latter month, the campaign would have resulted more brilliantly for our troops, and might have accomplished the total destruction of the hostiles in the field. As matters terminated, however, America cannot too highly respect the officers and soldiers whose combined heroism and endurance settled, in 1876, the great Sioux difficulty on the main portion of our long-harassed frontier.

APPENDIX

Echoes from the Little Big Horn

GENERAL SHERIDAN'S ACCOUNT OF THE CUSTER
TRAGEDY. COMPILED FROM THE OFFICIAL
DOCUMENTS AT MILITARY HEADQUARTERS.

THE following extracts from the account of the closing scenes of the battle of the Little Big Horn, taken from the official records of the late General Philip H. Sheridan, cannot fail to be of great interest to the readers of this volume:

"The valley of the creek was followed toward the Little Big Horn, Custer on the right of the creek, Reno on the left of it, Benteen off still farther to the left and not in sight. About 11 o'clock Reno's troops crossed the creek to Custer's column and remained with it until about half-past 12 o'clock, when it was reported that the village was only two miles ahead and running away.

"Reno was directed to move forward at as rapid a gait as he thought prudent and to charge, with the understanding that Custer should support him. The troops under Reno moved at a fast trot for about two miles, when they came to the river, crossed it, halted a few minutes to collect the men, and then deployed. Not seeing anything, however, of the subdivisions under Custer and Benteen, and the Indians swarming upon him from all directions, Reno took position dismounted in the edge of some timber which afforded shelter for the horses of his command, continuing to fight on foot until it became apparent that he would soon be overcome by superior numbers of Indians. He then remounted his troops, charged through the enemy, recrossed the river and gained the bluffs on the opposite side. In this charge First Lieutenant Donald McIntosh, Second Lieutenant B. H. Hodgson and Acting-Assistant-Surgeon J. M. DeWolf, were killed.

"Reno's force succeeded in reaching the top of the bluff, but with a loss of three officers and twenty-nine enlisted men killed and seven men wounded. Almost at the same time that Reno's men reached the bluff, Benteen's battalion came up, and a little later the pack-train, with Mac-Dougall's troop escorting it. These three detachments were all united under Reno's command, and numbered about 381 men, in addition to their officers.

"Meanwhile, nothing had been heard from Custer, so the reunited divisions, under Reno, moved down the river, keeping along the bluff on the opposite side from the village. Firing had been heard from that direction, but, after moving to the highest point without seeing or hearing

anything of Custer, Reno sent Captain Weir with
his troop to try and open communications. Weir
soon sent back word that he could go no farther;
that the Indians were getting around him. At the
same time he was keeping up a heavy fire from his
skirmish line. Reno then turned everything back
to the first position he had taken on the bluff,
which seemed to be the best for defense; had the
horses and mules driven into a depression; put
his men, dismounted, on the crests of the hills
which formed the depression, and had hardly
completed these dispositions when the Indians
attacked him furiously. This was about 6 o'clock
in the evening, and the ground was held, with a
further loss of eighteen killed and forty-six
wounded, until the attack ceased about 9 o'clock
that night.

"By this time the overwhelming numbers of
the enemy rendered it improbable that the troops
under Custer could undertake to rejoin those
with Reno, so the latter began to dig rifle pits,
barricaded with dead horses and mules and
boxes from the packs, to prepare for any further
attack which might be made the next day. All
night long the men kept working, while the Indians were holding a scalp dance within their hearing in the valley of the Little Big Horn below.

"About half past two o'clock in the morning of
June 26th a most terrific rifle fire was opened

upon Reno's position, and as daylight increased hordes of Indians were seen taking station upon high points which completely surrounded the troops, so that men were struck on opposite sides of the lines from where the shots were fired. The fire did not slacken until half-past nine o'clock in the morning, when the Indians made a desperate charge on the line held by Troops H and M, coming to such close quarters as to touch with a 'coup-stick' a man lying dead within Reno's lines. This onslaught was repulsed by a charge from the line assaulted, led by Colonel Benteen. The Indians also charged close enough to send their arrows into the line held by Troops D and H, but they were driven back by a counter-charge of those troops, led in person by Reno.

"There were now many wounded and the question of obtaining water was a vital one, for the troops had been without any from 6 o'clock the previous evening, a period of sixteen hours. A skirmish line was formed under command of Colonel Benteen to protect the descent of volunteers down the hill in front of the position to reach the water. A little was obtained in canteens, but many of the men were struck while obtaining the precious fluid. The fury of the attack was now over and the Indians were seen going off in parties to the village. . . . About two o'clock in the afternoon the grass in the bottom was extensively fired by the Indians, and behind the dense smoke thus created the hostile village began to move away. Between six and seven o'clock in the evening the village came out from behind this cloud of smoke and dust, the troops obtaining a full view of the cavalcade as it filed away in the direction of the Big Horn Mountains, moving in almost full military order. . . .

"During the night of June 26th the troops under Reno changed position so as to better secure a supply of water and prepare against another assault, should the warriors return in strong force, but early in the morning of June 27th, while preparing to resist any attack that might be attempted, the dust of a moving column was seen approaching in the distance. Soon it was discovered to be troops who were coming, and in a little while a scout arrived with a note from General Terry to Custer, saying that some Crow scouts had come into camp, stating that he had been whipped, but that their story was not believed. About 10:30 o'clock in the morning General Terry rode into Reno's lines and the fate of General Custer was ascertained.

"Precisely what was done by Custer's immediate command subsequent to the moment when the rest of the regiment last saw him alive has remained partly a matter of conjecture, no officer or soldier who rode with him into the valley of the Little Big Horn having survived to tell the tale. The only real evidence of how they came to meet their fate was the testimony of the field where it overtook them. . . .

"Custer's trail, from the point where Reno crossed the stream, passed along and in rear of the crest of the bluffs on the right bank for nearly or quite three miles. Then it came down to the bank of the river, but at once diverged from it again, as though Custer had unsuccessfully attempted to cross; then, turning upon itself and almost completing a circle, the trail ceased. It was marked by the remains of officers and men and the bodies of horses, some of them dotted along the path, others heaped in ravines and upon knolls, where halts appeared to have been made. There was abundant evidence that a gallant resistance had been offered by Custer's troops, but they were beset on all sides by overpowering numbers.

"Following up the movements of Custer's column from the Yellowstone, starting from Tullock's Creek soon after five o'clock on the morning of June 25th the infantry of Gibbon's command made a march of twenty-two miles over a most difficult country. In order that scouts might be sent into the valley of the Little Big Horn, Gibbon's cavalry and the battery [three Gatling guns] were pushed on thirteen or fourteen miles farther, not camping until midnight. Scouts were sent out at 4:30 o'clock on the morning of June 26th. They soon discovered three Indians, who were at first supposed to be Sioux, but who, when overtaken, proved to be Crows who had been with General Custer. They brought to Terry the first intelligence of the battle. Their story was not credited. It was supposed that some fighting—even severe fighting—had taken place, but it was not believed that disaster could have overtaken so large a force as twelve troops of cavalry. The infantry, which had broken camp very early, soon came up and the whole column entered and moved up the valley of the Little Big Horn.

"During the afternoon efforts were made to send scouts through to what was supposed to be Custer's position, in order to obtain information of the condition of affairs, but those who were sent out were driven back by parties of Indians, who, in increasing numbers, were seen hovering in front of Gibbon's column. At twenty minutes before nine o'clock that night the infantry had marched between twenty-nine and thirty miles; the men were weary, and daylight was fading. The column was, therefore, halted for the night at a point about eleven miles, in a straight line, above the mouth of the stream. On the morning of June 27th the advance was resumed, and after a march of nine miles the intrenched position was reached. The withdrawal of the Indians from around Reno's command and from the valley of the Little Big Horn was, undoubtedly, caused by the approach of Gibbon's troops. . . .

"On the 28th of June Captain Ball of the Second Cavalry made a reconnaissance along the trail of the Indians after they left the valley. He reported that they had divided into two parties, one of which kept the valley of Long Fork, making, he thought, for the Big Horn Mountains. The other turned more to the eastward. He also discovered, leading into the valley, a very heavy trail, not more than five days old. This was entirely distinct from the one which Custer had followed, and indicated that at least two bands had united just before the battle."

[NOTE. It would appear from the statements of Major Reno and other officers engaged in the battle on the bluffs that they were entirely ignorant of the fate of Custer and his five troops until the arrival of Generals Terry and Gibbon. The Author was told by some of the soldiers of the Seventh Cavalry, after the commands of Terry and Crook came together in the Rosebud Valley, August 10, 1876, that the savages had displayed Custer's guidons and other trophies of victory during the fighting on the 25th and 26th of June. Colonel Anson Mills' cavalry detachment recovered, at Slim Buttes, on September 9th of that year, as stated in Part I, one of Custer's guidons, Colonel Keogh's gauntlets and many blouses, etc., which were the property of the slaughtered battalion.

It seems strange that Reno could not comprehend Custer's fate until after the arrival of Generals Terry and Gibbon, when some of the private soldiers did. Where did Major Reno suppose the hostiles procured the uniforms, etc., which they displayed? Lieut. C. C. De Rudio of the Seventh Cavalry, who with Private O'Neill of Troop C was cut off from Reno's command during the retreat from the river to the bluffs on June 25th, says, in a letter to a friend, dated from Camp on the Yellowstone River, opposite the Big Horn, July 5, 1876: "The night (June 25–6), was passed and in the dim light of day I thought I saw some gray horses, mounted by men in military blouses, and some of them in white hats. They were, I thought, going out of the valley, and those who had already crossed the river were going up a very steep bluff, and others were crossing after them. I saw one man with a buckskin jacket, pantaloons and top boots, and a white hat, and felt quite sure I recognized him as Captain Tom Custer, which convinced me that the cavalry was of our command. With this conviction I stepped boldly out on the edge of the bank and called to Captain Custer: 'Tom, don't leave us here!' The distance was only a few yards, and my call was answered by an infernal yell and a discharge of three or four hundred shots. I then discovered my mistake, and found that the savages were clad in clothes and mounted on horses captured from our men."

Fortunately De Rudio and O'Neill were enabled to escape in the thick undergrowth, and finally succeeded in rejoining the remnant of the command.]

CROOK'S ACCOUNT OF ROSEBUD FIGHT.

General Sheridan forwarded the following dispatch, which contains General Crook's official report of the battle at Rosebud Creek, to the War Department on receipt:

CHICAGO, June 23, 1876.

GEN. E. D. TOWNSEND, Washington, D. C.:

The following dispatch from General Crook is forwarded for the information of the General of the Army:

CAMP ON THE SOUTH OF TONGUE RIVER, WYOMING, June 19th, via Fort Fetterman, June 23d.—LIEUT.-GEN. SHERIDAN, Chicago, Ill.: Returned to camp to-day, having marched as indicated in my last telegram. When about forty miles from here on Rosebud Creek, Montana, on

the morning of the 17th inst., the scouts reported Indians in the vicinity and within a few
moments we were attacked in force, the fight
lasting several hours. We were near the mouth of
a deep cañon, through which the creek ran. The
sides were very steep, covered with pine and apparently impregnable. The village was supposed
to be at the other end, about eight miles off. They
displayed a strong force at all points, occupying
so many and such covered places that it is impossible to correctly estimate their numbers. The
attack, however, showed that they anticipated
that they were strong enough to thoroughly defeat the command.

During the engagement I tried to throw a
strong force through the cañon, but I was obliged
to use it elsewhere before it had gotten to the
supposed location of the village. The command
finally drove the Indians back in great confusion,
following them several miles, the scouts killing a
good many during the retreat. Our casualties
were nine men killed and fifteen wounded of the
Third Cavalry; two wounded of the Second
Cavalry; three men wounded of the Fourth Infantry, and Captain Henry, of the Third Cavalry, severely wounded in the face.[81] It is impos-

[81][Note by the Author]: The General omits the friendly
Indians killed and wounded and also those of the soldiers
whose injuries did not place them *hors de combat.*

sible to correctly estimate the loss of the Indians, many being killed in the rocks and others being gotten off before we got possession of that part of the field, thirteen dead bodies being left.

We remained on the field that night, and having nothing but what each man carried himself we were obliged to retire to the train to properly care for our wounded, who were transported here on mule-litters. They are now comfortable and all doing well.

I expect to find those Indians in rough places all the time and so have ordered five companies of infantry, and shall not probably make any extended movement until they arrive.

The officers and men behaved with marked gallantry during the engagement.   Crook,
Brigadier-General.

The movement of General Terry, indicated in his dispatch of the 12th inst., leads me to believe that he is at or near the Rosebud about this time. He has formed a junction with Gibbon, and will, undoubtedly, take up the fight which Crook discontinued for want of supplies and to take care of his wounded. I communicated to General Crook by courier from Fort Fetterman the position and intentions of General Terry. He must have received it before this date.

P. H. Sheridan, *Lieutenant-General.*

Index

INDEX

AMERICAN Horse, killed, 287–88, 300.
Andrews, Capt.—, in Rosebud battle, 130,134; illness, 266.
Andrew's Creek, army examines, 270.
Antelopes, shot, 149–50, 308–309.
Arctic exploration, Lieut. Schwatka conducts, xxxiii, 36, 153.
Army, in Lieut. Grattan tragedy, xviii; Ash Hollow battle, xviii–xix; ; Sioux defeat, xxix–xxx, 124–51, 197–218, 342–53; Finerty joins, 15–19, 30–33; organization of Crook's command, 51–53; beauty on march, 73–74; monotony of camp life, 152–63; whiskey drinking, 220–21; night march described, 240–43; discourse on vermin, 249–50; ugliness of uniforms, 249; soldiers gripe, 263–64; forlorn condition of soldiers, 271–72; officers characterized, 273–74; lot of private soldiers, 161, 274–75; lack of rations, 276–79, 301, 306.
Arnold, —, scout, 89–90, 100.
Ash Hollow, battle, xix.

BAD Lands, army passes, 45, 55, 59.
Balaklava, battle, xxxiii.
Bassett, Sergeant —, adopts Calamity Jane, 54.
Bear Butte, sighted, 304.
Bear Springs, army encamps, 34–35.
Beaver Creek, route of army, 84, 86, 267–70.
Becker, John, mule packer, 173–96.
Beecher, Henry Ward, adultery scandal, 303.
Bell, James, carries dispatches, 221–22.
Belle Fourche River, Custer describes, xxvii–xxviii; army encamps, 311.
Benteen, Col. Frederick, in Little Big Horn battle, 207–208, 213–14, 345.
Bessie, Corporal —, hunting adventure, 309.

357